Poverty and Social Welfare in the United States

Poverty and Social Welfare in the United States

edited by
Donald Tomaskovic-Devey

Westview Press / Boulder and London

This Westview softcover edition is printed on acid-free paper and bound in
softcovers that carry the highest rating of the National Association of State
Textbook Administrators, in consultation with the Association of American
Publishers and the Book Manufacturers' Institute.

Published in 1988 in the United States of America by Westview Press, Inc.;
Frederick A. Praeger, Publisher; 5500 Central Avenue, Boulder, Colorado 80301

Library of Congress Cataloging-in-Publication Data
Poverty and social welfare in the United States/edited by Donald
  Tomaskovic-Devey.
     p.   cm.
  ISBN 0-8133-7458-8
  1. Public welfare--United States. 2. United States--Social
policy. 3. Poor--United States.   I. Tomaskovic-Devey, Donald,
1957-
HV95.P68   1988
362.5'8'0973--dc19   87-21311
                                                  CIP

Printed and bound in the United States of America

 The paper used in this publication meets the requirements of the
American National Standard for Permanence of Paper for Printed
Library Materials Z39.48-1984.

6   5   4   3   2   1

Contents

Preface vii
Acknowledgments ix

1   Poverty and Social Welfare
    in the United States,
    Donald Tomaskovic-Devey   1

PART ONE
THE POVERTY POPULATION AND POVERTY GENERATION:
SEX, RACE, AND LABOR MARKET STRUCTURE

2   The Feminization of Poverty: Nature,
    Causes, and a Partial Cure,
    Irwin Garfinkel and Sara McLanahan . . .   27

3   Unmarried Women in a Patriarchal Society:
    Impoverishment and Access to Health
    Care Across the Life-Cycle,
    Teresa Arendell   53

4   Local Labor Market Structure and the
    Poverty Vulnerability of Black and White
    Women in Large Metropolitan Areas,
    David J. Maume, Jr.   82

5   Industrial Structure, Relative Labor
    Power, and Poverty Rates,
    Donald Tomaskovic-Devey 104

PART TWO
IDEOLOGY, SOCIAL RESEARCH,
AND THE WELFARE SYSTEM

6   A Test of the New Structural Critique
     of the Welfare State,
     Jimy M. Sanders 130

7   Fighting Poverty by Reducing Dependency:
     The Dilemma of Policy Assumptions,
     Michael Morris 162

8   The Dynamics of Welfare Use:
     How Long and How Often?
     Mark R. Rank 177

9   Health and Poverty in Single-Parent
     Families: The Consequences of
     Federal Policy Change,
     Rosemary C. Sarri and
     Carol Crill Russell 194

PART THREE
POLITICS AND SOCIAL WELFARE POLICY

10   Ideology and Welfare Reform Under
     the Reagan Administration,
     Susan Gotsch-Thomson 222

11   Poverty, Policy, and Politics:
     Implications of the Research Findings
     for Social Welfare Action,
     Donald Tomaskovic-Devey 250

Preface

A society must come to grips at some point with its
failures. The United States is an affluent society
that tolerates the impoverishment of one-eighth of
its population. Our social welfare responses to
poverty are typically half-hearted and punitive.
We do not like or trust the poor, perhaps because
poverty is so incongruous in an affluent society.
Our ideological and academic predilections are to
"blame the victim" rather than to confront systemic
failings. This volume confronts our failings as a
society by focusing on the creation of poverty by
normal economic and demographic processes and the
activities of the welfare state and politics in
ameliorating and occasionally creating poverty.

This book was born of my surprise and excitement
at the sheer volume of academic work on poverty and
social welfare being reported at sociological
conferences around the United States in 1985 and
1986. It seems as if sociologists in particular
are paying more attention to these issues than has
been typical in the past. This is not to say that
this book is a purely sociological treatment of
poverty and social welfare. All of the chapters to
follow are profoundly interdisciplinary regardless
of the academic affiliation of the authors. All of
the papers display, however, a sociological insight
into the social embeddedness of poverty and social
welfare programs in broader political economic and
cultural systems. Within this volume the poor are
not incongruous deviations in an affluent society.
Rather, poverty and our social responses to poverty
are generated by larger social forces.

Hopefully, this book will have many audiences. Teachers may wish to use it in advanced undergraduate and graduate level courses to introduce students to current debates about poverty and social welfare and to analytic strategies for resolving those debates. Economists, the main social science investigators of poverty, will find a somewhat different set of explanations and assumptions guiding these more sociological approaches to poverty and social policy. Sociologists and political scientists will find a rich and varied source of inspiration for future research. Finally, politicians, social policy analysts and activists will find not only a framework for understanding a frustrating and seemingly intractable social problem but also a series of loosely integrated policy proposals for addressing the failings of an affluent society.

Donald Tomaskovic-Devey

Acknowledgments

This collection was made possible by the splendid cooperation and hard work of the contributors. All of these papers are original contributions to this volume, many of which were edited and/or rewritten to better fit the theme of the volume. Jean Pittman did the wordprocessing and composition that produced this manuscript. Without her efforts the project simply would not have succeeded. Carol Gilbert helped with the manuscript as well.

I owe a particular debt of gratitude and respect to S. M. (Mike) Miller who, although not among the authors in this volume, has influenced greatly my approach to poverty and social welfare. To the extent that I have done a good intellectual job as editor he certainly deserves some of the credit.

Donald Tomaskovic-Devey

1

Poverty and Social Welfare in the United States

Donald Tomaskovic-Devey

This volume is about poverty. The chapters that follow represent some of the most current and informative research being done on poverty in the United States. The topics covered include who is poor, the antecedents of poverty on both the individual and social structural levels, some consequences of poverty, the role and limitations of the current U.S. welfare state in both the amelioration and (occasional) creation of poverty, and a series of policy recommendations for more effective assaults upon the problem of poverty in the United States. As such it is an ambitious book which endeavors to give the student of poverty and social welfare a broad look at the processes and policies associated with poverty in this country. The papers are serious pieces of research, clear headed, generally empirical, and well presented. For readers new to the field many myths that surround poverty and the welfare state will be dispelled. For academics active in the field some new ways of understanding and dealing with poverty and social policy will be outlined.

This introductory essay has two purposes. First, it will serve as a broad overview and introduction to understanding poverty and social welfare in the United States. As such, it will cover much territory quickly in order to give the reader a perspective with which to evaluate and understand the more substantive chapters that follow. The second purpose of this essay is to give the reader a road map that makes clear the location of the

research to follow on the broad landscape of
poverty and associated social policies. These
purposes will be accomplished simultaneously as I
foreshadow the insights of the papers to follow in
this overview essay.

UNDERSTANDING AND DEFINING POVERTY

Understanding Poverty

When we speak about the 'poor' who are we speaking
of?   What images are called to mind, what life
experiences are implicated, and what social costs
does the existence of a poor population imply for
the non-poor?   In the United States we have a
general imagery of a population that has few
material possessions, low income, often derived
from an inability or reluctance to get a job, and
homes in substandard even dangerous places. Poverty
is understood as both a cause and result of a host
of social ills such as teenage pregnancy, crime,
drug abuse and other types of socially undesirable
behavior. [1]
    These general social images suggest that poverty
is often conceptualized as both material
deprivation and a lack of social integration.
Material deprivation is, of course, the dominant
consequence of poverty for the individuals and
families who are poor. The social problems that
transcend the poor population and involve the whole
society are a consequence of the violence to the
self and family that material deprivation visits
upon those who are poor, particularly those who are
persistently poor. From this perspective poverty is
best understood as a social relationship between
the poor and the standards of living and behavior
commonly expected in the larger society. The poor
are stigmatized, socially isolated and their sense
of self-efficacy threatened (if not destroyed) by
being unable to participate fully in a society
characterized by and which values highly affluence.
I do not mean the affluence of the very rich but
the simple affluence of normal social
participation. Having the money to spend on clothes
for school, church and social visiting is denied
the poor. Travel to work, to the homes of friends

and relatives, or to outings at the beach or lake on a hot summer day are denied to those without the money to afford a car or mass transportation. It is no wonder that we see large concentrations of the materially poor in cities with good mass transportation systems. Here at least mass transportation reduces the cost of social participation and so acts to ameliorate the social experience of material deprivation.

Poverty then is most damaging to the individual, and by extension to the society, when it is relative to the standards of the society, and acts to isolate the poor from normal social participation and so integration. This relative notion of poverty, first suggested by Victor Fuchs (1967) and more recently elaborated upon and empirically investigated by the British sociologist Peter Townsend (1979), suggests that it is not absolute levels of material deprivation which define the poverty experience but the social isolation that results from low income. The single mother or aged woman who is confined to a small apartment because she hasn't the resources to travel far from home, whose income is spent on rent, utilities and food (in that order) is relatively isolated from participation in the culture. The teenager who lives on the street hustling for money is similarly isolated from participation in mainstream culture. In the creative and occasionally dangerous business of finding alternative, perhaps even illegal, ways of surviving emotionally as well as physically, this young adult often threatens the sensibilities and occasionally the safety of the non-poor who encounter him or her.[2]

If we want to understand poverty then it should be as a social condition, characterized by isolation from participation in the culture. The poor are isolated primarily because their low level of material resources, makes normal social activity difficult at best. In the United States money is the key to social participation, people with little access to money spend everything they have on survival with little to spare for visiting friends, relatives and churches, much less in long term investments in education, travel to distant work places or the acquisition of stable job histories.

4

Social isolation does not imply, however, physical isolation from other people. The poor often work in paid jobs and form communities of their own. It is not total isolation from others that creates this social notion of poverty but rather the limited character of social participation.

Defining Poverty

The preceding discussion leads to a simple definition of poverty. The poor are those people whose income is below the level needed for normal social participation. People whose income is below this level will tend to be both materially deprived and socially isolated, which may lead to low levels of self-esteem and the potential for anti-social behavior.

This social definition of poverty is helpful in understanding the individual and social consequences of poverty. It is not, however, the definition of poverty commonly used in empirical studies of U.S. poverty, including those in this book, nor in the creation of social policies to deal with the poor. The definition of poverty in U.S. policy and research focuses not on relative but on absolute material deprivation in the population. The U.S. poverty line is, in fact, a nutritional baseline for physical survival. It was originally computed in the early sixties as three times the cost of an emergency economy food plan (Orshansky, 1965). The food plan covered the bare minimum of caloric intake for short term survival if the shopper was careful to buy only the cheapest foods with the highest nutritional payoff (e.g. rice and beans; milk and potatoes). The plan was multiplied by three on the assumption that about one-third of the typical American household income went to buy food. This nutritional survival definition remains the definition of U.S. poverty, it has been adjusted since its inception in 1964 only for inflation and how it treats farm families.

Does this mean that the 31 million people who are officially below the poverty line in the United States are slowly starving to death? In general it does not, although of course many are hungry at some time. The poor actually spend more than a

third of their income on food and so the official
definition understates the nutritional threat of
being officially poor. In addition, while the
social definition of poverty implies social
isolation, this isolation is relative rather than
absolute and the poor are often aided with gifts of
food and services from friends, relatives and
occasionally public and private agencies. These in-
kind transfers are not counted as income even
though they clearly act to support those who are
poor. From this point of view, the current poverty
line can be best understood as a minimal and harsh
standard of living. While a literal nutritional
interpretation of the poverty line probably
overstates the amount of hunger and physical
deterioration associated with poverty, the poor in
the United States are likely to be hungry regularly
(when money runs out or when in-kind transfers from
relatives or friends are unavailable) and the
physical health of the poor is lower than that of
the rest of the population. The poor die younger,
spend more time sick in bed, and are much more
likely to give birth to babies who will die in the
first year of life. See the extensive bibliography
in Chalfant (1985) and the Arendell (Chapter 3) and
Sarri and Russell (Chapter 9) contributions to this
volume for more on the relationship between poverty
and health.
    What then is the relationship between the
official absolute definition of poverty that most
studies and social policies use, and the relative
social conception of poverty developed above? In
general, the relative definition of poverty
suggests that many more people are "socially" poor
than are "officially" poor. That is, non-
participation in the culture, social isolation, and
the resultant violence to self, family and society
is common at incomes above those required for
physical survival. Physical survival requires a
quantifiable number of calories and protection from
environmental threats such as the weather. Social
survival is more expensive because it requires the
ability to participate as a member in the society.
As such the official poverty line understates the
amount of relative poverty in the society. On the
other hand, some of the officially poor, those who

live close to family, friends, and other cheap
sources of social support and social integration
may not be socially impoverished.

The gap between official and relative poverty
is probably one explanation of why the problems
commonly associated with poverty such as teenage
pregnancy, absent and irresponsible fathers, and
crime do not respond to social policies targeted at
physical survival. The fact that the social
problems associated with poverty have tended to
rise even in the face of social spending and social
policies targeted at the amelioration (if not
elimination) of material poverty probably has more
to do with the fact that the poor in the United
States are poorer now relative to the rest of the
population than they were when the poverty line was
originally set in 1964.

The distinction between the two definitions of
poverty can be overdone. The official poverty line
is a reasonable indicator of the level of material
deprivation in the society. As such it gives us a
low estimate of the amount of relative poverty, and
a high estimate of the level of malnutrition in the
population. When we compare the poverty rates of
demographic groups, or regions, the poverty line
gives us a reasonably accurate idea of who is at
greater risk for poverty, where poverty is
concentrated in the society, and the like. Like
many other analysts I find the official poverty
line a useful measure for research purposes as long
as it is treated as a rough estimate rather than a
precise one. The Garfinkel and McLanahan (Chapter
2), and Tomaskovic-Devey (Chapter 5) contributions
to this volume use the official poverty line as
their empirical indicator. Maume (Chapter 4), on
the other hand, uses a variable he calls a "poverty
buffer" in order to investigate the individual and
labor market factors that put people at risk for
poverty. His poverty buffer is basically a measure
of how far some one is from the poverty line. The
reasoning for a measure of this sort should become
clear in the next section of this essay.

EXPLAINING POVERTY

We needed a definition of poverty in order to study
it intelligently. The point is not, however, to
define poverty, but to explain it in terms of
ultimate causes. Why are people poor? Where does
poverty come from? There are a variety of answers
to these questions. I will discuss each briefly
starting with the view that is most widely embodied
in the practice and organization of the U.S.
welfare state.

Individual Level Explanations of Poverty

There have been three general theoretical
orientations prevalent in the study of poverty. In
the first, people are poor because of some personal
or cultural defect. Blacks, Puerto Ricans and the
poor in general have been characterized as
participating in a "culture of poverty" (Glazer and
Moynihan, 1970; Lewis, 1968; Banfield, 1970). In
this perspective people are poor because that is
all that they know how to be. The poor it is
argued have distinctive maladaptive values and
behaviors which are largely self perpetuating. As
such the culture of poverty explanation of poverty
is generally congruent with the widespread American
middle class impatience with and tendency to blame
the poor for their circumstances. As Gotsch-Thomson
shows in Chapter Ten, the Reagan administration has
done much ideological work to revive this notion.

In the second approach people are poor because
of some personal characteristic that makes them
less competitive in the labor market. Low
education credentials, primary allegiance to the
family rather than the workplace, inadequate
intelligence or motivation are some examples of
this type of analysis and it is quite consistent
with the culture of poverty explanation (e.g.,
Banfield, 1970). This approach to poverty is
implied although not investigated (Hodge and
Laslett, 1980) in the status attainment tradition
in sociology (e.g., Blau and Duncan, 1967; Hauser
and Featherman, 1976). In this tradition poverty
is merely a case of low income achievement (Hauser,
1980). Economists in the human capital tradition

(Becker, 1964) have been more directly involved in studying poverty and share with status attainment researchers the tendency to identify personal characteristics (particularly education, work experience and personal motivation) as they determine labor market competitiveness as the causes of poverty. See the review in Morgan (1980) of economists' research on poverty; see also Morgan (1974) and Duncan and Morgan (1978, 1979) for some of the central ongoing poverty research by economists. The labor market competitiveness approach differs, however, from the culture of poverty analysis in that non-cultural sources of individual level differences, such as racial discrimination and sex-role socialization are potential explanations for poverty as well.

Structural Explanations of Poverty

In a third approach to poverty, the poor are described as having limited economic opportunity, either because of present labor market segmentation based on sex and race or because of the amount of overall opportunity in the locality in which they reside (Wachtel, 1972; Gordon, 1972; Edwards, Reich, and Gordon 1975; Gordon, Edwards and Reich, 1982). Segmentation research has stressed the theoretical centrality of the demand side of the labor market in the creation of poverty. Labor market segmentation research has helped focus the awareness of researchers on the characteristics of jobs, industries, and labor markets and the concomitant realization that employment does not preclude poverty. The empirical research in this tradition has focused on the contextual effects of employment location; characteristics of industries, firms, and jobs that lead to the creation of good and bad jobs (see Bibb and Form, 1977; Beck et al., 1978, 1980; Kalleberg et. al, 1981; among many others). Some researchers (Morril and Wohlenberg, 1973; Gordon, 1972; Parcel and Mueller, 1983; Reif, 1986) have extended this line of reasoning to a focus on the geographic distribution of poverty, arguing that because of patterns of uneven industrial development and labor conflict localities and regions vary in their distribution of opportunity. In this volume Maume (Chapter 4) and Tomaskovic-Devey (Chapter 5) build directly upon the structural insights of segmentation and geographical researchers.

A few academics (Gans, 1972; Schiller, 1976; Gordon, 1972; Wachtel, 1971; Sackery, 1973), have argued either that the existence of a poor population is functional for the society in general or for economic elites, even though it is clearly dysfunctional for the poor. What are the positive functions that a poor population provides other populations in society? First, the unemployed poor provide a reserve labor force for employers. In times of employment expansion the unemployed poor can be drawn into the labor market at low wages. When the economy contracts across the business cycle these same people are fired. In addition to providing a variable labor force for the contraction and expansion of employment in a locality the unemployed poor by their presence in a labor market keep the wages of the employed from rising too quickly in periods of economic expansion (Marx, 1976:781-793). This analysis suggests that the elimination of poverty may not be a goal shared with equal enthusiasm by all members of U.S. society. If the elimination of poverty requires eliminaing low wage jobs than many employers (and some consumers) will suffer.

Of course, many poor people work. In 1979 over 30 percent of families in poverty across the United States participated in the labor force at some time, and for families with a member between the ages of twenty-five and sixty-four the figure was over 50 percent.[3] In some industries, according to both Hodson (1983) and Tomaskovic-Devey (1984), between 30 and 50 percent of available jobs typically pay poverty level wages. Thus, material poverty is not exclusively understood in terms of exclusion from the labor force but also in terms of the pattern of participation. See also Wachtel and Betse (1972), Gordon (1972), and Bluestone et al. (1973) for this argument. In 1985 a family of four with two wage earners at or near the minimum wage, working a combined sixty hours a week and fifty-two weeks a year would have earned a family income below the poverty line. The normal functioning of the private economy, benefits from the existence of an unemployed labor force as well as the creation of an array of low quality jobs. In sum, poverty level positions in the social structure are the product of the process of economic organization as they are currently constituted.

We can think of the individual level causes of poverty as being the interaction between personal characteristics (such as education, experience, sex, race and perhaps culture) and the intensity of sex and race segmentation of employment and the number of poverty level positions in a locality. The chapter by Maume tries to estimate an individual level model for the poverty buffer which includes both human capital, job and local industrial structure as antecedents to the poverty of individual women. The chapter by Tomaskovic-Devey explores the various causes of the amount of poverty in labor markets.

Race and Sex

The two best predictors of official poverty status in the United States are sex and race. Being female and being black vastly increase the probability of being poor. How can we understand these status associations with poverty? Individual level explanations suggest that we look for cultural, attitudinal or human capital differences between males and females, whites and blacks to account for aggregate differences in poverty rates. Structural level explanations suggest that we should focus on the different patterns of opportunity available to women and men, blacks and whites.

Discrimination in hiring by job and industry as well as structural barriers to labor force participation do seem to account for part of the higher rates of black and female poverty. In addition, blacks are much more likely to live in low opportunity, high poverty localities (the south and urban ghettos) and the degree of racial discrimination in a locality is associated with the size of the black population (Blalock, 1967; Szymanski, 1976; Lieberson, 1980; Reich, 1981). As the black population size rises (relative to the size of the white population), blacks pose an increasing economic threat and the level of

discrimination (particularly in terms of the types
of jobs that are available) rises. In addition, one
of the historical legacies of racial discrimination
is lower human capital for the black population
overall, both in terms of education credentials and
typical patterns of job histories. While structural
explanations of race differences in poverty are
widespread and receive a great deal of empirical
support, cultural explanations of race differences
are still alive and well in the academic as well as
popular conceptions of poverty (see particularly
Murray, 1984).

    For women the pattern is different. Everywhere
the amount of labor market discrimination against
women is high. The primary mechanism of labor
market sex discrimination is through the sex-
segregation of jobs (Treiman and Hartmann, 1981)
which is as high as 96 percent in the most recent
study using unusually detailed job-title and firm
level data (Bielby and Baron, 1986). Almost all
women are employed in "female" jobs which are
typically low wage. The effect is that it is
difficult for single women to earn a non-poverty
level wage. For single women with children the
difficulties are higher still. Socialization
(rather than cultural) explanations of female
poverty are still prevalent, as well, with
arguments that women have lower commitment to the
labor market then men because of sex-role
socialization.

    Many of the analyses in this volume (Garfinkel
and McLanahan, Maume, Arendell, Rank, Sarri and
Russell) focus on female poverty precisely because
both poverty and social welfare policy are
concentrated in and on single women and their
children. The analysis of patriarchal social
relations suggested in Chapter Three (Arendell)
helps us understand the unique place of single
female heads of households in the problems of
poverty. Low wages for women in the workplace
explains why single women are disproportionally
poor. Why are married women less likely to be
poor? Obviously, because they have access to the
higher wages of their husbands. Female poverty in
a patriarchal society directly reflects the
traditional subordination of women to men in the
household and the workplace. Employers have

traditionally paid low wages to women because they were seen (and often acted) as a temporary, secondary labor force with primary commitments and duties to their families. These low female wages keep women as a group dependent on their husbands earnings for survival. In addition women, but not husbands, have primary responsibility for maintaining the household including children. When male income is high enough the job of wife and mother can be a full-time one. When family finances are tight female labor force participation, often part-time and generally low waged, rises while household responsibilities remain. Males gain in the labor force through high wages and at home through female subordination.

What happens when families dissolve through divorce or never form (e.g. illegitimate births)? Women tend to continue to have household, particularly childcare, responsibility but no longer have access to high male earnings. The result is, of course, likely to be poverty. The poverty of single mothers can be either unemployed poverty or employed, but at low wage, poverty. The trade off between employment and unemployment has to do with the availability of child care, local wage rates, child support from the father, the woman's earning capacity and government income supports. Thus the high incidence of poverty among women with children, but without husbands, is a reflection of the patriarchal relations in both families and the labor market. In addition, as Arendell discusses in Chapter Three, efforts to ameliorate poverty have often tended to reflect those patriarchal relations as well.

THE WELFARE STATE AND POVERTY REDUCTION

The Deserving and Undeserving Poor

The role of government in responding to the material needs of poor people has always been limited and unenthusiastic in the United States.[5] This essay is not the place for a detailed history of the U.S. welfare state (see Patterson 1981 for a good recent history) but a quick overview is in order.

At the turn of the century there was no federal
level provision for the needs of poor people. What
programs were available tended to be local and in
most cases charitable rather than state run. These
attempts to deal with the poor focused on moral
reform, particularly the cultural integration of
immigrants from Europe. Income and food supports
were modest and discouraged as potential threats to
self-sufficiency. A common distinction was made
between the poor and paupers (the dependent poor).
While early poverty reformers were aware of the
structural sources of poverty in the economy their
solutions tended to focus on changing the
behaviors, attitudes and values of the poor
themselves.   Charity was generally restricted to
widows with children under the assumption that it
was better for families to be hungry with a working
father than pauperized. Similarly, charity to
abandoned or unwed mothers was discouraged because
if might threaten the integrity of the family. In
essence the operating theory behind early poor
relief was a culture of poverty one, in which the
poor rather than the system were to be reformed.
In addition, husband headed family forms and the
role of a strong work ethic were seen as having
higher priority than the subsidization of the poor
population, regardless of how destitute. Great
faith was placed in economic growth to eliminate
the structural sources of poverty.

The creation of the U.S. welfare state, as we
currently know it, was a response by the federal
government to the great depression and the
political agitation of the poor for income security
(Patterson, 1981; Piven and Cloward, 1971). The
three basic programs that were enacted --Social
Security for the aged and disabled, Unemployment
Insurance, and Aid to Dependent Children (ADC)--
while extended begrudgingly and after much
political agitation among elites as well as from
below (Quadagno, 1984), largely reproduced the
assumptions about the primacy of the work ethic and
family form of earlier in the century. In the case
of social security and ADC income supports were
extended only to the deserving poor, those too old,
too young or too incapacitated to work.
Unemployment insurance was only extended for a
limited period to adults who had already

demonstrated that they were committed workers. The limit on the time you could collect unemployment insurance insured that no non-aged, non-disabled adults would become dependent on welfare. The logic of the U.S. welfare state at its inception was to make distinctions between the deserving and undeserving poor, in order to extend some income supports without undermining the work ethic of adult men and women. Poor families without children, or poor families with fathers present were undeserving and excluded from participation.

A new profession of social workers arose in this context to administer the emerging welfare state. Social work has struggled to create an environment of professional control in the workplace, while attempting to screen out the undeserving poor and reform the culturally poor in an environment of low political support.

The War on Poverty

Beginning in the Kennedy administration, and vastly accelerated under Johnson and Nixon, the U.S. welfare state expanded greatly in the 1960's and early Seventies. There was a growing realization that economic growth would not eradicate all poverty and that a "war on poverty" would be necessary if the 39 million Americans estimated to be poor in the early sixties were to be reduced. At the same time the civil rights movement sensitized political elites to the needs of poor blacks in particular (Piven and Cloward, 1971). On the other hand, the level of political unrest and pressure was lower in the Sixties than it had been in the Thirties, when the modern welfare state was created. Another plausible source of the elite readiness to pursue the "war on poverty" can be found in the fear that government budget surpluses were permanent and potential threats to the long-term health of the economy. In short, the government had money to spend, ushering in an era of "cost free liberalism" (see Wilson and Aponte, 1985 and Miller and Tomaskovic-Devey, 1983 for this argument). While economic growth did not eliminate poverty positions it did provide the resources (via tax revenues) to mount a war on poverty.

The war on poverty included an increase in the amount of money spent on income transfers, with liberalization in eligibility requirements and the expansion of welfare benefits to adult members of poor households with children (Aid to Dependent Children became Aid to Families with Dependent Children), and the creation of new forms of income transfer, most prominent being medicaid (for the non-aged poor), medicare (for the aged regardless of poverty status), housing subsidies and the food stamp program. This extension of the range and generosity of the welfare state (although most poor families that receive benefits remain under the poverty line in terms of household income) largely reproduced the deserving/undeserving poor distinction of the earlier programs. Benefits were, however, increased, and to some extent the definition of deserving was broadened to include the mothers of poor children, the nutritional needs of the near poor, and in a few states AFDC payments were extended to families with husbands present. New programs tended to extend benefits in kind (e.g. food stamps or medicaid) rather than in cash, mirroring the suspicion that the poor were culturally or morally deficient and could not be trusted with cash.[6]

A second thrust of the "war on poverty" was into job training programs. Initially funded by the Manpower Development and Training Act in 1962, job training programs operated on the assumption that the poor needed to be given the human capital and motivational equipment necessary for stable employment. It was, again an individualist level solution to poverty in which the goal was to reform the culturally poor into good stable working class workers. Since the enactment of the Manpower Development and Training Act there has been a constant tension in the creation of social welfare policy between policies targeted at income transfer and those designed to teach skills. Skill training is attractive in that it attempts to give the poor the skills necessary for economic independence. Unfortunately its assumptions about the antecedents of poverty are entirely individualistic. Training ignores the availability of jobs and the quality of jobs for which the poor are being trained. As Michael Morris points out (Chapter Seven) job or

skill training programs tend to make a long chain
of dubious assumptions about the sources of poverty
which in practice make their payoff uncertain at
best.

The War on the Poor

The "war on poverty" has been roundly criticized as
an expensive experiment that failed. While poverty
was reduced (see the data presented in the
Garfinkel and McLanahan, and Tomaskovic-Devey
chapters) it was not eliminated, and poverty began
to grow again both absolutely and as a proportion
of the U.S. population in the mid-seventies. In a
series of labor market experiments to test the
feasibility of a guaranteed minimum income some
politically disturbing findings surfaced. In
general, as the security and size of the guaranteed
income went up, husbands and wives reduced their
hours of work and the divorce rate went up as well
(see Robbins, 1985 for a good recent summary of
this research). This data has been interpreted by
conservative critics of the welfare state as
evidence that transfer payments destroy families,
reduce work effort and ultimately will create a
dependent population. Although this argument has
been made in many places it has been most
forcefully and best presented by Charles Murray
(1984).   His argument is that generous welfare
payments have undermined the work ethic,
particularly for young black males, leading to high
rates of single female headed households, who
become dependent upon the state and culturally
isolated.   These female headed households in turn
produce a new generation of dependent, culturally
poor children. Intergenerational welfare families,
rising crime, illegitimacy and single mothers are
all symptoms for Murray of the (to use the turn of
the century term) "pauperization" of the poor. The
worst fears of critics of the welfare state, the
creation of a dependent, subculture of poverty, are
argued to have been the unanticipated consequence
of the war on poverty. The specter of a crime
infested, morally degenerate, (black) underclass
haunts the nightmares of conservative analysts.

Did the war on poverty create poverty? The empirical research seems to say no. (See especially the arguments in McLanahan et al., 1985 for this evidence.) First and probably most importantly as Chapter Eight by Rank demonstrates, almost all AFDC participants are short term. Even the most long-term poor, young single women with two or more young children, are generally poor for less than eight years. Recent research has demonstrated that poverty is widespread in the society, with up to fifty percent of the population being officially poor at some time during their lifetime. The greatest exposure to poverty occurs during childhood, when often all that stands between children and poverty is the presence of a father. When households dissolve through desertion or divorce (and almost half of new marriages fail) children and their mothers are quite likely to spend some time poor. Other times of high exposure to poverty for men and women are during periods of unemployment associated with the business cycle and regional patterns of industrial change.

The fact that the poor are not a stable population (although some people are poor for long periods), and that many people are at risk to be poor at some point in their life time explains Maume's use (in Chapter 4) of a "poverty buffer" rather than the poverty line as his indicator of poverty. The "poverty buffer" indicator helps sensitize the researcher and the reader to the reality that poverty is a widespread experience, not limited to some culturally deprived sub-population.

While the income maintenance experiments did show some reduction of work effort associated with higher government income guarantees, as the conservatives have argued, those reductions were typically small. In the most extreme cases they amounted to husbands reducing their work effort by one week a year, and wives as well as single mothers reducing their work effort by three weeks a year (Robbins, 1985). These are small reductions in work effort and the income maintenance experiments were much more generous and unrestricted than AFDC is, suggesting that any work reductions from current government aid are small indeed. Chapter Five by Tomaskovic-Devey, as well

as Chapter 9 by Sarri and Russell suggest that the
level of AFDC payments is only weakly associated
with work effort. In addition, Tomaskovic-Devey
finds that cities with higher welfare payments also
create better quality jobs, thus offsetting any
labor supply effect. Sanders' contribution to this
volume (Chapter Six) shows, contrary to the
conservative argument, that increases in welfare
support levels are unassociated with growth in the
poverty rate for the fifty U.S. states in the 1960-
1970 period but may have inceased marginally the
level of poverty in the 1970-1980 period.

Sanders research also shows an association
between increases in the level of AFDC payments and
the formation of single female headed households
with children. This is consistent with the evidence
in the income maintenance experiments, and with the
great rise in single female headed households in
the last twenty years among both blacks and whites
(see Garfinkel and McLanahan, Chapter Two). Is it
possible that welfare payments targeted at women
with children but without husbands increases the
formation of single female households? The
evidence is by no means conclusive on this question
but the relationship seems plausible. Danziger et
al. (1982) report a small increase in the formation
of female headed households associated with
increases in welfare payments. While raising the
level of income supports does not seem to increase
the level of poverty much if at all, it is quite
possible to argue that it increases the
independence of young women from subordination to
their husband's and father's households. If this is
the case, it may or may not be disturbing depending
on your point of view. On the other hand, low
earnings opportunities for young men, particularly
in the seventies (Dooley and Gottschalk, 1985), and
an increasing emphasis on the potential and rights
of the individual may, as Ehrenreich (1985) has
suggested, have already reduced the commitment of
men to their families and welfare supports merely
make it easier to walk away. In general, the
conservative attack on the generosity of the
welfare state as anti-work, anti-family may be
correct in form but not in emphasis. That is,
raising welfare payments may reduce work effort and
encourage the formation of single female headed

families but very little of the variation in poverty or household composition is a function of welfare payment levels.

It is not necessary for the conservative interpretation of the "war on poverty" to be correct for it to be persuasive to policy makers, particularly conservative governments like that of the Reagan administration. Conservatives have never been enthusiastic about support for the poor as both Morris (Chapter Seven) and Gotsch-Thomson (Chapter Ten) suggest. The Reagan administration in particular, has been aggressive in promoting a conservative ideological attack upon the welfare state as it is currently constituted.

The conservative ideological attack has, of course, had concrete impacts on the current constitution of U.S. social welfare policy. During the Carter years average AFDC payments were allowed to decline relative to inflation scaling back the level of income transfers to the poor (Miller and Tomaskovic-Devey, 1983). During the Reagan administration many families, particularly the working poor have been disqualified from participation in the food stamp and AFDC programs (see Chapter Nine). Poverty has been rising sharply since 1981, although Reagan attacks on the welfare state must share the blame with a weak economy that has been unusually effective at producing poverty level jobs and unemployment. Sarri and Russell (Chapter Nine) report on one aspect of a larger project that evaluates the effect of the Reagan budget and eligibility cuts in support of the poor. Their findings of clear health related damage caused by the Reagan attacks on the welfare state undercut substantially the argument that the safety net remains for the "truly needy."

CONCLUSION

Currently the welfare state is under attack because (among other reasons) its promises remain unfulfilled.[7] The failure to eradicate poverty confirms the fear of critics of the welfare state that income transfers cause more problems than they cure. Did the "war on poverty" accomplish anything? Of course it did. Gottschalk and Danziger (1985) demonstrate that in the 1969-1979 period that the effect of income transfers (the welfare state) upon the poverty rate was roughly equivalent to that of changes in the distribution of income from the economy. As Garfinkel and McLanahan (Chapter Two) show the dramatic initial reductions in poverty across the 1960s primarily reflect the expansion of social security to nearly all old people. The poverty rate for those over sixty-five is now lower than it is for those under sixty-five. The tone of this essay may have implied to the reader that the welfare state cannot address the needs of the poor. This is not my intent and would clearly be an incorrect conclusion. Social Security is a perfect example of how the welfare state can eliminate much poverty. In this program eligibility is widespread and transfer payments are high enough to lift most recipients above the poverty line.

The welfare state has lifted many of the elderly out of poverty while being much less effective with the non-elderly. This is understandable, however, if you take into account the low level of support actually available as income transfer payments. In no state are income transfers alone (for the non-aged) high enough to lift a poor family up to the poverty line, and in only a few states can AFDC, food stamps, and housing subsidies combined bring a family above the poverty line. Most importantly, the welfare state has never addressed the structural economic antecedents of poverty and what benefits are extended to the working age poor are pegged at levels low enough to insure that welfare does not undermine the incentive to work. In conservative, low wage states, particularly in the south, AFDC payments are extremely low. Many of the chapters to follow provide us with clues and suggestions for more effective anti-poverty policies than either the "war on poverty" or the "war on the poor" have provided. The concluding chapter summarizes these policy implications and places them in a wider political context.

Notes

1. This essay is necessarily brief in character. For the reader interested in more inclusive overviews of the social, economic and political history of poverty and social welfare in the United States I would recommend Patterson (1981), Piven and Cloward (1971), Murray (1984), Wilson and Aponte (1985) and Chalfant (1985) and the references therein. This essay has a definite point of view. It stresses the structural antecedents of poverty and to some extent neglects more individual based explanations. These individual based explanations are, however, dominant in most discussions and don't require another champion here.

2. While poverty is associated with various social ills it would be grossly misleading to argue either that all poor people are criminals or that all criminality stems from poverty. Social behaviors, such as illegitimacy, crime or unemployment, always have a variety of antecedent causes. Similarly, social conditions (e.g. poverty) can lead to a variety of behaviors.

3. My calculations from the 1980 Public Use Sample of the United States Census.

4. It would be misleading to imply that structural and individualist perspectives on poverty are mutually exclusive. Rather, the structure of local opportunity defines the likely level of poverty in a locality, and the individual level distribution of human capital and perhaps cultural motives sorts people into or out of poverty.

5. The same cannot be said for social work professionals who have always had a broad intellectual and political committment to the welfare state. In addition, social workers while generally emphasizing individual level antecedents of poverty have always had a broader structural perspectives as well.

6. Some have argued that in-kind benefits, particularly medicaid and medicare, if counted as income would eliminate poverty. This seems absurd because the sicker you get the richer you seem. See Wilson and Aponte (1985) for a good discussion of in-kind transfers and the definition of poverty.

7. This statement is somewhat simplistic. As Gotsch-Thomson argues in Chapter Ten the ideological attack upon the welfare state is clearly important. On the other hand, the U.S. has never enthusiatically supported the poor. A useful political model of the U.S. welfare state is a cyclic one, in which the needs of the poor are responded to after periods of unrest, protest, and electoral threat (Piven and Cloward, 1979; Schram and Turbett, 1983), and contract in more stable periods (Piven and Cloward, 1979) or when business needs "crowd out" welfare spending (O'Connor, 1973; Piven and Cloward, 1982; Miller and Tomaskovic-Devey, 1983).

Bibliography

Banfield, Edward C. The Unheavenly City. Boston: Little Brown. 1970.

Beck, E. M., Patrick M. Horan and Charles M. Tolbert, II. "Stratification in a dual economy: a sectoral model of earnings determination." American Sociological Review 43:704-20. 1978.

_____ "Industrial segmentation and labor market discrimination." Social Problems 28:13-30. 1980.

Becker, Gary. Human Capital. New York: Columbia. 1964.

Bibb, Robert and William Form. "The effects of industrial, occupational and sex stratification on wages in blue-collar markets." Social Forces 55:974-96. 1977.

Bielby, William T. and James N. Baron. "Men and women at work: sex segregation and statistical discrimination." American Journal of Sociology 91:759-799. 1986.

Blalock, Hubert. Toward a Theory of Minority Group Relations. New York: Wiley. 1967.

Blau, Peter and Otis D. Duncan. The American Occupational Structure. New York: Wiley. 1967.

Bluestone, Barry, William M. Murphy and Mary Stevenson. Low Wages and the Working Poor. Ann Arbor, MI: University Publications, University of Michigan. 1973.

Chalfant, Paul H. The Sociology of Poverty in the United States. Westport, CT: Greenwood Press. 1985.

Danziger, Sheldon, G. Jackson, S. Schwartz, and E. Smolensky. "Work and welfare as determinants of female poverty and household headship." Quarterly Journal of Economics 97:519-34. 1982.

Dooley, Martin and Peter Gottschalk. "The increasing proportion of men with low earnings in the United States." Demography. 22:25-34. 1985.

Duncan, G and J. Morgan (eds.). Five Thousand American Families: Patterns of Economic Progress, Vol. 6. Ann Arbor, MI:Institute for Social Research. 1978.

_____ Five Thousand American Families: Patterns of Economic Progress, Vol. 7. Ann Arbor, MI: Institute for Social Research. 1979.

Ehrenreich, Barbara. The Hearts of Men: American Dreams and the Flight From Commitment. NY: Doubleday. 1984.

Edwards, Richard, Michael Reich, and David Gordon (eds.). Labor Market Segmentation. Lexington, MA: D.C. Heath. 1975.

Fuchs, Victor. "Redefining poverty and redistributing income." The Public Interest 8:88-95. 1967.

Gans, Herbert. "The positive functions of poverty." American Journal of Sociology 78:275-289. 1972.

Glazer, Nathan and Daniel P. Moynihan. Beyond the Melting Pot. Cambridge, MA :MIT Press. 1970.

Gordon, David. Theories of Poverty and Unemployment. Lexington, MA:D.C. Heath. 1972.

Gordon, David, Michael Reich and Richard Edwards. Segmented Work, Divided Workers: The Historical Transformation of Labor in the United States. New York: Cambridge University Press. 1982.

Gottschalk, Peter and Sheldon Danziger. "A framework for evaluating the effects of economic growth and transfer on poverty." American Economic Review 75:153-161. 1985.

24

Hauser, Robert and David Featherman. The Process of Stratification. New York: Academic Press. 1977.

Hauser, Robert. "On 'stratification in a dual economy'." American Sociological Review 4:702-712. 1980.

Hodge, Robert and Barbara Laslett. "Poverty and status attainment," in V. Covello (ed.) Poverty and Public Policy: An Evaluation of Social Science Research. Cambridge, MA: Schenkman. 1980.

Hodson, Randy. Worker's Earnings and Corporate Economic Structure. New York: Academic. 1983.

Kalleberg, Arne, Michael Wallace, and Robert Althauser. "Economic segmentation, worker power, and income inequality." American Journal of Sociology 87:651-83. 1981.

Lewis, Oscar. LaVida. New York:Vintage. 1968.

Lieberson, Stanley. A Piece of the Pie: Black and White Immigrants since 1880. Berkeley, CA: University of California Press. 1980.

Marx, Karl. Capital: A Critique of Political Economy, Volume 1, Ben Fowkes (tr.), New York: Random House. 1976.

McLanahan, Sara, Glen Cain, Michael Olneck, Irving Piliavin, Sheldon Danziger and Peter Gottschalk "Are we losing ground?" Focus. 8,3:1-12. 1985.

Miller, S. M. and Donald Tomaskovic-Devey. Recapitalizing America: Alternatives to the Corporate Distortion of National Policy. Boston, MA: Routledge and Kegan Paul. 1983.

Morgan, James N. "Poverty research on economic status and inequality." in Vincent Covello (ed.) Poverty and Public Policy: An Evaluation of Social Science Research. Boston: National Academy of Sciences, G.K. Hall. 1980.

_____ Five Thousand American Families: Patterns of Economic Progress, Vols 1-4. Ann Arbor, MI: Institute for Social Research. 1974.

Morrill, Richard and Ernest H. Wohlenberg. The Geography of Poverty in the United States. New York: McGraw-Hill. 1971.

Murray, Charles. Losing Ground: American Social Policy, 1950-1980. New York: Basic Books. 1984.

O'Connor James. The Fiscal Crisis of the State. New York: St. Martins Press. 1973.

Orshansky, Molly. "Counting the poor: another look at the poverty profile." Social Security Bulletin 28:3-29. 1965.

Parcel, Toby L. and Charles W. Mueller. Ascription and Labor Markets: Race and Sex Differences in Earnings. New York: Academic Press. 1983.

Patterson, James T. America's Struggle Against Poverty, 1900-1980. Cambridge, MA: Harvard University Press. 1981.

Piven, Francis Fox, and Richard A. Cloward. Regulating the Poor: The Functions of Public Welfare. New York: Academic Press. 1971.

_____ Poor Peoples Movements. New York: Vintage Press. 1979

_____ The New Class War. New York: Basic Books. 1982.

Quadagno, Jill S. "Welfare capitalism and the Social Security Act 1984 of 1935." American Sociological Review 49:632-647.

Reich, Michael. Racial Inequality: A Political Economic Analysis. Princeton, NJ: Princeton U. Press. 1981.

Reif, Linda. Farming and The Nonfarm Sector: An Analysis of Farm, Industry, and Socioeconomic Interrelationships. Ph.D. Dissertation, Department of Sociology, North Carolina State University. 1986.

Robins, Philip. "A Comparison of the labor supply findings from four negative income tax experiments." Journal of Human Resources. 20:567-582. 1985.

Sackrey, Charles. The Political Economy of Urban Poverty. New York: Norton. 1973.

Schiller, Bradley R. The Economics of Poverty and Discrimination. Engelwood Cliffs, N.J.: Prentice Hall. 1976.

Schram, Sanford F. and J. Patrick Turbett. "Civil disorder and the welfare explosion: a two-step process." American Sociological Review 48:408-414. 1983.

Szymanski, Albert. "Racial discrimination and white gain." American Sociological Review 41:403-414. 1976.

26

Tomaskovic-Devey, Donald. Good Jobs, Bad Jobs, No Jobs: The Stratification Consequences of U.S. Industrial and Occupational Structure and Change, 1960-1980. unpublished Ph.D. dissertation, Boston University. 1984.

Townsend, Peter. Poverty in the United Kingdom : A Survey of Household Resources and Standards of Living. London: Allen Lane Books. 1979.

Treiman, Donald and Heidi Hartmann. Women, Work and Wages. Washington D.C.: National Academy Press. 1981.

Wachtel, Howard M. "Looking at poverty from a radical perspective." The Review of Radical Political Economy 3:1-19. 1971.

Wachtel, Howard M. and Charles Betsy. "Employment at low wages." The Review of Economics and Statistics 54:121-129. 1972 .

Wilson, William Julius and Robert Aponte. "Urban poverty." Annual Review of Sociology. 11:231-58. 1985.

2

The Feminization of Poverty: Nature, Causes, and a Partial Cure

Irwin Garfinkel and Sara McLanahan

The proportion of the poor who were women increased rapidly during the 1970s. This phenomenon was termed "the feminization of poverty" and was interpreted by many to mean that the economic condition of women was deteriorating. This paper demonstrates that this was not the case. The feminization of poverty resulted almost equally from the rapid growth in the prevalence of single mothers and from the decline in poverty rates among other groups, such as the aged. Nevertheless, poverty has been and continues to be widespread among female-headed families.

Poverty among single mothers can be attributed to the low earnings capacity of these women, the limited contributions that absent parents make to the households in which their children live, and inadequate public transfers.

One way in which the economic situations of female-headed families can be improved is by adoption of a Child Support Assurance System. Such a system would assure that those who parent children share their income with them; it would collect child support equitably; it would increase the economic well-being of children with a living absent parent; and it would reduce welfare costs and caseloads.

INTRODUCTION

In 1967 52% of the poor consisted of women, both married and single, and children living with single mothers. By 1978, the comparable figure was 63%.[1] This trend has attracted considerable attention in recent years among social scientists as well as the general public and has been labeled "the feminization of poverty." Some analysts have even predicted that if present trends continue ". . . the poverty population will be composed solely of women and their children by the year 2000."[2]

Although the term is catchy and the prediction startling, there has been surprisingly little analysis of the underlying nature and causes of the "feminization of poverty." Thus it is not clear whether the trend is due to declines in the standard of living of women (the popular interpretation) or to other causes, such as increases in the relative well-being of other groups or increases in the prevalence of female-headed families. To make the analysis manageable, we focus specifically on poverty among female-headed families with children. Although related, the trends and underlying causes of poverty among aged widows and single women without children are far from identical to those for single mothers. And therefore, a comparable analysis for these other groups would take us well beyond the scope of a single paper. (Chapter Three looks at poverty among other types of female headed households)[3]

We begin by looking at trends in poverty from 1967 to 1983. We address the following questions: (1) What are the trends underlying the increase in the proportion of the poor who live in female-headed families? (2) To what extent is the increase due to changes in the relative economic status of different groups and to what extent is it due to shifts in composition? And finally, (3) to what extent are the underlying trends likely to continue so as to produce what some have naively projected -- a poor population by the year 2000 which consists entirely of persons living in female-headed families?

The second section of the paper looks at the sources of income of female-headed families and asks to what extent their poverty is due to (1) the low earnings capacity of single mothers, (2) the inadequacy of private child support payments, and/or (3) the inadequacy of public transfers. The final section of this chapter discusses one potential cure for the feminization of poverty: the adoption of a new Child Support Assurance System.

THE FEMINIZATION OF POVERTY

In Table 2.1, the composition of the poverty population between 1967 to 1983 is broken down into four major demographic groups: female-headed families, two-parent families, the aged, and non-aged individuals without children.

The numbers in Table 2.1 clearly show that during the late 1960s and early 1970s poverty increasingly became associated with female-headed families. In 1967, 21% of the poor were living in female-headed households with children, whereas by 1978 the number had grown to 36%.

In view of all the attention devoted to the feminization of poverty, what is most striking about Table 1 is the reversal of the trend after 1978. Between 1978 and 1983 the proportion of the poor in female-headed families actually declined from 36% to 32%. Projecting from the more recent trend, we might conclude that somewhere around the year 2025, poverty among single mothers would be extinct. The conflicting predictions suggest that little is gained from looking at and crudely projecting trends in the demographic composition of the poor. If we want to understand what is at the root of the feminization of poverty and how far it is likely to go, we must look at the dynamics behind the shift in composition.

Trends in Poverty Rates: 1967-1983. Trends in the prevalence of poverty among female-headed families, two-parent families, the aged, and non-aged without children are reported in Figure 1 for the years 1967 through 1983. The prevalence

TABLE 2.1 Breakdown of Poverty Population by Household Type, 1967–1983

	Total Poor (in millions)	Female-Headed Households with Children	Two-Parent Households with Children	Aged Households	Nonaged Households without Children
1967	28.0	21.4%	41.4%	23.5%	13.7%
1968	25.4	24.0	39.8	22.2	13.9
1969	24.4	24.7	36.8	23.7	14.8
1970	25.6	26.7	36.1	22.1	15.1
1971	25.6	27.1	36.3	20.5	16.1
1972	24.5	30.0	34.7	18.7	16.6
1973	22.9	32.4	31.8	18.5	17.3
1974	20.3	32.4	34.3	16.8	16.5
1975	25.9	32.0	35.9	15.4	16.7
1976	25.0	33.6	32.6	15.9	18.3
1977	24.7	34.6	31.7	15.4	18.3
1978	24.5	35.6	29.8	15.7	18.8
1979	25.4	34.4	30.3	16.6	18.3
1980	29.3	33.2	33.2	15.9	17.7
1981	31.8	32.8	33.1	14.8	19.3
1982	34.5	32.5	36.3	13.0	20.4
1983	35.3	31.6	35.4	13.0	19.9

Source: Current Population Surveys, 1967–1983. Tables prepared by Christine Ross of Institute for Research on Poverty as background for the conference, "Poverty and Police-Retrospect and Prospects," Williamsburg, Va., December 1984.

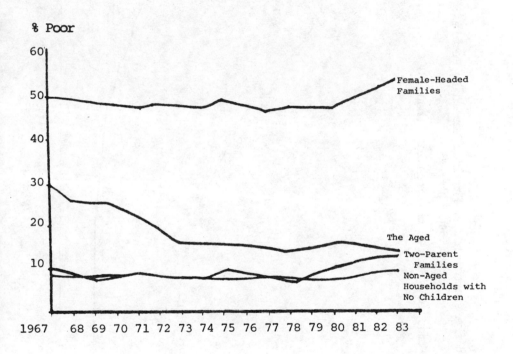

Figure 2.1
Poverty Rates for Female-Headed Families,
Two-Parent Families, the Aged, and Non-Aged with No Children
1967-1983

32

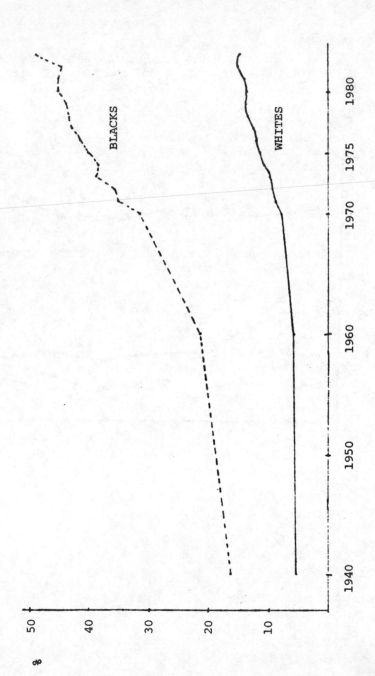

Figure 2.2

Trends in the Proposition of Families Headed by Females:
1940-1983

(Families with own children less than 18)

figures are based on the official definition of poverty and include income from cash transfer programs such as AFDC, Social Security, and Disability Insurance.

According to Figure 2.1, women and children in female-headed families have had the highest poverty rates in the country, at least since 1967. Indeed their lead has widened during the past 15 years. This is not to say that their absolute income position has deteriorated. In 1982, the proportion of single mothers who were poor was a little over 50%, just barely higher than in 1967. Note also that this figure actually declined during the early seventies only to rise again after 1979.

If the proportion of female-headed families who are poor has not increased, why do we observe the "feminization of poverty"? There are two reasons. The first is that while the economic status of single-mother families more or less stood still during this period, the situation of other groups improved substantially. Poverty among the aged dropped by about half between 1967 and 1974 in response to major increases in social security benefits.[4] Poverty among two-parent families and other groups also declined during the early part of the seventies. Because two-parent families are the most numerous group, a 30% decline in poverty for this group means a huge decrease in the absolute number of families in poverty. Figure 1 also indicates that the proportion of two-parent families who are poor have increased sharply after 1979. The 1980-1982 recession appears to be the principal cause. As normal economic growth resumes, most and perhaps all of this reversal may prove to be temporary. In contrast, past experience suggests that economic growth by itself is unlikely to be of much help to female-headed families.

The second reason for the increasing feminization of poverty is the tremendous growth in the prevalence of female-headed families. Figure 2.2 depicts the proportion of all families headed by women from 1940 through 1983. It shows that the proportion grew dramatically from 1960 through 1979, increasing from 6% to 14% among whites and from 16% and 46% among blacks. [By the late 1970s, however, there is some suggestion that the

growth rate in female headship had leveled off.]
If the growth ceases or the trend reverses, the
prediction that all poverty will be in female-
headed families by the year 2000 will obviously not
materialize.

A simple decomposition of the shifts in the
poverty population suggests that the feminization
of poverty between 1967 and 1978 was due to both
the decrease in poverty rates among other groups
and the increases in prevalence of female-headed
families. About half of the increase was due to
increased prevalence and about half was due to
decreases in the poverty rates of other groups.[5]

Our major findings may be briefly summarized as
follows:

- The increasing feminization of poverty which
  characterized the 1960s and 1970s was reversed
  by the 1980s.
- Poverty has been and continues to be widespread
  among   female-headed families.
- But, the feminization of poverty was not due to
  an increase in the impoverishment of female-
  headed families.
- Rather, the feminization of poverty was due
  almost equally to the rapid growth in the
  prevalence of single mothers and to the decline
  in poverty rates among other groups.
- The increase in poverty rates among male-headed
  families between 1979 and 1983 led to the
  defeminization of poverty in the 1980s.

CAUSES OF POVERTY

In this section we attempt to answer the question
of why female-headed families are so poor. This
will provide clues for what can be done to reduce
or eliminate their poverty, the question addressed
in the final section. We begin by looking at the
sources of income available to female-headed
families and by comparing their incomes to those of
two-parent families. We also compare the incomes
of different types of female-headed families based
on whether the mother is widowed, divorced,
separated, or never-married. The comparisons
suggest that female house-holders are poor for

three reasons: first because the primary breadwinner (the mother) has relatively low earnings; second, because the contribution of other family members, and in particular the absent father, is low; and finally, because public transfers to single-mother families, with the exception of widows, are quite meager and substitute for, rather than supplement, income from work and remarriage.

The sources of income for two-parent and female-headed families are reported in Tables 2.2 and 2.3 for whites and blacks. The top row in each table contains the average income of different family types and the remaining rows contain a breakdown of specific sources of income.

According to Tables 2.2 and 2.3, the average income of two-parent families in 1982 was about 2.5 times as large as the average for female-headed families. Total income was $30,814 for white two-parent households as compared with $12,628 for white female-headed households. For blacks, the pattern was much the same, although income levels were lower in all households. The average income for black two-parent families was $23,913 as compared with $9,128 for female-headed families.

Low Earnings Capacity of Household Head

With the exception of widows, the major source of income for both two-parent and female-headed families is the earnings of the head of household. Approximately 60 to 70% of total income is accounted for by the head's earnings, which suggests that the ability of single mothers to earn income is a critical determinant of their economic status.

When we compare the earnings of female householders with those of the fathers in two-parent families, we find that female breadwinners bring in only 35% as much income as male breadwinners. This discrepancy is due to differences in labor force participation and to differences in wages.

TABLE 2.2 Income Receipts of White Families with Children in 1982 by Type and Amount

	Husband-Wife Families	All Female-Headed Families	Marital Status			
			Widowed	Divorced	Separated	Never Married
Total Cash Income	$30,814	$12,628	$17,799	$13,845	$10,122	$7,812
Head's earned income	$21,932	$7,666	$5,098	$9,556	$6,070	$4,568
% who report income	94	70	54	81	64	52
Mean for those who report	$23,230	$10,866	$9,359	$11,833	$9,475	$8,709
Pensions	$273	$119	$851	$37	$30	$31
% who report income	4	2	15	1	0.4	2
Mean for those who report	$7,187	$5,059	$5,613	$4,472	$5,571	$2,885
Other unearned	$1,609	$702	$2,878	$524	$385	$258
% who report income	77	47	61	52	40	26
Mean for those who report	$2,049	$1,493	$4,687	$1,004	$961	$978
Others' earnings	$6,377	$928	$2,132	$874	$755	$511
% who report income	70	22	41	23	19	8
Mean for those who report	$9,159	$4,283	$5,239	$3,850	$4,072	$6,044

Alimony and Child Support	$ 227	$ 1,246	$ 174	$ 1,797	$ 1,022	$ 238
% who report income	13	40	9	55	33	13
Mean for those who report	$ 1,814	$ 3,129	$ 1,968	$ 3,260	$ 3,099	$ 1,763
Social Security	$ 289	$ 961	$ 6,493	$ 273	$ 414	$ 369
% who report income	5	15	86	6	7	7
Mean for those who report	$ 5,843	$ 6,471	$ 7,574	$ 4,306	$ 5,890	$ 5,075
Public Assistance	$ 107	$ 1,007	$ 173	$ 784	$ 1,445	$ 1,837
% who report income	3	29	9	23	40	53
Mean for those who report	$ 3,076	$ 3,430	$ 1,878	$ 3,392	$ 3,608	$ 3,496
Food Stamps	$ 67	$ 392	$ 176	$ 299	$ 575	$ 642
% who report income	7	32	17	26	44	52
Mean for those who report	$ 1,022	$ 1,205	$ 1,056	$ 1,158	$ 1,293	$ 1,205

Source: 1983 Current Population Survey.

Note: Total cash income is the sum of all categories shown except food stamps. For some unknown reason this sum differs from the original total variable in the CPS data tape for some groups. The biggest difference is found among the white male-headed households, where our figure is $220 higher. For black male-headed households the difference is $50. For female-headed households the differences are either zero or within the margin of rounding error.

Looking at the rows which report the percentage of single mothers who work, it is clear that female breadwinners work substantially less than males. Labor force participation ranges from a low of 34% for black widows to a high of 81% for white divorcees. The significance of not working is profound. Mary Jo Bane, for example, has shown that less than 10% of single mothers who worked full-time/full-year during the past decade were poor in any given year as compared to over 75% of nonworking mothers.[6] Note, however, that these findings should not be interpreted to mean that if all single mothers worked full time, only 10% would be poor. To some extent, the apparent advantage of working mothers reflects the selection process that channels women with higher earnings capacity into the labor force and women with lower capacity into homemaker and welfare status. Isabel Sawhill finds that women on welfare have very low wage rates, and that even if they worked full time, more than half would still earn less than their welfare grant. Another quarter would earn up to $1000 more than their grant, and only one-quarter would earn over $1000 more than their grant (Sawhill, 1976). Sawhill's results do not obviate the conclusion that work is important. Rather they suggest that a significant minority of single mothers would remain poor or near poor even if they worked full time (see the analysis in Chapters Four and Five for more on this essential insight).

Why are the wages of female breadwinners so low? In part this is due to the fact that they are women. In general, females who work full time earn less than 60% of what full-time male workers earn, a fact that is attributed both to sex discrimination in the labor market and to sex differences in human capital. In addition, many single mothers are teenagers who have not completed high school and who have very little employment experience. Moreover a substantial portion of older single mothers were teenager mothers in the past. Numerous studies have shown that early pregnancies have a strong negative effect on earnings capacity and increase the risk of poverty over the life course (Wertheimer and Moore, 1982; Holferth and Moore, 1982; Furstenberg, 1976).

Limited Contributions from Absent Parents

A second major cause of low income among female-headed families is the fact that only one parent contributes to the family income. Tables 2 and 3 show that a substantial portion of family income in two-parent households comes from "others' earnings," which measures primarily the earnings of the mother/wife. Wife's earnings account for about 12% of the total income of white two-parent families and for about 34% of the total income of black two-parent families.

In single-mother families, the contribution from the second parent is recorded under child support and alimony.[7] According to our estimates, payments from the absent father account for about 10% of the income of white single-mother families and for about 3.5% of the income of black single mothers. There is considerable variation in the amount of child support received. White divorced mothers are most likely to receive support and to receive the largest payments, whereas never-married mothers receive the least. In no case do child support payments begin to equal the contribution of the second-earner parent in two-parent families, much less the wages of male heads of household.

Why does child support account for such a small share of income? And to what extent should absent fathers contribute more than they do to the family income of single-mother families? Consider the two-parent situation. Parents are obligated by law to support their children. When parents live with their children this obligation is normally met through the course of everyday sharing. When a parent doesn't live with his or her child, the obligation is supposed to be discharged via private child support, a transfer of income from the noncustodial parent to the custodial parent.

If noncustodial fathers paid a very large portion of their income in child support, the presence of only one adult in the female-headed family would have less dire economic consequences. But it is unrealistic to expect noncustodial fathers to transfer most of their income to children with whom they do not live. Even parents who live with their children do not spend most of their income on the children. And when a family

TABLE 23 Income Receipts of Black Families with Children in 1982 by Type and Amount

	Husband-Wife Families	All Female-Headed Families	Marital Status			
			Widowed	Divorced	Separated	Never Married
Total Cash Income	$23,913	$ 9,128	$ 9,489	$11,187	$ 8,221	$ 8,517
Head's earned income	$13,508	$ 5,363	$ 2,454	$ 7,660	$ 4,967	$ 4,939
% who report income	86	58	34	71	56	56
Mean for those who report	$15,710	$ 9,276	$ 7,207	$10,736	$ 8,825	$ 8,821
Pensions	$ 232	$ 93	$ 568	$ 61	$ 79	$ 36
% who report income	4	2	9	1	1	1
Mean for those who report	$ 5,670	$ 4,946	$ 6,510	$ 4,745	$ 5,571	$ 2,885
Other unearned	$ 849	$ 251	$ 367	$ 389	$ 184	$ 196
% who report income	54	25	20	38	23	21
Mean for those who report	$ 1,559	$ 1,000	$ 1,808	$ 1,027	$ 792	$ 954
Others' earnings	$ 8,096	$ 827	$ 1,818	$888	$ 511	$ 783
% who report income	75	17	34	19	15	13
Mean for those who report	$10,732	$ 5,002	$ 5,409	$ 4,693	$ 3,328	$ 5,958

Alimony and Child Support	$ 253	$ 322	$ 123	$ 613	$ 284	$ 236
% who report income	13	19	11	28	18	16
Mean for those who report	$ 1,940	$ 1,698	$ 1,145	$ 2,150	$ 1,610	$ 1,431
Social Security	$ 639	$ 563	$ 3,207	$ 315	$ 384	$328
% who report income	11	15	69	8	12	10
Mean for those who report	$ 5,743	$ 3,873	$ 4,679	$ 3,734	$ 3,142	$ 3,420
Public Assistance	$ 336	$ 1,710	$ 952	$ 1,264	$ 1,813	$ 1,999
% who report income	12	50	36	34	53	59
Mean for those who report	$ 1,940	$ 1,698	$ 1,145	$ 2,150	$ 1,610	$ 1,431
Food Stamps	$ 1,502	$ 832	$ 581	$613	$ 1,001	$963
% who report income	15	57	47	43	61	63
Mean for those who report	$ 1,502	$ 1,514	$ 1,241	$ 1,425	$ 1,636	$ 1,514

Source: 1983 Current Population Survey.

Note: Total cash income is the sum of all categories shown except food stamps. For some unknown reason this sum differs from the original total variable in the CPS data tape for some groups. The biggest difference is found among the white male-headed households, where our figure is $220 higher. For black male-headed households the difference is $50. For female-headed households the differences are either zero or within the margin of rounding error.

splits, it loses the economies of scale that result from living together in one household. Two homes must be bought or rented, furnished, heated, and maintained, rather than one. Even if all noncustodial fathers paid a reasonable amount of child support, such payments would not compensate fully for the economic contributions of a father in the house. Unfortunately, most noncustodial fathers do not pay reasonable amounts of child support.

National data on child support awards and payments indicate that only about 60% of the women with children potentially eligible for child support even have an award. Of those with an award, only half receive the full amount due. Nearly 30% receive nothing. Furthermore, even when ability to pay child support is held constant, the award amounts vary dramatically. Some children are well provided for; others get nothing (Sorenson and MacDonald, 1983; McDonald, Moran and Garfinkel, 1983).

Exactly what share of the cost of raising the child should be borne by the absent father depends, of course, on value judgments. To get an idea of what the poverty status of female-headed families (excluding widows) would be if the noncustodial father bore a bigger share, we simulated the effect of collecting child support equal to 17% of the absent father's income for one child, 25% of his income for two children, 29% for three children, 31% for four children, and 33% for five or more children. Our estimates indicate that the poverty gap -- the difference between the incomes of poor female-headed families and the amount of money they would need to reach the poverty level -- would be reduced by 27%. Of course, additional payments might also result in behavioral changes that further reduced the poverty gap. For example, by providing a stable source of income that is not means-tested, child support might help a welfare mother to obtain a job, gain work experience, and eventually work her way out of poverty.

Inadequate Public Transfers

A final cause of low income in female-headed
families is the relatively meager transfer benefits
provided to single mothers and their children.
By comparing public transfer benefits available to
widows with those available to families headed by
divorced, separated and never-married mothers, the
inadequacy of the latter becomes starkly obvious.
Since 1935, poor female-headed families have been
eligible for cash welfare assistance under the Aid
for Families with Dependent Children (AFDC)
program. Since 1938, widows and their children
from all income classes also have been eligible for
benefits from the Survivors Insurance (SI) program.
Whereas 51% of all female-headed families are poor,
only 34% of widowed families with children are in
such financial straits. The difference is in large
part directly traceable to the difference between
SI and AFDC. To see this we return to Tables 2.2
and 2.3 again. Note that white widows are far
better off than any other single-parent group. Not,
however, because they earn more. Whereas all other
groups get well over half of their income from
earnings, white widows get only 29% of their income
from work. The big difference is that white widows
get 36% of their income from Social Security. The
average white widow in 1983 received $6500 in SI
benefits. Without this income, the proportion of
white widows who were poor would have been much
closer to that of the other groups. Table 2.2
indicates that subtracting the $6500 in Social
Security income from the nearly $17,800 total
income of widows would leave them only $11,300:
less than divorced women, about equal to black
divorced women and barely more than separated and
never-married women. (Of course, if widows did
not receive the Survivors Insurance benefits, they
would work and earn more.)
   Welfare plays a much smaller role for nonwidowed
female heads than Survivors Insurance plays for
widowed heads. Nearly 90% of all white widows and
70% of all black widows receive survivors
insurance. Only 23 and 43% of white and black
divorced women receive welfare, and the proportion
for separated and never-married whites and blacks

ranges from 40 to 59%.   In addition the average level of benefits in Survivors Insurance is more than double the average level of welfare benefits.

Benefits for divorced, separated, and never-married mothers and their children could be made more similar to benefits to widows either by substantially increasing benefit levels, or by making benefits available to single mothers of all income classes, or by doing both.   Increasing benefit levels would be consistent with a policy decision to enable poor single mothers to stay home and raise their children.   Making benefits available to single mothers without income limits would be consistent with a policy decision of expecting poor single mothers to work and of supplementing their earnings.

By drastically reducing benefits as earnings increase, welfare programs replace rather than supplement earnings.   Even when the AFDC program contained work-incentive provisions, as it did between 1967 and 1982, the gains from working were slight. After deductions for work-related expenses, families lost 66 cents in AFDC for each dollar earned (the figure is now 100 cents).   In addition, they lost about 25 cents in Food Stamp benefits. If they lived in public housing their rents increased. And if they were fortunate enough to be able to earn enough to leave welfare, they faced the prospect of losing a very valuable health insurance policy in the form of Medicaid.   In short, from the perspective of poor single mothers who contemplate working, what welfare programs give with one hand, they take away with the other.   The consequence is that female heads with low earnings are faced with an all-or-nothing situations: become dependent on welfare or work full time and achieve a marginally better economic position-- assuming a full-time job and suitable child care can be found.   With sub-poverty benefit levels, either choice leads to poverty or near poverty. Under these circumstances, it is not surprising that a large minority of poor single mothers do not work and remain poor and on welfare.

A PARTIAL SOLUTION TO POVERTY IN FEMALE-HEADED FAMILIES: THE CHILD SUPPORT ASSURANCE SYSTEM

In the last section we saw that the poverty of female-headed families is due to the low earnings capacity of the mothers, limited contributions from absent parents, and inadequate public transfers. Increasing the earnings capacity of single mothers will require a multi-faceted approach including changes in socialization of women and men, reductions in labor market discrimination against women, and reductions in early childbirth. A separate paper could easily be drafted to analyze the potential effectiveness of each of these strategies. We make no attempt here to even address the complex issues that would be raised by such an evaluation. Our purpose is more modest. We suggest that adoption of a new Child Support Assurance System would simultaneously increase the incomes and reduce the dependence of female-headed families.

Under the program all parents who live apart from their children would be liable for a child support tax. The child support tax base would be gross income. The tax rate would be proportional and depend upon the number of children owed support. For example, the tax rate might be 17% for one child, 25% for two children, and 30% for three or more children. The child support tax would be collected through a wage withholding system, like payroll and income taxes. All children with a living absent parent would be entitled to a child support benefit equal to the child support tax paid by the absent parent or a socially insured minimum benefit. In cases where the absent parent pays less than the minimum, the difference would be financed out of general revenues now devoted to the AFDC program.[8] Finally, in cases where the absent parent pays less than the minimum, the custodial parent would be subject to a surtax up to the amount of the public subsidy. The surtax rate would be one-half the tax rate of the absent parent.

The new Child Support Assurance System would achieve the objectives of (1) assuring that those who parent children share their income with them; (2) establishing and collecting child support

equitably and efficiently; (3) increasing the
economic well-being of children with a living
absent parent; while (4) simultaneously reducing
welfare costs and caseloads. How much would a
child support program cost? And how much would it
reduce poverty and welfare dependence?

Both the benefits and the costs of a Child
Support Assurance Program would depend upon the
level of the minimum benefit, the tax rates on noncustodial and custodial parents, and the
effectiveness of child support collections. In
Table 2.4 estimates of net savings or costs and
reductions in poverty and AFDC caseloads are
presented for programs with four different minimum
benefit levels. The minimum benefits for the
first child range from $2000 to $3500. Minimum
benefits for the second, third, fourth, fifth, and
sixth child respectively are $1500, $1000, $500,
$500, and $500. The tax rates for noncustodial
parents are 17% for one child, 25% for two
children, 29% for three children, 31% for four
children, 32% for five children, and 33% for six or
more children. Tax rates for custodial parents
are equal to one-half those for noncustodial
parents.

The estimates in Table 2.4 are for all children
potentially eligible for child support including
those in remarried, two-parent families.[9] The
estimates in the top panel assume 100% collection
effectiveness. The most striking finding is that
if we collect 100% of the non-custodial parents'
child support obligation, three of the four Child
Support Assurance programs would actually save
money. That is, the extra dollars paid out under
the new program would be more than offset by
increased child support collections and consequent
reductions in welfare expenditures. Even the most
generous plan costs less than a quarter of a
billion dollars.

At the same time, all the programs would reduce
the poverty gap (the difference between the income
of a poor family and the income the family would
need to reach the poverty line) and the number of
families on welfare. The reductions in the
poverty gap for families eligible for child support
are quite large -- ranging from a low of 39% to a
high of 53%. Similarly, reductions in welfare

caseloads are very large, ranging from 48 to 64%.[10] In short, all of the programs would substantially reduce poverty and welfare dependence, and three of four would actually save money.

No matter how efficient the collection system is, less than 100% of potential revenue will be collected. Consequently, the second and third panels in Table 4 present estimates of the effects of the two middle plans if we collected only 80% and 70% respectively of the noncustodial parents' child support obligation. If we collected only 80% of potential revenue, the $2500 minimum benefits plan would still save $.59 billion. But the $3000 minimum benefit plan instead of saving $.87 billion (with 100% collection) cost an additional $.33 billion. If we collect only 70% of potential revenue, both plans cost more, though the extra cost of the $2500 plan is very small. Note also that collecting less than 100% of the noncustodial parent obligation also reduces the effectiveness of a child support program in reducing poverty and welfare dependence. The effects are not so large as on costs, however, because for poor families the minimum benefit makes up for most of the loss in private child support.

SUMMARY AND CONCLUSION

The term "feminization of poverty" has helped to draw attention to the serious plight of single-mother families. No other major demographic group has such a large proportion of its members who are poor and no other group experienced so little economic progress during the late 1960s and the 1970s. But the feminization of poverty has mistakenly led some to believe that the composition of the poor became increasingly female because female-headed families were becoming increasingly impoverished. Quite the contrary. The proportion of female-headed families who were poor was declining throughout the period that poverty was becoming increasingly feminized. Rather the proportion of the poor in female-headed families increased between 1967 and 1978 because the prevalence of such families increased dramatically

TABLE 2.4 Estimated Costs or Savings and Effects on Poverty and AFDC Caseloads of Alternative Child Support Assurance Programs in 1983 Dollars

Minimum Benefit Level for First Child	Net Savings or Costs (billions)	Reduction in Poverty Gap	Reduction in AFDC Caseloads
100% collection effectiveness			
$2000	$2.37	39%	48%
2500	1.72	43	54
3000	0.87	48	59
3500	-0.18	53	64
80% collection effectiveness			
$2500	$0.59	40%	49%
3000	-0.33	45	56
70% collection effectiveness			
$2500	$-0.06	38%	48%
3000	-1.83	43	54

NOTE: The estimates are derived from the 1979 Current Population Survey-Child Support Supplement (CPS-CSS). The CPS-CSS is a match file which contains data from both the March annual demographic and income survey and the April 1979 child support supplement. On the basis of the March survey, 3,547 women who were eligible to receive child support were identified and interviewed in April. In order to estimate savings per costs and reductions in poverty and AFDC caseloads, it was necessary to impute incomes of noncustodial parents. Estimates of the noncustodial fathers' income are derived from regressions relating wives' characteristics to husbands' incomes. For a more detailed description of the data and methodology, see Donald Oellerich and Irwin Garfinkel, "Distributional Impacts of Existing and Alternative Child Support Systems," Policy Studies Journal, 12(1) (Sept. 1983): 119-129.

during this period and because other groups,
especially the aged, were lifted out of poverty.
When the poverty rates of other groups increased in
But this does not mean that poverty became a less
serious problem for female-headed families.

Analyzing the poverty rates and causes of
poverty among female-headed families is more
fruitful and informative than analyzing the
increases or decreases in the proportion of the
poor who are female.   Poverty among single-mother
families is widespread because they have low
earnings capacity, receive limited contributions
from absent parents, and get inadequate public
transfers.   Due to differences in socialization
and discrimination, women on average earn only 60%
as much per hour worked as men.   About three-
fourths of the single mothers on welfare -- a large
minority of all single mothers -- can earn no more
or just barely more than they receive on welfare.
Four out of ten women with children eligible for
child support have no awards.   Of those with
awards, only 50% receive the full amount due them,
while 28% receive nothing.   In all, over half of
the women with children potentially eligible for
support receive none.   Finally, the welfare
system provides near-poverty level benefits that
are reduced drastically in response to earnings
increases.   The consequence is that poor single
mothers are faced with the all-or-nothing choice of
relying upon welfare or working full time for a
marginal economic gain.   Either way they will
remain poor.

If we expect poor single mothers to work and
wish to increase their incomes to above poverty
levels, we must invent a program that, unlike
welfare, will supplement rather than replace
earnings.   A new Child Support Assurance System
would both increase contributions from absent
parents and restructure public transfers so that
they supplemented rather than replace the earnings
of single mothers. As such, it directly affects the
second two causes of poverty. Legislating a child
support standard and with-holding the obligation
from wages and other sources of income would
substantially increase private child support
payments from noncustodial parents.   Assuring that

50

the child receives the higher of either what the
noncustodial parent pays or a socially insured
minimum benefit will enable single mothers with low
earnings capacity to combine child support benefits
with modest earnings to remove them from welfare
and lift them out of poverty.

NOTES

1. For 1967 and 1978, the figures are from U. S.
Department of Commerce, Current Population Reports,
Series P-60, No. 124, "Characteristics of the
Population Below the Poverty Level 1978," Table 1.
The 1983 figures are from U. S. Department of
Commerce, Current Population Reports, Series P-60,
NO. 145. "Money Income and Poverty Status of
Families and Persons in the United States: 1983,"
Table 15. In arriving at the number of females
in poor male-headed households, the assumptions are
made that all male heads are married with wife
present and that there is no other adult female in
the family. These two assumptions have opposite
effects on the estimation. We use the total number
of individuals in female-headed households rather
than just the female head and her children.
2. National Advisory Council on Economic
Opportunity, 12th Report: Critical Choices for the
1980s (Washington, D. C.: (August, 1980) pp. 7-19.
3. By restricting our attention to trends in
female-headed families with children, we ignore sex
difference in poverty among the aged and non-aged
individuals without children.
4. The numbers reported in Figure 1 are based on
the official definition of poverty which counts
only the cash income of families. Since a large
proportion of female heads receive noncash benefits
in the form of food stamps, medical assistance, and
housing subsidies, many people have argued that the
official definition underestimates the true
economic position of single mothers as well as the
improvements in their standard of living which have
occurred during the past decade. If the value of
in-kind benefits is counted, the overall decline in
poverty between 1967 and 1979 is greater than
Figure 1 suggests, and the proportion of female-
headed families that are poor in 1983 is lower.

poorer than all other groups. The Census Bureau estimates that in 1983, depending upon how in-kind benefits are valued, the proportion of female-headed families classified as poor ranges from 29 to 41%. Even the lower estimate implies that more than one of every four families, is poor, a proportion that far exceeds the rates for the aged (2.5 to 6.0%) or for two-parent households (15 to 18%). In short, no matter how poverty is measured, no other group has such a large proportion of its members who are poor and no other group has experienced less economic improvement from the late 1969s to the late 1970s.

5. Between 1967 and 1978 the proportion of the poor living in single-mother families increased from 21 to 36%. If the 1978 poverty rates of the four groups had been the same as they were in 1967, but the prevalence of each group changed as it actually did, 28% of the poor would have lived in female-headed families in 1979. Similarly, had the 1979 prevalence of each group been the same as the 1967 prevalence, but the poverty rates changed as they actually did, then 28% of the poor would have lived in female-headed families.

6. M. J. Bane, unpublished manuscript, Harvard University, Cambridge, Mass., 1984.

7. We should note that some widows receive child support because of a marriage prior to the one that ended in widowhood.

8. A few words about the rationale for three major features of this new system are warranted. First, why establish child support obligations by legislation rather than judicial discretion? The principal argument is that because of the large financial obligation already borne by the state, the apportionment of support for poor children among the custodial parent, the absent parent, and the public is more appropriately a legislative function. Moreover, a legislated formula would reduce inequity. Finally, the use of courts is too costly to society and the families affected. Second, why use general revenues to supplement inadequate child support payments from absent parents? The answer is that doing so will insure children against the risk that their noncustodial parent's income declines or is permanently low and will also reduce welfare costs and caseloads.

Third, why treat child support as a tax and use the withholding system in all cases? Because wage withholding is the most effective collection tool we have, and effective and efficient collection of child support is essential.

9. About one-third of children eligible for child support live in two-parent families.

10. The welfare caseload reductions are too high because they are based on annual data, whereas eligibility is based on monthly income. On the other hand, they are too low because they do not take account of the increases in work that would result from the improved incentives of a Child Support Assurance program.

BIBLIOGRAPHY

Furstenberg, Frank, Jr. 1976. Unplanned Parenthood: The Social Consequence of Teenage Childbearing. New York:Free Press.

Holferth, Sandra and Kristin Moore. 1982. "Early Childbearing and Late Economic Well-Being." American Sociological Review 44:784-815.

McDonald, Tom, James Moran and Irwin Garfinkel. 1983. Wisconsin Study of Absent Fathers Ability to Pay Child Support. Institute for Research on Poverty Special Report #34, Madison, WI.

Sawhill, Isabel. 1976. "Discrimination and Poverty Among Women Who Head Families." Signs 2:201-212.

Sorenson, Annemette and Maurice MacDonald. 1983. "An Analysis of Child Support Transfer," in Judith Cassetty (ed.). The Parental Child Support Obligation. Lexington, MA: Lexington Books.

Wertheimer, Richard F. and Kristin Moore. 1982. "Teenage Childbearing: Public Section Costs." Final Report to Center for Population Research, National Institutes of Child Health and Human Development. Washington, D.C.

3

Unmarried Women in a Patriarchal Society: Impoverishment and Access to Health Care Across the Life-Cycle

Teresa Arendell

This paper focuses on life-cycle causes of female poverty and the associated restrictions of access to health care. The forces that lead women in all stages of the life-cycle to be more likely than men to be poor are discussed. Three life-cycle types of female poverty -- young women with children, middle-aged displaced homemakers, and the elderly -- and their causes and consequences are explored in this chapter. The health and health care realities of female poverty are explored throughout the paper, weaving together the effects of low income and inadequate social welfare programs on women's health care. In general, for all stages of the female life-cycle both the structure of labor markets and the rules associated with social welfare programs assume that the normal condition of women is one of dependency on males. When women are not protected and supported by the higher wages, savings, pensions, and social security payments available to men then the threat of poverty and ill-health loom large.

How can we understand the poverty vulnerability of single women? The approach that this chapter takes is to examine how female dependence on males is linked to their access to income, health insurance, and even transfer payments. In a very real sense most of the major institutions in the United States are organized from within a patriarchal value system. This refers to a general

social framework or perspective in which male
primacy over females is assumed and made manifest
not only in the household but in all institutional
realms as well. In the United States patriarchal
assumptions are embedded in the sex segregated
economic structure of opportunity, which itself is
sex segregated, and so we can speak of patriarchal
capitalism as well.

WOMEN AND POVERTY

Patriarchal capitalism refers to the dual
subordination of women to men that takes place in
advanced capitalist societies such as the United
States. The first, and historically older,
subordination is the direct subordination of women
to men in the household and family. The second
subordination is in the labor market, where
"women's work" is consistently devalued, insecure
and likely to be low waged (Hartmann, 1976,1981).
Both aspects of patriarchal social relations figure
prominently in the high rates of female poverty
across the life-cycle and the inadequacy of most
social programs for meeting women's needs. As we
will see in this paper this second subordination of
women to men in the labor market leads to sex based
inequality in access to health care as well.
    Being female in a patriarchal capitalist
society, which devalues women's labor and often
neglects their needs, has a variety of adverse
consequences throughout the life-cycle. Since
marriage generally obscures women's economic
vulnerability and subordinate status in the labor
market, being unmarried exposes women to the
disadvantages of occupying the lower stratum in a
society organized along gender lines. Women's
subordinate status is itself evidenced by women's
vulnerability to poverty and, as we shall see, by
inadequate health care access.
    The number of women living in conditions of
poverty or low income is increasing (see Chapter
Two for the nature of this change). This
"feminization of poverty" includes three kinds of
women: young adult women with dependent children,
mid-life women who are displaced homemakers, and
aged women. Whereas old women and young unmarried
mothers have long been at risk for being poor, they

are joined today by women "in the middle," largely as a result of divorce. Women's poverty occurs then across a cross-section of adult life.

Each of the three broad categories of impoverished women (women with children, displaced homemakers, and the elderly), has limited access to health care due to financial constraints. Most low income and poor women, a category made-up largely of unmarried women, have little or no health insurance coverage. Further, contrary to public stereotypes, the majority of the poor have no health care coverage through public programs.

POVERTY AND ACCESS TO HEALTH CARE

Medical care costs have increased at rates faster than overall inflation (US House, 1984; Estes et al., 1984). Rising health costs exacerbate the stresses associated with living in or near poverty. The plight of the medically uninsured or inadequately insured worsens as health care costs rise and poverty increases. "The vast majority of women are low-income and are further impoverished by health costs and insurance practices" (Kasper and Soldinger, 1983:86).

Substantial gaps exist in health care insurance. Neither public nor private insurance or public health programs provide the poor or near poor with adequate access to care. Despite the expanded health coverage provided by the Medicare and Medicaid programs, primarily for the aged and poor respectively, some 25 million Americans at any one time have no health insurance coverage at all. Nearly 35 million Americans are without health insurance coverage at some point during the course of a year. Approximately 18 million Americans are without insurance for an entire year and another 16 or so million are without coverage for a portion of the year (Davis and Rowland, 1983). Another 20 million people are inadequately insured (Kasper and Soldinger, 1983).

The poor are twice as likely to be uninsured as middle class people and three times as likely to have no insurance as those in the upper income brackets (Davis and Rowland, 1983). Since most private health insurance coverage is a benefit of employment, the unemployed or low wage employees

who receive relatively few benefits -- "pink collar
workers" -- are the most likely to have no private
health insurance coverage. "The lack of health
insurance is most common among those least able to
afford the consequences of poor health or lack of
preventive health care." And "it is women who are
the least likely to have insurance in their own
right, or the money to buy it" (Kasper and
Soldinger, 1983:77).

Most women's private health insurance is derived
from their status as dependent wives. Unless they
are among the relatively small proportion who have
employment with decent wages and/or benefits
comparable to men's, unmarried women are likely to
be without health insurance. Women's marital
status is a more significant predictor of their
health insurance coverage than is their employment
status (Berk and Taylor, 1983). Yet,
proportionately, fewer women are married today then
in the past.

Public health coverage through the Medicaid
program reaches only about 40 percent of the poor,
including fewer than 40 percent of poor children
(Davis and Rowland, 1983; CDF, 1985). Eligibility
requirements and numerous state program and policy
variations prevent many poor and marginally poor
from being eligible for Medicaid coverage (Davis
and Rowland, 1983; US Congress, 1984; CDF, 1985).
Over four billion dollars were cut from the
Medicaid program between 1982 and 1985 (see
Chapter Nine for indepth discussion of the
consequences for poor women's health of these
cuts). Virtually every state reduced its
provisions for health care for the poor and
reduced the numbers of persons eligible as a
response to these federal reductions (US Congress,
1984). These reductions were made at the same
time as the numbers in poverty rose.

We know more about the impoverishment of women
and the health consequences of being poor
generally than we know about the relationship
between the impoverishment of women and women's
health and access to care. Research has simply not
focused on this specific area, although anecdotal
stories abound among those working with and
knowing these women. (An important exception is
Chapter 9 by Sarri and Russell in this volume).

Yet some data are available about the effects of changes in family compositions, program changes and budget cuts on women's access to health care. Each of the three broad categories of economically disadvantaged women has somewhat different factors contributing to its poverty, somewhat unique health care needs, and is affected by different federal and state programs and policies.

Female-Headed Families

Female-headed families with children make-up approximately one-fifth of American families. However, this 20 percent of families make-up over half, 55 percent, of all poor families (USBC, 1985). More than 36 percent of all female-headed families are in poverty and 45 percent are below the 125 percent poverty line (USBC, 1985). Minority women are at greater risk for impoverishment than are white women: while 31 percent of families headed by white women are in poverty, 60 percent of families headed by a Hispanic woman and 59 percent of families headed by a black woman are poor (USBC, 1985). Central to the recent increase in numbers of poor women, and decreased access to public health care programs, was the Reagan Administration's welfare reform package, the Omnibus Budget Reconciliation Act of 1981. Policy changes cut the majority of poor working women off of all public assistance. Twenty-seven percent of the adult AFDC population were in the labor force, either working or actively seeking employment, when the program changes took effect in 1982 (Zinn and Sarri, 1984). Many working women lost income assistance, food stamps, and child care assistance, and became ineligible for Medicaid coverage as a result of the program changes.

Health care needs of young women are particularly related to reproductive processes, birth control, pregnancy and childbirth (Kasper and Soldinger, 1983; Boston, 1984). Access to these kinds of health care needs is limited both by low income and reductions in available public programs for the economically disadvantaged.

Over half of the states provide no maternity medical coverage to poor women who are married. Ten states provide no Medicaid coverage to poor women who are pregnant for the first time. And even in the states providing maternity coverage, federal restrictions require that no Medicaid coverage be used for pregnant women before the third trimester of pregnancy. No Medicaid dollars can be used for abortions (Hadley, 1982; Petchesky, 1985). Budget cuts and program reductions have occurred across the board so that states and communities have not generally compensated for health care cuts in some programs by increasing others. For example, 47 states have reduced their services to large numbers of women and children as a result of cuts in the Maternal and Child Health (MCH) program (Coalition, 1984; US Congress, 1984).

Cuts in the WIC program (the Special Supplemental Food Program for Women, Infants, and Children) have made women's and young children's health situations even more precarious. Fewer than one-third of the potentially-eligible low income nine million women and preschool aged children are reached by the WIC program; nearly a half million beneficiaries were cut as a result of recent administrative budget cuts (US Congress, 1984; Coalition, 1984). The consolidation of 22 categorical health programs into four block grants and the overall 25 percent cut in funding resulted in present federal health block grant funding remaining below the 1981 level, despite some recent funding increases (NHLP, 1985; US House, 1985). Viewed together, these cuts in health care provisions and increased restrictions in access to health care paint a bleak picture indeed for the health care of pregnant women, mothers, the unborn and newborn.

Health risks of pregnancy are greatest for women of lower socioeconomic status (Petchesky, 1985; USCCR, 1984). Largely reflecting their disadvantaged income status, black pregnant women had a maternal death rate more than three times that of white pregnant women in 1981, 20.4 maternal deaths per 100,000 live births compared to 6.3 maternal deaths (USBC, 1985). The proportion of black pregnant women receiving no or late prenatal care is double that of white women's (Kasper and Soldinger, 1983; Hadley, 1982).

Teenaged unmarried mothers are a sub-group of single women with children. They are important not only because of their numbers and health care needs, but because teenaged mothers are likely to be poor and to remain handicapped by poverty throughout their lives (Hofferth and Moore, 1978). Over a million teenagers become pregnant (Kasper and Soldinger, 1983) and nearly 600,000 teenaged women give birth annually. Almost one in six U.S. births is to a teenaged woman (USBC, 1985).

Health risks to pregnant teenaged women significantly exceed health risks to pregnant women generally. Anemia, malnourishment, emotional stress, toxemia, and premature or prolonged labor are health conditions affecting teenaged pregnant women at disproportionate rates. Infants born to teen mothers are at significantly greater risk also. Low birth weight and high infant mortality rates are directly related to socioeconomic status and age of mother. The lower the income, education, and occupational level, and mother's age, then the higher the infant mortality rates (Hadley, 1982). Lack of adequate and early prenatal care jeopardizes the health of both mother and child and increases the risks of ultimately incurring exceptionally large maternity and neonatal medical bills.

Legalized abortion has meant better reproductive health, especially for poor, teenaged, and minority women (Petchesky, 1985; Hadley, 1982). Several legislative actions have limited women's ready access to abortion, particularly during the first weeks of pregnancy when abortion is safest. The Hyde Amendment of 1977 cut off federal Medicaid funds for abortion. And cuts in funding for family planning agencies and community clinics and hospitals have further limited pregnant and poor women's access to reproductive and maternity health care. Nearly a quarter of community family planning centers have been closed in the last several years, as a result of federal budgetary reductions (Coalition, 1984).

Parental notification and consent laws add to
the delay by teenaged pregnant women in obtaining
early abortion (Petchesky, 1984). Additional
legislative restrictions are expected to deter even
more young women from reproductive planning.
Nearly eight percent of births to white teen
mothers and 30 percent of births to black teens are
unwanted (USBC, 1985). While these figures are
probably underestimated the racial discrepancy
between them point toward a conclusion that lower
income teenagers' are likely to depend on public
programs and funding for birth control and
abortions. Evidently, little account is taken at
policy-setting levels of the direct relationship
between teenaged pregnancy and long term poverty.

Pregnancy economically affects working women in
other health-related ways, particularly low income
women. Fewer than 49 percent of working women have
maternity coverage to take as much as even six
weeks off for delivery and postpartum recovery.
Only five states have temporary disability laws
which cover childbirth (US House, 1984). Low
income working women who become pregnant are at
great economic risk: lack of health insurance
coverage and lack of paid leave add to the jeopardy
of pregnancy and child rearing.

Single women with children are particularly
susceptible to high levels of stress and stress-
related health problems (McLanahan, 1981). Added
to the stress of single parenting are the stresses
associated with living in conditions of economic
hardship and the effects of downward mobility.
Many of the new poor are frustrated in their
attempts to give their children the experiences and
lifestyle consistent with the values and
expectations of their former middle or upper-middle
class lifestyle (Arendell, 1986). Inadequate
income and health problems interact with and
contribute to emotional stress, worsening women's
overall health and adding further to the degree of
emotional stress.

Low income and poor single women with dependents
are caught in a vicious cycle of economic
uncertainties and hardships, restricted access to
health care, and emotional stress. Reductions in
income supports, supplementary food programs, and
public health care programs, among numerous other

changes affecting women in less direct ways during the Reagan years, affected millions of American women and children and contributed to their impoverishment. The immediate savings in the national budget derived from these domestic program changes may well evolve into far greater social expenses as the effects of poverty and limited access to health care take hold over the long-term.

Displaced Homemakers

Displaced homemakers, mid-life and older women who have lost their homemaking and family roles as a result of marital separation, divorce, or death of their husband, are estimated to number between four and six million (King and Marvel, 1982). Due to the rapid increase in long-term marriages ending in divorce and the low remarriage rate for mid-life and older women, this estimate is undoubtedly low. These women invested their early adult years caring for their families, expecting economic security within their marriages. As displaced homemakers, many of these women find themselves living in poverty, victims of ageism, wage discrimination, a lack of recent employment experience, and inadequate (if any) spousal support payments after divorce or inadequate widow's benefits after a husband's death.

The increased numbers of mid-life and older women who suddenly find themselves needing to be fully self-supporting after having been economically dependent during marriage is due largely to the continued high divorce rate. Over a third of the over one million divorces annually occur between couples married ten or more years and 20 percent of all divorces involve couples married 15 or more years. Nearly half a million divorces occur between people aged 45 and older each year (NCHS, 1984). And the divorce rate both among couples of long term marriages and among those middle aged or older continues to rise (NCHS, 1985). Divorce is revoking the relative economic security that women "in the middle" have traditionally had in comparison to unmarried young and elderly women.

Divorce has profound, often lasting, effects on women' standards of living. The economic effects of divorce impact on women of all ages. But mid-life and older women have even fewer options for reversing the downward mobility prompted by divorce than younger women (Arendell, 1986). Studies show that men recover economically from divorce, having in fact, an improvement in their finances after divorce. Women, however, generally experience no such recovery unless they remarry (Weitzman, 1981a; 1981b; Johnson and Minton, 1982; Hill, 1981). For example, Weitzman's 1981 California study showed that following divorce women experience a 73 percent loss in standard of living and men experience a 42 percent improvement in their standard of living (Weitzman, 1981b). Other studies found similar trends (Duncan and Morgan, 1979; Hill, 1981; Chambers, 1979). Substantial employment advancement is less likely for older women re-entering the labor market than for their younger counter-parts. Remarriage, the surest route for women's economic recovery (Duncan and Morgan, 1979; Johnson and Minton, 1982) is inversely related to age for women. Thus, older women are much less likely to remarry than are younger women although remarriage rates are declining for all women over age 30 (Norton and Glick, 1979; NCHS, 1979; 1983). Especially after age 40, relatively few divorced women remarry: indeed, fewer than 15 percent of women whose marriages end after age 40 remarry (Wattenberg and Reinhardt, 1979). Men's remarriage rates, however, do not vary significantly by age and men tend to remarry younger women (NCHS, 1979; 1984). These differential remarriage patterns along gender lines points to the double-standard of aging in which women experience both sexism and ageism and carry lesser value in the marriage market than do men.

Divorce settlements generally do not provide divorced women with economic security. Fewer than 17 percent of divorcing women are awarded any spousal support and fewer than six percent actually receive any support (USBC, 1985; Weitzman, 1981b). Less than half of currently divorced women received any property settlement (USBC, 1981). Homemakers divorced after long marriages are likely to receive little or none of their husband's pensions so the economic hardship following divorce is likely to continue throughout these women's lives. The transfer of wages from the family wage earner to former economic dependents seldom occurs in reality despite legislative mandates to the contrary and "the dramatic increase in divorce, especially in the marriages of long duration, predicts an increase in the number of older women living alone and in poverty in the next generation" (King and Marvel, 1982:44).

Becoming widowed also puts some women into the status of being displaced homemakers. The average age at which a woman becomes widowed in this country is about 56 years yet no Social Security widow's benefits are available until age 60 (Block, 1981; Marksun, 1984). One in six women over age 21 is a widow (O'Laughlin, 1984). The time between being widowed and turning age 60, referred to as the "widow's gap," frequently leaves many widowed women who were economic dependents in marriage with no economic protection. Coupled with the unfavorable labor market for mid-life and older re-entry women, this lack of protection adds to the pushing of once economically secure women into harsh economic realities. At greatest risk for being mid-life and poor are the women who fulfilled traditional marital and family roles common to middle class families. After the birth of a child, these women typically did not pursue occupational development or advanced education. Their employment histories were sporadic and earned incomes low. These homemakers earned few, if any, Social Security credits in their own right so have little or no individual eligibility. Displaced homemakers qualify for no unemployment compensation since their family and home work is unpaid. Nor do they qualify for Social Security Disability benefits. These social programs are geared to protect paid workers. Essentially there are no public funds available for providing temporary support to women who suddenly lose their economic base, are not seriously disabled, and have no minor dependents.

Even married women who maintain more active employment patterns are at risk for being impoverished if divorced or widowed. Working married women contribute less than 25 percent of

the total family income so these women are also
largely economically dependent on their husband's
higher earnings (Chapter 2;Rainwater, 1984; USBC,
1984). Few mid-life and older married women earn
wages comparable to men's or earn what can be
considered to be a family wage with relevant
benefits (USCCR, 1983; King and Marvel, 1982; Rix,
1984). Women's economic dependency in marriage
puts them at great economic risk when they are no
longer married, for whatever reason. Prospects for
substantial employment advancement are slim for
most displaced homemakers who do find paid work and
most women will accrue only minimal retirement
funds, if any. Vesting requirements common to
private pension funds further hamper re-entry mid-
life and older women's chances for securing
adequately for their old age (Rix, 1984).

Despite the increase in numbers of displaced
homemakers, no programs have been initiated to
provide economic support for these women, no matter
how desperate their economic situations. Women of
all ages hold only a small fraction of
apprenticeships and older women are virtually
unrepresented in paid occupational training (USDL,
1982). Instead, federal cuts in employment and
training have brought these programs to their
lowest funding levels in 15 years (US Congress,
1984). By 1984 funding for employment and training
programs had been cut 57 percent below 1980
funding, despite the high unemployment rates of the
early and mid-80s (US Congress, 1984).
Specifically, employment and training reductions
have occurred in each of the major programs: the
Job Training Partnership Act (which replaced the
larger CETA program, which had specifically
targeted older women in late 1982), Title V of the
Older Americans Act, and the Targeted Jobs Tax
Credit program (Coalition, 1984; Block, 1982).
Women attempting to re-enter the employment sector
during mid-life or later years are directly harmed
by the lack of training programs.

Health Care. The aging process involves physical
and physiological changes, some of which require
health care and medical attention (Verbrugge, 1983;
Wantz and Gay, 1981, Marieskind, 1980; Kerzner,
1984). Despite health care needs, many mid-life
and older women have limited access to care because

of financial constraints.   These women fall
between the gaps in medical care coverage, private
and public.   Displaced homemakers are likely to
have no private health insurance since most medical
insurance is a benefit of husbands' employment
(Berk and Taylor, 1983).   Divorced women are twice
as likely as any other group to be without any kind
of health insurance coverage (Berk and Taylor,
1983).   Despite proposals put forth by some women's
organizations for insurance companies to offer
conversion plans for retaining health insurance,
most women who divorce lose their coverage unless
they can afford to purchase it, generally at much
higher private rates.   Widows also have little
choice about maintaining their health insurance
coverage; they too lose their dependent's benefits
when the husband's employment ceases.   Women
attempting to obtain new coverage are also
disadvantaged if they have a pre-existing medical
condition because most companies exclude coverage
for pre-existing health conditions.   Lack of money
and the presence of certain medical conditions
simply precludes having private health insurance
for many unmarried mid-life and older women.
     No public health coverage exists for non-
disabled mid-life and older women prior to age 65
regardless of their economic destitution or health
care needs, except for the very minimal and
restrictive county-level program for medically
indigent adults.   Women below the age of 65 and
past the years of raising minor children qualify
for no Medicaid coverage unless they are severely
disabled.   Medicaid is restricted to parents of
minor children who qualify for Aid to Families with
Dependent Children, disabled adults, and the
elderly poor.   Medicare requires that its
beneficiaries be eligible for Social Security
benefits and be age 65 (Coalition, 1984; Rix, 1985;
Social Security, 1985).
     Further, both married and unmarried women face
possible responsibilities for providing care to an
older person.   The vast majority of caregivers of
aged family members are women; fewer than about ten
percent of caregivers are men.
     Women's family activites of nurturing and caring
for children extend into caring for disabled and
infirm adults and elderly.   Tradition and social

norms prescribe that women provide these services
within the family, generally with neither private
nor public assistance and often at great personal
costs to themselves.

Mid-life and older employed women confronted
with caregiving tasks frequently must give up their
wage earning activities in order to provide
necessary caregiving. Limited earnings prevent
caregivers from hiring services to provide care
during their own working hours. A national survey
revealed that only 25 percent of middle aged female
caregivers under age 65 were in the labor force
compared to over half their male counterparts (Hess
and Waring, 1984). For displaced homemakers who
must rely on their own earning abilities, the
demands of caregiving can be an additional burden.
Social isolation, emotional and physical drain,
lack of attention to personal health care needs,
and despair related to a sense of limited options
combine with economic hardships to worsen
caretaking women's situations and possibilities
(Hess and Waring, 1984; Cicirelli, 1980; Brody,
1981; Finch and Groves, 1982). Foregoing paid
employment in order to provide elderly parents care
worsens unmarried women's retirement income
possibilities, including social security benefit
levels.

As the population ages and as the aged live
longer, more women will be faced with caregiving
responsibilities. In all probability, the
proportions of women involved in giving home care
to the elderly will steadily increase (Hess and
Waring, 1984; Baruch, 1984; Brody, 1981). Social
funding of programs giving supports for in-home
caregiving has been reduced. Substantial funding
shifts have occurred together with a steady
increase in demand for support in giving care
outside of institutions. How these will be
reconciled and basic needs met remain unclear
(Vladeck; 1980; Hess and Waring, 1984; Wood et al.,
1983). Yet the economic and social dilemmas facing
caretaking mid-life and older women persist.

Caretaking women's health care needs, present
and future, remain insufficiently addressed.
Particularly for displaced homemakers who already
confront fundamental economic struggles, the trend
for increased home caretaking will produce greater

personal and economic havoc. Physical and emotional stress will add to and create health care needs. Yet without money and private or public health insurance
coverage, these women will be forced to delay obtaining timely and adequate health care. Preventive health care will be an unaffordable luxury.

The raising of the minimum age of eligibility for Social Security and Medicare in 1987 ignored the plight of the displaced homemaker. Eligibility requirements for Medicaid also neglect this segment of poor women. Prospects for preventive health care and necessary medical treatment for the unmarried and poor mid-life and older women are bleak. And the ranks of women sharing the characteristics of displaced homemakers will continue to swell if present family, social, and policy trends persist.

Older Women, 65 and Over

Women aged 65 and over are the third group of women lodged disproportionately in poverty. Little recognition has been directed at the feminization of poverty among the old, even though older women have traditionally been disproportionately poor. Many recent articles and volumes addressing the topic of women's poverty simply ignore the plight of aged (and aging) women. Yet the numbers of old women who are poor rise daily and a no exit situation exists for the vast majority of older women who find themselves in poverty (see Chapter Eight for the low rates of exit from welfare programs of the elderly).

Despite the overall relative improvements in recent years for the aged, due largely to Social Security cost of living increases (Grad, 1984; Crystal, 1982), the proportion of older women living in poverty has risen. In 1979, 13 percent of aged female household heads were poor. The percentage had risen to almost 18 in 1984, compared to less than 10 percent for men (USBC, 1985). Nearly three-quarters of all aged poor are women. More than 56 percent of women over age 65 have a total income of less than 6000 dollars annually,

well over twice the proportion of older men living
in such limited economic conditions (Rix, 1984).
Women are 83 percent of all elderly people living
alone and in poverty (WEAL, 1985).

Racial differences in the economic status of
older women are significant: elderly black women
have a poverty rate of 42.4 percent, elderly
hispanic women 31.4 percent, and white women 15.1
percent. Elderly men's poverty rates are: 31.8
percent for blacks, 19.7 percent for hispanics, and
8.3 percent for whites (USBC, 1985).

Older women are the fastest growing segment of
the American population. The factors which
presently put older women into poverty appear
likely to persist for at least some years. The
continued increase in the number of displaced
homemakers and low income mid-life women suggests
that the proportion of women entering old age
already poor will increase as will the proportion
of women who get thrust into poverty during the
latter years of their lives.

The most serious problem confronting older women
is a lack of economic resources (King and Marvel,
1984; Marksun, 1984). Widowhood is accompanied for
many by a dramatic drop in income and a substantial
number of women will experience poverty or near
poverty during their widowed years (Rix, 1984;
WEAL, 1985). Poverty in women's older years is a
direct outcome of their lifelong subordinate social
and economic status and their loss of access to a
husband's greater earnings and pension benefits.

Marital status and living arrangements differ
between older men and women. The demographic
realities facing older women are that they outlive
their husbands, maintain independent living
arrangements, and live into their 80s. Because
women outlive men, the majority of older women are
widowed while the majority of older men are
married. Over 70 percent of older men live with
their wives while fewer than one-third of older
women have a living spouse. Ninety percent of
married women outlive their husbands and by age 75,
more than 80 percent of women are widowed (Block et
al., 1981; Marksun, 1984). Yet marriage is a key
determinant for older women's economic status, as
it is for women of every age. For example,

unmarried women between the ages of 65 and 69 have about 40 percent the total income as have their married counterparts (Uhlenberg and Salmon, 1984).

Older women's poverty is at least partially a result of their dependency on Social Security as the primary, even only, source of income (O'Rand, 1983). Older women's dependency on Social Security is much greater than men's. About three-quarters of all older unmarried women depend on Social Security for at least half of their income (Rix, 1984). The average Social Security monthly benefit to widows is 379 dollars (USBC, 1985). The gender inequities of the Social Security system, and built-in penalties for women's efforts in family caretaking (WEAL, 1985; Rix, 1984), contribute to the impoverishment of older women and the lack of escape options. The fundamental assumption of the Social Security program that men's greater benefits -- based on their histories of higher earnings and greater labor force participation -- are shared with wives, ignores the demographic reality that many women are either unmarried or will become widowed.

Social Security benefits taken at age 62 are less than three-quarters' the monthly amount they are if taken at age 65. Although the benefits remain at the lower amount no matter how long the woman lives, nearly 70 percent of women begin drawing their benefits early (King and Marvel, 1982; Coalition, 1984). Not surprisingly, older women have about three-fifths the total income that men have (USBC, 1985). Affecting the lowest Social Security beneficiaries, the minimum Social Security benefit of 122 dollars monthly has been abolished for persons retiring after January 1982 (US Congress, 1985). The poorest elderly women are those most affected by recent and proposed changes in Social Security. Yet these women are relatively powerless in the political arena to make their needs and situations known and to effect change.

Only about 13 percent of older women receive income from private pensions and even then the amounts received are about half men's benefits (King and Marvel, 1982; WEAL, 1984). Assets contribute relatively little to older women's overall income (King and Marvel, 1982; Rix, 1984). Few older women improve their financial situations through employment (Coalition, 1984; Rix, 1984). Social security disincentives for earning substantial income together with the combined processes of ageism and sexism thwart women's earning possibilities. Thus, the amounts of income derived by older women from pensions, assets, and employment are generally not significant additions to Social Security benefits.

Women comprise over three-quarters of aged recipients of the federal-state cash assistance program for the poor elderly, disabled, and blind (USBC, 1985). This means-tested program, Supplemental Security Income, the only income assistance support for the poor elderly, is so minimal that its recipients remain well below poverty level (US Congress, 1985). The average monthly SSI stipend is 212 dollars (USBC, 1985) and only 26 states supplement the federal stipend. Nearly a quarter of a million elderly women had SSI as their only source of income in 1984 (USBC, 1985). Eligibility requirements for SSI are so rigid that once a woman becomes a beneficiary, few options for moving herself off exist (Chapter Eight; Vladeck, 1980; Crystal, 1982). Coupled with older women's low incomes is the likelihood of increased need for medical care. Medical and health care costs increase with age (Rice and Estes, 1984) while income remains relatively fixed for aged women. Older women are more subject to chronic disease with advancing age than are younger women generally (Verbrugge, 1983). And women (who live longer than men) are also more likely to experience more chronic health problems (Block et al., 1981; Rice and Estes, 1984). Older women also tend to have nutritional deficiencies, at least some of which is undoubtedly related to limited financial resources.

The vast majority of women over age 65 are covered by Medicare. However, only 44 percent of the elderly's health care costs are covered through the Medicare program (NHLP, 1985). Few private insurance dollars, less than 16 percent, go to health services for the aged (Kasper and Soldinger, 1983). Since older women make-up the majority of the older poor and have lower incomes than elderly men, it is women who are least able to cover out-of-pocket medical costs or supplementary private health coverage. Yet a House Aging Committee report in March of 1984 reported that the average out-of-pocket costs for doctors' bills was "virtually the same for older persons with incomes under $5000 as for those few older persons with incomes of $35,000" (Coalition, 1984:63). Due to escalating health care costs, aged persons actually pay a greater share of their incomes to health care costs now than they did prior to the enactment of Medicare and Medicaid (US Congress, 1984; US Congress, 1985).

Medicare does not cover preventive health care. And it is geared toward acute rather than chronic illness even though a majority of older people suffer from at least one chronic illness. Many chronic illnesses affecting older women, such as: osteoporosis, breast cancer, arthritis, and osteoarthritis, can be treated at home if regular health care is available. But lack of Medicare coverage for home treatment and services increases older women's chances of being institutionalized (Block, 1982). The Medicare gaps in coverage are numerous. For example, prescription drugs are not covered by Medicare. Nor are eyeglasses or hearing aids covered. Counseling services for the emotional traumas of loss of spouse through death or other losses associated with increasing age are also not covered. Although both men and women are affected by the gaps in Medicare coverage, it is women's low economic status which distinguishes them from their male counterparts. Men's higher income levels provides them better access to necessary and timely care.

The poorest of the elderly who qualify for and receive SSI are covered by Medicaid in addition to Medicare. Thus, the nearly two million older women SSI recipients have a more comprehensive health coverage than do most poor women. However, many physicians will not accept patients covered by Medicaid (see Chapter Nine for evidence to this effect) so older poor women have difficulty obtaining desired medical care. And the recent legislative act requiring co-payments for medical services received through Medicaid further deters women from obtaining timely and needed health care.

The older a woman becomes, the greater the risks of her being institutionalized in a nursing home for custodial and medical care. Although fewer than five percent of people over 65 are in nursing homes at any one time, the proportion increases to 22 percent after age 85. Since women outlive men, more than three-fourths of nursing home residents are women (Vladeck, 1980). Most institutionalized women are impoverished or become impoverished due to the high costs of long-term care.

The stress of living with economic uncertainties and fears knows no proper age and older women's financial and basic survival anxieties interact with physical and mental health. High costs and stringently restricted income are major detergents to older women's good health, adequate and preventive health care, and timely medical treatment.

SUMMARY AND IMPLICATIONS

The impoverishment of women, a result of a complex interaction of factors inherent in a society organized along gender lines and discriminating against women, affects their access to health care in different ways at each stage of the life cycle. Although both the proportion and number of women who are self-supporting, often with financial responsibilities for dependents, have increased dramatically, society remains fundamentally stratified along gender lines. Both the labor market and social welfare programs reinforce male self-sufficiency and female dependency. Policies and programs are premised on the assumption that women are married and have access to a husband's higher earnings and employment-related benefits. Unmarried women with children, displaced homemakers, and aged women are the primary victims of the "feminization of poverty." While their health needs vary across the life course, access to health care is restricted for most women who are not married or employed in a relatively high status professional position with adequate benefits coverage.

Social programs which serve to "mop-up" but not to prevent poverty only worsen the situation facing those on or near the bottom. Radical budget cuts made in domestic programs in apparent oblivion of changes in typical family structure, a sex-segregated labor market, and inequitable policies for the aged perpetuate economic gender stratification.

Despite the growing size of the class of impoverished women, this group remains poorly represented in the public sphere, having limited power and access to resources. Adequate policy attention simply has not been given to the growing numbers of economically disadvantaged women.

The dilemmas faced by unmarried women, as a result of their secondary placement in a gender-stratified society, point to the broad scope of the problem. These issues could take many years to fully redress. Yet, immediate corrective action can, and should be, taken. Programs and policies can be implemented to ease the lives of unmarried women; examples of relatively successful programs from other industrial countries show that such corrective action is possible (Kamerman, 1984). Ultimately, to end the undermining of women's status requires altering the gender-based organization of society. Needed programs and policy reforms fall into six broad categories: income supplements, housing, health care, child care and caregiving support services, legal reforms in divorce laws, and retirement pension coverage. More specifically, program needs include the following:

a) Strategies to close the gender wage gap and to bring about pay equity; ending discrimination on the basis of both sex and age;

b) Expansion of job opportunities for women and increased job training programs, for women of all ages;

c) Affordable, high-quality child care programs;

d) Flexible work schedules that recognize the need to and permit the reasonable coordination of family and employment needs;

e) Welfare program reforms and implementation of a truly adequate and guaranteed minimum family allowance;

f) Guidelines and mandates for determining and setting adequate child support awards; mechanisms for automatic cost of living increases and for children's increased needs as they grown older;

g) Enforcement of child support awards, including administrative collection mechanisms;

h) Increased availability of adequate, affordable, and safe housing;

i) Legal reforms resulting in more equitable definitions of marital (and family) property, and divorce settlements which recognize men's and women's different family and work roles;

j) Expansion of programs that serve the displaced homemaker, including increased access to supplementary income and other forms of public assistance;

k) Protected access to all types of health care;

l) Protected access to retirement coverage, including continued reforms of private pension programs and implementation of earnings sharing in the Social Security program;

m) Ending the Social Security program's penalizing of women for every year beyond five taken out of the paid labor force to care for family dependents;

n) Financial and material compensation for women who provide care in the home to aged relatives, and protection of health and retirement benefits for caregivers;

o) Expanded and affordable caregiving support services.

The impoverishment of women is not some abstract phenomenon. We are not talking about some distant process about which we can remain scientifically objective, reviewing data and social trends. We know these women who are among the poor: they are our sisters, mothers, neighbors, friends, grandmothers, daughters, nieces, patients, clients, and students. Some of us will appear among these numbers; a few of us have been there already and managed to escape. In a society which remains organized along gender lines and which discriminates against women, all women remain at risk for impoverishment. We must end women's relegation and vulnerability to poverty if we are to secure for all the full rights of citizenship and equality, including decent access to health care.

BIBLIOGRAPHY

Arendell, T. 1986. Mothers and Divorce: Legal, Economic, and Social Dilemmas. Berkeley: University of California Press.

Baruch, G. 1984. "The Psychological Well-Being of Women in the Middle Years," in G. Baruch, ed., Women in Midlife. New York: Plenum Press.

Berk, M. and A. Taylor. 1983. "Women and Divorce: Health Insurance Coverage, Utilization, and Health Care Expenditures." National Health Care Expenditures Study. Paper presented at Annual Meeting of the American Public Health Association. November.

Block, M. ed. 1982. The Direction of Federal Legislation Affecting Women Over Forty. College Park, Maryland: National Policy Center on Women and Aging.

Block, M, J. Davidson, and J. Grambs. 1981. Women Over Forty: Visions and Realities. New York: Springer Publishing Company.

Boston Women's Health Collective. 1984. The New Our Bodies, Ourselves. New York: Simon and Schuster, Inc.

Brody, E. 1981. "Women in the Middle." The Gerontologist. 21(5).

_____. 1985. "Parent Care As a Normative Family Stress," The Gerontologist, Vol. 25(1).

Butler, L., P. Newacheck, D. Piontkowski, A. Harper, and P. Francks. 1981. Low Income and Illness: An Analysis of National Health Policy and the Poor. University of California, San Francisco, School of Medicine, January.

Califano, J. Jr. 1984. "The Challenge to the Health Care System: Can the Third Biggest Business Take Care of the Medically Indigent? A Personal Perspective," in D. Yaggy, ed. Health Care for the Poor and Elderly: Meeting the Challenge. Durham, North Carolina: Duke Press Policy Studies.

Chambers, D. 1979. Making Fathers Pay: The Enforcement of Child Support. Chicago: University of Chicago Press.

Children's Defense Fund. 1985. Children and Federal Health Care Cuts. Washington, D.C.

Cicirelli, V. 1980. Personal Strains and Negative Feelings in Adult Children's Relationships with Elderly Parents. Lafayette, Indiana: Purdue University Press.

Coalition on Women and the Budget. 1984. Inequality of Sacrifice: The Impact of the Reagan Budget on Women. March. Washington, D.C.: National Women's Law Center.

Corcoran, M., G. Duncan, and M. Hill. 1984. "The Economic Fortunes of Women and Children: Lessons from the Panel Study of Income Dynamics," in Signs, 10(2).

Crystal, S. 1982. America's Old Age Crisis: Public Policy and the Two Worlds of Aging. New York: Basic Books, Publishers.

Davis, K. and Rowland, D. 1983. "Uninsured and Undeserved: Inequities in Health Care in the United States." in Securing Access to Health Care. Vol. 3. Presidential Commission for the Study of Ethical Problems in Medicine and Biomedical and Behavior Research. March. Washington, D.C.: Government Printing Office.

Diamond, I. ed. 1983. Families, Policies, and Public Policy: A Feminist Dialogue on Women and the State. New York: Longman.

Duncan, G. and J. Morgan (eds). 1979. Five Thousand Families, Vol. 7. Ann Arbor: University of Michigan.

Estes, C., L. Gerard, J. Zones, and J. Swan. 1984. Political Economy, Health, and Aging. Boston: Little, Brown, and Company.

Finch, J. and D. Groves. 1982. "By Women for Women: Caring for the Frail Elderly," Women's Studies International Forum, Vol. 5(5).

Grad, S. 1984. "Incomes of the Aged and Nonaged, 1950-82," Social Security Bulletin. Vol. 47(6). Washington, DC.

Hadley, J. 1982. More Medical Care, Better Health? An Economic Analysis of Mortality Rates. Washington, D.C.: The Urban Institute.

Hartmann, Heidi. 1981. "The Family as the Locus of Gender, Class, and Political Struggle: the Example of Housework." Signs 6:366-394.

_____. 1976. "Capitalism, Patriarchy and Job Segregation by Sex" in Martha Blaxall and Barbara J. Reagan (eds.). Women in the Workplace. Chicago: University of Chicago Press.

Hess, B. and J. Waring. 1984. "Family Relationships of Older Women: A Women's Issue," in E. Marksun, ed. Older Women: Issues and Prospects. Lexington, Massachusetts: Lexington Books.

Hill, M. 1981. "Some Dynamic Aspects of Poverty," in G. Duncan and J. Morgan (eds). Five Thousand Families, Vol. 9.Ann Arbor: University of Michigan.

Hofferth, S. and K. Moore. 1978. The Consequences of Age at First Childbirth: Causal Models. Working Paper. Washington, D.C.: The Urban Institute.

Howe, L. 1977. Pink-Collar Workers: Inside the World of Women's Work. New York: Avon Books.

Johnson, W. and M. Minton. 1982. "The Economic Choice in Divorce: Extended or Blended Family?" Journal of Divorce. 5(1-2).

Kamerman, S. 1978. "To Consider Planning for the White House Conference on Families," U. S. Congressional Report. February 2.

Kamerman, S. 1984. "Women, Children, and Poverty: Public Policies and Female-Headed Families in Industrialized Countries," in Signs, 10(4).

Kasper, A. and E. Soldinger. 1983. "Falling Between the Cracks: How Health Insurance Discriminates against Women," Women and Health. Vol. 8(4).

Kerzner, L. 1984. "Physical Changes after Menopause," in E. Marksun, ed. Older Women: Issues and Prospects. Lexington, Massachusetts: Lexington Books.

King, N. and M. Marvel. 1982. Issues, Policies, and Programs for Midlife and Older Women. Washington, D.C.: Center for Women's Policy Studies.

Luft, H. 1978. Poverty and Health: Economic Causes and Consequences of Health Problems. Cambridge, Mass: Ballinger Publishing Company.

78

McCarty, L. 1985. The Feminization of Poverty. Report of the State of California's Lieutenant Governor's Task Force on the Feminization of Poverty. January. Sacramento, California.

McLanahan, S. 1981. Family Structure and Stress: A Longitudinal Comparison of Male and Female-Headed Families. Institute for Research on Poverty. University of Wisconsin, July.

Marieskind, H. 1980. Women in the Health System: Patients, Providers and Programs. St. Louis: The C.V. Mosby Company.

Marksun, E. ed., 1984. Older Women: Issues and Prospects. Lexington, MA: Lexington Press.

National Advisory Council on Economic Opportunity (NACEO). 1981. The American Promise: Equal Justice and Economic Opportunity. Washington, D.C.

National Center for Health Statistics. 1979. Monthly Vital Statistics Report: Marriage and Divorce. Vol. 3. U.S. Department of Health and Human Services.

_____. 1985. Monthly Vital Statistics Report. February. U.S. Department of Health and Human Services.

National Health Law Program (NHLP). 1985. In Poor Health: The Administration's 1985 Health Budget. Los Angeles, California.

Norton, A. and P. Glick. 1979. "Marital Instability: Past, Present and Future," in G. Levinger and O. Moles (eds.) Divorce and Separation, New York: Basic Books.

O'Laughlin, K. 1984. "The Final Challenge: Facing Death," in E. Marksun (ed.) Older Women Lexington, Mass.: Lexington Books.

O'Rand, A. "Women," in E. Palmore (ed.) Handbook of the Aged in the United States, New York:Greenwood Press.

Petchesky, R. 1985. "Abortion in the 1980s: Feminist Morality and Women's Health," in E. Lewin and V. Olesen, (eds.) in Women, Health, and Healing: Toward a New Perspective, New York: Tavistock Publications.

Rainwater, L. 1984. "Mothers' Contributions to the Family Money Economy in Europe and the United States," in P. Voydanoff (ed.) Work and Family, Palo Alto: Mayfield Publishing Company.

Rice, D. and C. Estes. 1984. "Health of the Elderly: Policy Issues and Challenges," Health Affairs, vol. 3(4) (Winter):25-49.

Rix, S. 1984. Older Women: The Economics of Aging. Women's Research and Education Institute of the Congressional Caucus for Women's Issues.

Rogers, D. 1984. "Providing Health Care to the Elderly and Poor: A Serious Problem for the Downsizing 1980s," in D. Yaggy, ed. Health Care for the Poor and Elderly: Meeting the Challenge. Durham, North Carolina: Duke Press Policy Studies.

Sabin, T. 1982. "Biologic Aspects of Falls and Mobility Limitations in the Elderly," Journal of American Geriatrics Society. 30.

Slater, C. 1984. "Concepts of Poverty," The Journal/The Institute for Socioeconomic Studies. Autumn.

Social Security Handbook. 1985. Baltimore, Maryland: Social Security Administration.

Uhlenberg, P. and M.A. Salmon. 1984. "Change in Relative Income of Older Women, 1960-1980." Paper presented at the American Sociological Association Meeting.

United States Bureau of the Census. 1981. "Money Income and Poverty Status of Families and Persons in the United States: 1981," Current Population Reports. Series P-60, Number 134. Washington, D. C.: Government Printing Office.

_____. 1983. "Money, Income, and Poverty Status of Families and Persons in the United States: 1983," Current Population Reports. Series P-60. No. 140. Washington, D. C.: Government Printing Office.

_____. 1984. Statistical Abstract of the United States, 1983-84. National Data Book and Guide to Sources. Washington, D. C.: Government Printing Office.

United States Commission on Civil Rights. 1983. A Growing Crisis: Disadvantaged Women and Their Children. Washington, D. C.

United States Congress. 1984. "Problems of Working Women." Hearing before the Joint Economic Commissions. April 4. Washington, D.C.: U.S. Government Printing Office.

80

_____. 1985. "An Analysis of the President's Budgetary Proposals for Fiscal Year 1986." Congressional Budget Office. February. Washington, D. C.: U.S. Government Printing Office.

United States Department of Labor. 1983. Employment in Perspective: Working Women. First Quarter, Report 683. Bureau of Labor Statistics. Washington, D. C.

United States House Budget Committee. 1984. A Review of President Reagan's Budget Recommendations, 1981-85. Committee on the Budget. August 2. Washington, D. C.: U.S. Government Printing Office.

United States House Select Committee on Aging. 1980. The Status of Mid-Life Women and Options for Their Future, Washington, D. C.: U.S. Printing Office.

Verbrugge, L. 1983. "Women and Men: Mortality and Health of Older People," in M. Riley, B. Hess, and K. Bond (eds.) Aging in Society: Selected Reviews of Recent Research, London: Lawrence Erlbauns Association, Publishers.

Vladeck, B. 1980. Unloving Care: The Nursing
    Home Tragedy. New York: Basic Books.
Wantz, M. and J. Gay. 1981. The Aging Process. A
    Health Perspective. Cambridge, Mass: Winthrop
    Publishers, Inc.
Wattenberg, E. and H. Reinhardt. 1979. "Female-
    Headed Families: Trends and Implications,"
    Social Work. 24.
Weitzman, L. 1981a. The Marriage Contract:
    Spouses, Lovers, and the Law. New York: The
    Free Press.
_____. 1981b. "Economics of Divorce: Social
    and Economic Consequences of Property, Alimony
    and Child Support Awards," UCLA Law Review.
    28.
Women's Equity Action League (WEAL). 1985. WEAL
    Facts: Letter To the Editor, Equity for Women.
    Washington, D. C.
Wood, J., C. Estes, P. Lee, and P. Fox. 1983.
    Public Policy, the Private Nonprofit Sector and
    the Delivery of Community-Based Long Term Care
    Services for the Elderly. San Francisco: Aging
    Health Policy Center.
Zinn, D. and Sarri, R. 1984. "Turning Back the
    Clock on Public Welfare," in Signs, 10(4).

4

Local Labor Market Structure and the Poverty Vulnerability of Black and White Women in Large Metropolitan Areas

David J. Maume, Jr.

As female household heads become a larger component of the poverty population, concern for the determinants of women's poverty grows. This paper argues that one should consider "poverty vulnerability" to include not only those women whose earnings are below the Census definition of poverty, but women who are near-poor as well. Using the Panel Study of Income Dynamics, the difference between a woman's earnings in 1976 and the government's poverty threshold is measured. The size of this "poverty buffer" is predicted using variables suggested by the human capital and structural research traditions. Regarding structural measures, three features of the local labor market of residence are controlled--industry mix, the economic power of dominant industries, and the extent of government participation in local labor and product markets. OLS results show these variables to have significant effects on the size of the poverty buffer, and that individual characteristics interact with local labor market variables. The policy implications of these findings are briefly discussed.[1]

INTRODUCTION

A cursory glance at recent literature on earnings inequality shows a growing concern for the origins and implications of poverty among women who head households (e.g., see Duncan, 1984; McLanahan,

1985; Smith, 1984). The attention given to this problem is due to the fact that women are becoming a larger component of the poverty population. In 1959, 23 percent of all poor families were headed by women; by 1976 this figure had increased to 48 percent (U.S. Bureau of the Census, 1978) (see the preceding two chapters for more on these trends). Clearly, these numbers have important implications for children who grow up in poverty and must attempt to escape it as adults. McLanahan (1985) finds that children who grow up in families headed by a woman are less likely to finish high school, suggesting that an increase in female poverty at present may portend a larger poverty population in the future.

Two perspectives underpin the research which has investigated the reasons for women's low earnings. One, the human capital approach, argues that women's low earnings are due to low educational attainment, fewer years of work experience, and a weak attachment to the labor force (Mincer and Polachek, 1974). Recent work casts some doubt on this argument, yet there is empirical support for the notion that women's lower stock of human capital is partly responsible for their low pay (for a review, see Corcoran and Duncan, 1979).

A complement to the supply-oriented human capital approach is the structural perspective, adopted by sociologists in the late 1970s. Despite differences in emphasis, structural researchers agree that features of the job setting affect earnings net of labor supply. For example, union membership has been found to affect pay, as has the market structure of the employing industry (e.g., see Bibb and Form, 1977; Beck et al., 1978a; Kalleberg et al., 1981). Collective organization is an important resource available to workers in the wage-bargaining process with management. Moreover, workers employed in competitive industries work in firms which have lower pay scales because they are unable to pass workers' wage demands on to the consumer (Galbraith, 1967). Thus, one reason for women's low pay (and high poverty rate) is because of underrepresentation in unions and overrepresentation in competitive-sector industries (Beck et al., 1980).

these researchers assume that the labor market--the
area in which people search for work--is defined by
the nation's boundaries. Yet, most individuals
look for work in their local areas of residence,
and these areas can differ from each other in ways
that affect individual earnings.

A recent study by Parcel and Mueller (1983)
incorporated the structure of the local labor
market of residence into earnings attainment
models.   Parcel and Mueller (1983) found that
women's earnings were higher when they lived in
areas with complex and growing tertiary sectors
(retail and service industries). They interpret
(p. 272) local labor effects on earnings as
reflective of differences in job opportunities
which vary by race and gender groups. Presumably,
living in service-based areas provide women with a
greater range of occupational choice (compared with
residence in manufacturing areas) and a better
chance of maximizing their earnings potential.

Parcel and Mueller's (1983) book provides a
point of departure for this paper, yet this study
extends their work in two ways. First, this paper
takes into consideration other aspects of local
market structure, namely the extent of government
participation in the local economy. Secondly, the
earnings effect of interactions between individual
characteristics and local labor market structure is
given explicit attention in this study. The
potential effect on earnings of a "match" or
"mismatch" between personal characteristics (such
as educational attainment) and local market
characteristics (e.g., industry mix) has been
ignored in past research.

STUDY DESIGN

The Panel Study of Income Dynamics (Survey Research
Center, 1978) was the data source for this paper.
The Panel Study (hereafter, PSID) provided
information on a woman's state and county of
residence which allowed me to identify the
metropolitan area (i.e., the labor market) in which
she lived. Then, measures of the industrial
features of 90 SMSAs (recorded from secondary data
sources) were merged into the PSID file (see the
section on local labor market variables below).

The Sample

The sample for this paper consists of female household heads who were between the ages of 20--64, and employed (but not self-employed) at the time of the interview in 1977.[2] Self-employed women were excluded from the sample because they do not participate in local labor markets (i.e., they do not sell their labor power for a wage), and jobless women were excluded because the PSID did not ask these women questions about their length of tenure with their last employer. Employer tenure has been shown to be a significant determinant of earnings (Mincer, 1974). The exclusion of jobless women does not yield a biased sample. After imposing age restrictions on the sample, only 22 women were jobless at the time of the survey. Moreover, recent research suggests that samples consisting only of employed women do not bias income determination equations (Corcoran et al., 1984).

Additionally, women had to have lived in one of the metropolitan areas greater than 150,000 in 1976 to be included in the sample. It is possible to make erroneous inferences concerning labor market effects on earnings if women live outside the SMSA but work inside it (or vice versa). Selecting women who live in large SMSAs minimizes this problem. One advantage of this selection criterion, however, is that poor women who head families tend to live in large metropolitan areas (Gifford, 1982), making this sample of women an appropriate one for investigating the general problem of poverty among female household heads.

The Dependent Variable--Poverty Vulnerability

Women whose earnings are above the poverty line at present may face a high probability of being poor in the future. A recent study of the economic fortunes of more than 5000 American families between 1968-1977 (Duncan, 1984:42) found that only three percent of all families were poor more than eight years of the study (yet, women who headed families made up 61 percent of the persistently poor). However, 22 percent of these families were poor between one and seven years during this interval. Women who divorced, suffered a debilitating accident, or were laid off from their jobs were likely to experience temporary poverty. Because the poverty line is easily crossed, the poverty threshold should be viewed more like a band than like a line. Women whose earnings are just above the poverty line may still be within the band of poverty vulnerability.

Taking these arguments into account, the dependent variable for this study is the difference between a woman's annual earnings.[3] in 1976 and the Census Bureau's official poverty threshold (which is adjusted for family size and place of residence).[4] Before taking the natural logarithm of this difference score (to correct for skewness), negative and zero values (about 25 percent of the cases) were recoded to one. An ordinary least squares multiple regression model was estimated to assess the strength of the predictor variables in determining the size of the poverty buffer.

Individual-Level Variables

Table 4.1 provides a list of variables in the PSID file used as predictors of poverty vulnerability (see the Appendix for descriptive statistics). These variables include the number of years of completed education,[5] a woman's stock of general skills manifested in work experience,[6] the acquisition of firm-specific skills measured by the length of employer tenure, the respondent's race, and the socioeconomic status index (SEI) of the woman's job.[7]

In addition, because annual earnings are determined by the product of wage rates and time spent working, total hours worked during 1976 was controlled. Sørensen (1983) claims that many earnings determination models are misspecified (especially for women) when they fail to control for time spent working.[8]

Finally, unearned income during 1975 could affect earned income during 1976. For example, past welfare state support might stigmatize a woman in the eyes of an employer, increasing the difficulty of her earning high wages. Similarly,

TABLE 4.1: Descriptions of Independent Variables
Provided by the Panel Study of Income Dynamics Data
Source

Variable Name	Description
EDUCATION	R's number of years of completed education.
EXPERIENCE	R's number of years of work experience. Following Mincer (1974), EXPERIENCE is computed by subtracting completed education (plus five) from R's age. This figure is then adjusted for women's discontinuous labor force participation by multiplying it by a constant less than one. Following Beck et al. (1978b), the constant is .55 for white ever-married women; .88 for white never-married women; .62 for black ever- married women; and .77 for black never-married women.
TENURE	The number of months R had worked for her current employer.
HRS WORKED	The total number of hours R worked during 1976. Estimated by computing the product of the number of weeks worked and the number of hours worked per week.
INCOME '75	Natural logarithm of unearned income, 1975.
SEI	Data from Duncan's (1961) socioeconomic index scale were matched to PSID occupation codes.
UNION MEMBER	Coded 1 if R was a union member; zero otherwise.
COMPETITIVE	Coded 1 if R was employed in a competitive industry; zero otherwise.
RACE	Coded 1 if R was black; zero otherwise.

income originating from family and friends might
result in a woman accepting work in which the main
concern in taking the job is some factor other than
the wage rate (like hours or location). Thus, the
natural logarithm of unearned income in 1975 is
controlled   in   the   model   of poverty
vulnerability.[9]

   Job-Specific Variables. The dual labor market
and dual economy literatures posit that the
structure of the work setting affects earnings net
of labor supply. Therefore, union membership and
employment in the competitive industrial sector
were controlled. Women who were union members in
1976 should have a larger buffer against poverty,
as should women who were employed in non-
competitive industries.

   Local Labor Market Variables. The main variables
of interest in this paper are those tapping local
labor market structure. These measures were first
recorded at the SMSA level and then merged into the
PSID file.

   Industry Mix. Following Parcel and Mueller
(1983) the mix of industries in the area of
residence was controlled. This variable was
measured by the percentage of SMSA employment in
service industries and was taken from the U.S.
Bureau of the Census (1979). I assume that in
service-based labor markets women can exercise a
greater degree of occupational choice (relative to
living in manufacturing areas), and have a better
chance of finding a high-paying job.

   Clearly though, not all women have the skills to
successfully compete in a service-oriented economy.
Research shows that unskilled workers or workers
with unstable work records are more likely to
experience unemployment and live in poverty when
they live in service-based areas (Harrison, 1972;
Betsey, 1978). These people either lack the skills
to find jobs in office-related services (finance,
insurance, real estate, law, advertising, data
processing, etc.) or they shun jobs in competitive
services (recreation, food and delivery services,
retail, personal services) which do not pay enough
to support their families (Kasarda, 1983; Wilson,
1980). As a result, some workers will drift in and
out of the labor force when they are between jobs,
and this work record prevents them from securing

better paying jobs (Piore, 1975). Moreover, living in a service-oriented labor market (with a large number of unattractive jobs) reinforces this pattern of employment.

In order to test this argument, I created two dummy variables: one was indicative of an unstable work record and the second tapped the extent of a woman's skills. Workers who were employed at the beginning of 1976 and whose length of employer tenure at the end of 1976 was less than 11 months, were assumed to have changed employers during 1976. These women were given a score of one on a dummy variable.

To measure the relative proportion of unattractive jobs, the service base of SMSAs was decomposed into two components--the percentage of employment in office-related and competitive service industries.[10] The articulation of the two service sectors is based on the discussion above (for a detailed list of industries in each sector, see Maume, 1985:298). The changed employers dummy variable was then multiplied by the proportion of employment in competitive service industries.[11]

Educational credentials were used as an indicator of a woman's stock of skills. Women at the tails of the educational distribution (high school dropout; college graduate) were given scores of one on separate dummy variables. The high school dropout dummy was multiplied by the percentage of employment in competitive services, while the college graduate dummy was multiplied by the percentage of employment in office-related services.

Following the dual labor market theorists (Harrison, 1972; Betsey, 1978), I predict that unstable and unskilled workers still have a smaller cushion against poverty when they live in areas with a large sector of employment in competitive service industries. But, college-educated women should earn more (and enjoy a larger poverty buffer) when they live in areas where those skills are in demand--i.e., in areas where the employment base is dominated by office-related services.

Economic Power. Another important feature of local market structure is the economic power of an area's principal industries. Export-base theory in economics suggests that regional economies can be divided into two sectors--the export base sector which sells its products primarily in national and international markets, and the local sector whose continued viability is dependent on the income stream generated by the export base. Thompson (1973) argues that the more productive the export base, the more likely it is to enrich the local area--directly, by paying high wages to its workforce, and indirectly, through inter-employer competition for labor. This "wage roll-out effect" hypothesized by Thompson (1973) has been empirically verified by Parcel (1979).

To measure the economic power of an area's principal industries, IRS data (U.S. Department of the Treasury, 1977) were used to measure the proportion of sales by industry (at the 2-digit SIC level) going to large firms (greater than $50 million in assets). An average score for the SMSA was computed by weighting the industrial sales figures by the proportion of SMSA employment in each industry (U.S. Bureau of the Census, 1979) and summing across industries. (For an example of measuring industrial concentration at the state level using this procedure, see Jacobs, 1982.) When women live in an area dominated by a concentrated industry (for example, as do residents of Detroit in this sample), they should enjoy a larger cushion against poverty due to wage roll-out dynamics which boost earnings for all workers in the area.

A preliminary scan of the values on the economic power measure revealed that residents of manufacturing areas had higher scores on this variable. Thus, it might be true that women in skilled blue-collar occupations enjoy higher earnings when they live in these areas. That is, inter-employer wage competition might operate with greater effectiveness among occupations which are in greatest demand by the area's principal employer(s). To control for this possibility, women employed in craft and operative occupations were given a score of one on a dummy variable, which was then multiplied by economic power.

Government Participation in the local Economy. Government participation in the local economy can be direct (in which the public sector hires from the local labor pool), or indirect (in which government purchases the products of industries housed in the local area). In either case, wage scales should rise throughout the region because of an increase in the aggregate demand for goods and services and a reduction in unemployment (Tobin, 1962; Wilson, 1980). Government spending should create income multipliers which boost the earnings of workers in the local economy and increases the size of the poverty buffer for individual women.

Direct government involvement in an area's economy was operationalized as the percentage of employment in the public sector (U.S. Department of Labor, 1979). Government participation in the local product market was measured in a fashion similar to the economic power variable. The U.S. Department of Commerce (1979) provided information on the share of output sold to the public sector by industry (2-digit SIC level). A weighted average for the SMSA was computed by multiplying the proportion of SMSA employment in an industry by its appropriate government sales figure. These products were then summed across all industries. Because the hypothesized effects on earnings are the same for both variables, a composite measure was created by summing the standardized values for these two variables.

One could argue that when the public sector hires from the local labor pool or purchases the output of local area firms, affirmative action policies are implemented which increase the demand for minority labor, and thereby increase the chances that a black woman will find a high-paying job. That is, these policies may create more job opportunities for black women who represent a "double minority" (Epstein, 1973). To test for this possibility, the race dummy variable was multiplied by the composite measure tapping government participation in the local economy.

RESULTS

Table 4.2 presents the specification of the model of female poverty vulnerability. Since the dependent variable is measured in logarithmic form, each variable's effect (b) can be interpreted as

Table 4.2 The Individual-level, Job-specific and Local Labor Market Determinants of the Size of the Poverty Buffer* (log), Female Household Heads, 1976 (N=256)

	b	B	t	Sig t
Constant	-15.65	---	-4.89	.0000
Individual-level Characteristics				
Years of Completed Schooling	.251	.16	2.70	.0075
Years of Labor Force Experience	.072	.12	2.29	.0230
Months Worked for Current Employer	-.002	-.03	-.65	.5148
Socioeconomic Status of Job (SEI)	.050	.29	5.23	.0000
Total Hours Worked	.004	.55	11.55	.0000
Log of Unearned Income, 1975	-.045	-.04	-.89	.3712
Race (1=Black)	-.764	-.09	-1.90	.0592
Characteristics of the Job Setting				
Union Member (1=yes)	1.577	.16	3.51	.0005
Competitive Industry	-1.176	-.14	-2.88	.0043
Local Labor Market Characteristics				
% Employed in Service Industries	.085	.09	1.81	.0711
Economic Power of Principal Industries	.119	.18	3.85	.0002
Gov't Participation in Local Economy	.373	.13	2.49	.0133
Unadjusted R^2	.55607			

*Poverty Buffer = Annual Income - Poverty Threshold

the proportionate change in the size of the poverty buffer given a one-unit increase in the independent variable. For example, a one-year increase in completed education increases the size of the poverty buffer by 25 percent. The standardized coefficient (B) shows the standard deviation change in the size of the poverty cushion given a one standard deviation change in the independent variable. The next two columns present the test statistic "t" and the associated probability of obtaining the observed metric coefficient if in fact there is no association between the independent and dependent variables (i.e., b=0).

Table 2 shows that only two variables are insignificant predictors of the size of the poverty buffer: employer tenure and unearned income during 1975. All other variables have significant effects on poverty vulnerability and are consistent with past research findings.

The strongest predictor of the size of the poverty buffer is total hours worked. This is not surprising given that the dependent variable is earned income (relative to the poverty line). Nevertheless, this finding is important because institutional economists argue that it is through stable employment that workers accumulate the skills necessary for high pay and job promotion (Thurow, 1970). Additionally, dual labor market theorists argue that it is weak job attachment coupled with intermittent labor force participation which prevents secondary workers from moving into high-paying jobs in the primary sector.

Given the importance of hours worked in determining earnings, one can ask, "Is weak job attachment a function of women's family responsibilities or do limited opportunities in the labor market prevent women from working as much as they would like?" Shaw (1985) has found evidence for both answers, but her study was conducted with a sample of married women. Researchers should make hours worked the dependent variable in a sample of female household heads and contrast the predictive strength of human capital and structural variables (as they have done in predicting earnings).

Importantly, the indicators of local labor market structure significantly predict the size of the poverty cushion. Consistent with the findings

of Parcel and Mueller (1983), the larger the
service base in the area of residence, the larger
the poverty buffer. However, the earnings effect
of the service base is only marginally significant.

Of the three local labor market variables, the
measure of the economic power of the area's
principal industries has the strongest effect on
the size of the poverty cushion (B=.18). The
results suggest confirmation of the wage roll-out
hypothesis.

Finally, I find support for the hypothesis that
government participation in local labor and product
markets increases the size of the poverty buffer
for women who head households. Clearly, this
finding has important policy implications.
Government spending tightens local labor markets
and improves the earnings power of the most
vulnerable segment of the population, women who
head households. But this finding also suggests
that when governments cut spending, women's
earnings may drop, possibly exacerbating gender-
based income inequality.

Interactions. Table 3 presents the net effects
of the interaction terms on the size of the poverty
buffer. Three of the five interaction terms are
significant at the .05 level, and each of these
adds about one percent to explained variation in
the model. Finally, it appears that living in an
area in which the government is an active
participant in the local economy does not
significantly boost the earnings for black women
any higher than is the case for white women.
Perhaps, though, a different or a larger sample
would produce an interaction term which is
significant at the .05 level.

Whereas past research has pointed to the wage-
enhancing effect of residence in an area dominated
by a powerful industry (Parcel, 1979), this paper
suggests that the effectiveness of the wage roll-
out is greater for women who occupy skilled blue-
collar jobs (term number 2). On the one hand,
gaining entry into these male-dominated jobs is
likely to result in women drawing higher wages
(Hartmann, 1976). But if women can, in addition,
live in areas where these job skills are needed by
key employers who operate in concentrated markets,
they will receive even higher job rewards. In

other words, when there is a match between one's skills and the skill requisites of the dominant employers in the area of residence, a woman's earnings will be higher.

Supposedly, such a match would exist when college-educated women live in areas where high skills are in demand by employers in office-related services. While the sign for this interaction term is in the expected direction, the coefficient is statistically insignificant. Perhaps because there are so few college-degree women in this sample (approximately 15 percent), the variance on the interaction term is constricted, making it less likely that this variable will predict the size of the poverty buffer.

The next two interaction terms test for the arguments of the dual labor market theorists. I find support for the notion that living in an area with large numbers of unattractive jobs (in competitive service industries) results in a smaller cushion against poverty for women with unstable work histories and/or women who dropped out of high school. It appears unlikely that women will escape poverty or near-poverty when they suffer from personal deficiencies and live in places which lack meaningful job opportunities.

If this interpretation is correct, it suggests that anti-poverty policy must simultaneously upgrade the skills women bring to the labor market, as well as improve the working conditions in competitive service industries. Regarding the latter, both Glazer (1975) and Kammerman (1984) argue that children's allowances could be used to increase pay in these industries. Such a policy would allow women to become self-sufficient while learning job skills that might lead to upward mobility at some future time.[12]

SUMMARY AND DISCUSSION

Female household heads are becoming a larger proportion of the poverty population and as Chapter Eight points out spend longer periods poor than any other group. Research which investigates the determinants of poverty for this group is important not only for developing and revising theories about

Table 4.3 The Effects of the Interactions Between Personal and Labor Market Characteristics*

	b	B	t	Sig t	R^2 change
1. Race (1=Black) x Gov't participation in economy	.566	.17	1.67	.0958	.00507
2. Craft, operative occupation (=1) x Economic Power of Principal Industries	.020	.10	2.01	.0458	.00727
3. College Diploma (=1) x % employed in office-related services	.047	.07	1.17	.2421	.00251
4. High school dropout (=1) x % employed in competitive services	-.049	-.14	-2.22	.0275	.00885
5. Changed employers, 1976 (=1) x % employed in competitive services	-.080	-.18	-2.92	.0039	.01507

* The effect of each interaction term is net of the effects of the variables in Table 2.

poverty in the America, but also for informing policy debates about how best to reduce poverty which might extend across generations.

The Panel Study of Income Dynamics was used to measure the distance between a woman's earnings in 1976 and the poverty threshold (the poverty buffer). After identifying the SMSA in which a woman lived, the structural features of that area were merged into the panel file. Results show that local labor market structure affects women's earnings. Women enjoyed a larger cushion against poverty when they lived in areas where government was an active participant in the local labor and product markets. This statement is also true of women who in places where the principal employer(s) operated in concentrated markets. Service-oriented economies provide a weak buffer against poverty as well.

Especially noteworthy, though, is that evidence was found for the interaction between personal and local labor market characteristics. For example, women who suffer personal deficiencies (such as an unstable work history or who dropped out of high school) live closer to the poverty line when they also live in areas with large base of employment in competitive service industries.

The problems of women (and men) who lack skills and who are trapped in local economies which offer little in the way of meaningful job opportunities will require special governmental attention. It is doubtful that skills training alone will enable these workers to attain economic self-sufficiency. Policies stressing government job provision and federalized child care will be needed to improve the earnings power of women who head households.

While this paper has pointed to the importance of understanding local market structure as a determinant of women's earnings, it is true that total hours worked was the most important determinant of women's poverty vulnerability. Future research should address whether deficiencies in women's labor supply are the result of individual choices made by women; constraints on women placed by child care responsibilities; or because of slack demand for women's labor. It is appropriate that sociologists should begin to investigate the determinants of job attachment from

98

the structural perspective. This research effort is likely to produce knowledge relevant to the wage attainment and mobility processes in American society.

FOOTNOTES

1. I would like to thank Bill Bridges, Toby Parcel, Rachel Rosenfeld, and Charles Tolbert for their comments on earlier versions of this paper.

2. The PSID defines the husband as the head of a household when a married couple live under the same roof. In this sample women who head households are unmarried and have dependent children living with them.

3. Excluded from the measure of annual earnings is income from governmental transfers, investments, alimony, child support, and aid from family and friends. Additionally, regional differences in the cost of living were controlled by inflating the earnings of non-Northeastern residents to reflect those of Northeastern residents.

4. There are some who claim that the poverty threshold overstates the true extent of poverty in the U.S. because non-cash transfers are not included in the family's income to which the poverty line is compared. Others argue that the poverty threshold is set too low because the government establishes the cost of a minimally nutritious diet and multiplies this figure by three. But increased fuel prices have forced American families to spend a lower proportion of their income on food. Thus, the government's food budget should be multiplied by a factor greater than three to arrive at the poverty threshold (for a review of these issues, see Harrington, 1983). I use the government's poverty threshold (despite its problems) because of its widespread use and ready availability. See Chapter One for more discussion of this issue.

5. A set of categorical measures of completed education (reflecting the attainment of various credentials) was substituted into the models of poverty vulnerability. The results did not change when controlling for education in this manner.

6.   The square of the experience measure was added into the poverty model but its effect on the dependent variable was insignificant.

7.   I did not control for the number of children a woman had (even though this variable affects earnings--see Hill, 1979) because the poverty threshold is adjusted for family size. To have included the number of children in the model would have resulted in a non-zero correlation between the regressor and the error term, thereby biasing the other coefficients in the model. Additionally, marital history (1=ever married) was controlled, but this dummy variable was an insignificant predictor of the size of the poverty buffer and was dropped from the analysis.

8.   A dummy variable controlling for health status (1=poor health) was investigated but it did not change the results.

9.   The previous year was used to avoid simultaneity bias with earnings in 1976. Originally, I separated transfer income from the global measure of unearned income, but without a change in the results. Lastly, zero values were recoded to one before computing the natural logarithm of unearned income.

10. Competitive sector industries are narrowly defined in this paper. They include industries which have traditionally employed large numbers of women in manufacturing (non-durable) and service (wholesale, retail, repair, business, recreation, and personal services) industries.

11. In addition, a term was entered into the model testing for the interaction between employment in a competitive industry and the proportion of employment in competitive service industries. This interaction term was too highly intercorrelated with its components to yield interpretable results.

12. Of course, women will not realize earnings gains from improved working conditions unless they have at their disposal adequate and low cost child care (Moore and Sawhill, 1978).

100

REFERENCES

Beck, E. M., Patrick M. Horan, and Charles M. Tolbert, III. 1978a. "Stratification in a Dual Economy: A Sectoral Model of Earnings Determination." American Sociological Review 43:704-720.

_____. 1978b. "Labor Market Discrimination Against Minorities: A Dual Economy Approach." Paper presented at the Annual Meeting of the American Sociological Association, San Francisco.

_____. 1980. "Industrial Segmentation and Labor Market Discrimination." Social Problems 28:13-30.

Bibb, Robert, and William H. Form. 1977. "The Effects of Industrial, Occupational, and Sex Stratification on Wages in Blue-collar Markets." Social Forces 55:974-996.

Betsey, Charles. 1978. "Differences in Unemployment Experiences Between Blacks and Whites." American Economic Review 68:192-197.

Corcoran, Mary, and Greg J. Duncan. 1979. "Work History, Labor Force Attachment, and Earnings Differences Between Races and Sexes." Journal of Human Resources 14:3-20.

Corcoran, Mary, Greg J. Duncan, and Michael Ponza. 1984. "Work Experience, Job Segregation, and Wages." in Barbara Reskin (ed.), Sex Segregation and the Workplace. Washington, D.C.: National Academy of Sciences Press.

Doeringer, Peter B., and Michael J. Piore. 1971. Internal Labor Markets and Manpower Analysis. Lexington, MA.: D.C. Heath.

Duncan, Greg J. 1984. Years of Poverty, Years of Plenty: The Changing Fortunes of American Workers and Families. Ann Arbor: Institute for Survey Research.

Duncan, Otis Dudley. 1961. "A Socioeconomic Index for All Occupations." in A. J. Reiss, Jr. (ed.), Occupations and Social Status. New York: Free Press.

Epstein, Cynthia. 1973. "Positive Effects of the Multiple Negative: Explaining the Success of Black Professional Women." American Journal of Sociology 78:912-935.

Galbraith, John Kenneth. 1967. The New Industrial
    State. Boston: Houghton-Mifflin.
Gifford, Bernard. 1982. "The Urbanization of
    Poverty." Paper presented at the Annual Meeting
    of the American Sociological Association, San
    Francisco.
Glazer, Nathan. 1975. "Reform Work, Not Welfare."
    The Public Interest 40:3-10.
Harrington, Michael. 1983. The New American
    Poverty. New York: Holt, Rhinehart and
    Winston.
Harrison, Bennet. 1972. Education, Training, and
    the Urban Ghetto. Baltimore: Johns Hopkins
    Press.
Hartmann, Heide. 1976. "Capitalism, Patriarchy
    and Job Segregation by Sex." in M. Blaxall and
    B. Reagan (eds.), Women and the Workplace.
    Chicago: University of Chicago.
Hill, Martha. 1979. "The Wage Effects of Marital
    Status and Children." Journal of Human
    Resources 14:579-593.
Jacobs, David. 1982. "Competition, Scale and
    Political Explanations for Inequality: An
    Integrated Study of Sectoral Explanations at the
    Aggregate Level." American Sociological Review
    47:600-614.
Kalleberg, Arne L., Michael Wallace, and Robert P.
    Althauser. 1981. "Economic Segmentation,
    Worker Power, and Income Inequality." American
    Journal of Sociology 87:651-683.
Kammerman, Sheila B. 1984. "Women, Children and
    Poverty: Public Policies and Female-headed
    Families in Industrialized Societies." Signs
    10:249-271.
Kasarda, John D. 1983. "Entry-level Jobs,
    Mobility and Urban Minority Unemployment."
    Urban Affairs Quarterly 19:21-40.
McLanahan, Sara. 1985. "Family Structure and the
    Reproduction of Poverty." American Journal of
    Sociology 90:873-890.
Maume, David J. 1985. "Government Participation
    in the Local Economy and Race- and Sex-based
    Earnings Inequality." Social Problems 32:285-
    299.
Mincer, Jacob. 1974. Schooling, Experience, and
    Earnings. New York: National Bureau of
    Economic Research.

Mincer, Jacob, and Solomon Polachek. 1974. "Investments in Human Capital: Earnings of Women." Journal of Political Economy 82:576-608.

Moore, Kristin A., and Isabel V. Sawhill. 1978. "Implications of Women's Employment for Home and Family Life," in A. H. Stromberg and S. Harkess (eds.), Women Working. Palo Alto: Mayfield.

Parcel, Toby L. 1979. "Race, Regional Labor Markets and Earnings." American Sociological Review 44:262-279.

Parcel, Toby L., and Charles W. Mueller. 1983. Ascription and Labor Markets: Race and Sex Differences in Earnings. New York: Academic Press.

Piore, Michael J. 1975. "Notes for a Theory of Labor Market Stratification," in R. C. Edwards et al. (eds.), Labor Market Segmentation. Lexington, MA.: D.C. Heath.

Shaw, Lois B. 1985. "Determinants of the Increasing Work Attachment of Married Women." Work and Occupations 12:41-57.

Smith, Joan. 1984. "The Paradox of Women's Poverty: Wage-earning Women and Economic Transformation." Signs 10:291-310.

Sørensen, Aage.. 1983. "Conceptual and Methodological Issues in Sociological Research on the Labor Market." Work and Occupations 10:261-289.

Survey Research Center. 1978. A Panel Study of Income Dynamics: Wave X Documentation. Ann Arbor: Institute for Survey Research.

Thompson, Wilbur. 1973. "The Economic Base of Urban Problems," in Neil W. Chamberlain (ed.), Contemporary Economic Issues. Homewood, IL.: R. D. Irwin.

Thurow, Lester. 1970. Investments in Human Capital. Belmont, CA.: Wadsworth.

Tobin, James. 1972. "Inflation and Unemployment." American Economic Review 62:1-18.

U. S. Bureau of the Census. 1978. Characteristics of the Population Below the Poverty Level: 1976. Current Population Reports. Series P-60. no. 115. Washington, D.C.: Government Printing Office.

_____. 1979. County Business Patterns. Parts 1-53. Washington, D.C.: Government Printing Office.

U. S. Department of Commerce. 1979. Input-Output Structure of the U.S. Economy, 1972. Washington, D.C.: Government Printing Office.

U. S. Department of Labor. 1979. Employment and Earnings: States and Areas, 1939-1978. Bureau of Labor Statistics. Washington, D.C.: Government Printing Office.

U. S. Department of the Treasury. 1977. Statistics on Income: Corporation Returns, 1976. Washington, D.C.: Government Printing Office.

Wilson, William J. 1980. The Declining Significance of Race. Chicago: University of Chicago Press.

Appendix

Means and Standard Deviations of Variables in the Analysis of Poverty Vulnerability, Female Household Heads, 1976 (N=256)

	Mean	S.D.
Size of the Poverty Buffer (log)	5.58	3.807
Years of Completed Education	11.82	2.380
Years of Labor Force Experience	13.51	6.569
Months Worked for Current Employer	69.68	67.481
Socioeconomic Status (SEI) of Job	36.33	21.772
Total Hours Worked	1585.06	544.980
Log of Unearned Income, 1975	5.29	3.565
Race (1=black)	.66	.426
Union Member (=1)	.19	.390
Competitive Industry (=1)	.26	.441
% Employed in Service Industries	46.66	4.005
Economic Power of Principal Industries	56.64	5.731
Government Participation in Local Economy	.092	1.298

5

Industrial Structure, Relative Labor Power, and Poverty Rates

Donald Tomaskovic-Devey

This paper develops a structural analysis of poverty which focuses on the creation of poverty positions within local labor markets. As such, it stands in contrast with most poverty studies which focus on the characteristics or behaviors of poor populations. Poverty rates are argued to be primarily a function of local industrial structure and the relative power of labor to extract from employers good quality jobs. Individual qualities of sex, race and education are seen as the cues that allocate people into poverty positions.

Social scientists have been relatively successful in identifying those individual characteristics that are most likely to land a person in poverty. Low education, physical handicaps, female gender and minority status are all generally associated with labor market opportunity, and when coupled with the absence of alternative earning capacity in the household, with poverty. The focus on "individual poverty credentials" is congruent with human capital and status attainment explanations of earnings. The poor are less productive in jobs because they have lower human capital investments (Becker, 1964; Mincer, 1970) or in Thurow's reformulation (1975) are at the tail end of a labor market queue where jobs are scarce and pay poorly.

The argument that the least productive or least credentialed/most discriminated against have high probabilities of poverty is a reasonable one, as far as it goes. Unfortunately, for those in

poverty and those whose goals include lowering the
incidence of poverty, it does not go far enough.
The fact that we can identify individual
characteristics generally associated with poverty
does not demonstrate that they are the causes of
poverty. On the contrary, the individual qualities
that sort people into poverty positions are
reactive to the amount of opportunity to be poor
that inhabitants of a community, or labor market,
face.   Between 1979 and 1983 the official U.S.
poverty rate rose from 11.7 percent of the
population to 15.2 percent. No one would seriously
argue that deterioration in the human capital
investments of almost ten million people was
responsible for this unprecedented (at least since
data have been available) rise in the U.S. poverty
rate. Most would agree that some combination of
lower transfer payment support and deteriorating
job opportunities created this jump in economic
misery.
    A more striking example can be found by
examining the pre-transfer poverty rate time-series
recently produced by Sheldon Danziger and
associates at the Institute for Research on
Poverty. Table 5.1 reports data on the time trend
for pre-transfer or market income poverty rates for
the U.S.. The official U.S. poverty rate includes
transfer income such as social security and AFDC
payments in its computation. The pre-transfer
poverty rate is calculated on all forms of income
prior to federal and state transfer payments. As
such it roughly represents the amount of poverty
that is produced by normal labor market
operation.[1] The most startling aspect of the data
is the lack of trend. From 1965 until 1980 the
market poverty rate fluctuated minimally around 20
percent of the U.S. population. Since 1980 that
rate has climbed to 24 percent. As Table 1
indicates, the same period has seen quite marked
trends in female headed households, per capita
income and median education of the U.S. population.
As per capita disposable income, female headed
households, and general education went up the
market poverty rate barely moved, fluctuating with
the business cycle, but not the "poverty
credentials" of the population. Even economic

106

growth as represented by per capita income does
not seem to have changed the underlying market
incidence of poverty.

Table 5.1 Time Trends in Pre-Transfer Poverty Rates
and Selected Indicators 1965-1983.

Year	Pre-Transfer Poverty	Disposable Per-Capita Income[a]	Female-Headed Households (%)	Median Education (25 years+)
1965	21.3%	$3171		10.6[b]
1967	19.4	3290		
1968	18.2	3389	20.4%	
1969	17.7	3493		
1970	18.8	3665	21.1	12.2
1971	19.6	3752		
1972	19.2	3860		
1973	19.0	4080	22.6	
1974	20.3	4009	22.9	
1975	22.0	4051	23.6	12.3
1976	21.0	4158	24.2	
1977	21.0	4280	24.6	
1978	20.2	4441	25.4	
1979	20.5	4512	25.8	
1980	21.9	4472	28.1	12.5
1981	23.1	4538		
1982	24.0	4544		
1983	24.2			

Source: Sheldon Danziger in Danziger, Peter
Gottschalk, Robert J. Rubin, and Timothy Smeeding,
"Recent Increases in Poverty: Testimony before the
House Ways and Means Committee," IRP Discussion
Paper no. 740-83, p. 6.; Economic Report of the
President, 1985 Table B-24 page 191; Statistical
Abstracts of the United States, Selected Years and
Tables.

a. 1972 dollars.
b. Data for 1960.

POVERTY AS OPPORTUNITY

The lack of relationship over time or for that matter across geographical space between "poverty credentials" and poverty rates should not be surprising. The poverty rate is a function of local opportunity. A town or region can have dramatic growth in poverty rates if an important industry or firm fails. In a capitalist labor market the incidence of poverty is primarily a function of the availability of non-poverty labor market positions and the redistribution of income by the State.

If there are enough good jobs, that is jobs that pay sufficient wages to support a family, there will be little poverty.[2] The extent of poverty then is most directly a function of the ratio of households to good quality, non-poverty level jobs. Presently in the United States the minimum wage is set so low ($3.35/hour) that a household of four must work about 70 hours per week just to rise to the poverty line. Clearly a female headed household, particularly with the added expense of childcare, can not rise above the poverty line at the minimum wage even if working full time. Even a two earner family must work many hours to rise above poverty at the minimum wage. Household composition and human capital investments are secondary and reactive to the quality of available employment. A high school diploma will not prevent poverty if the only jobs available are at the minimum wage. Conversely, single women with children are not doomed to poverty if jobs that pay enough to cover childcare are available. (See Chapter Four for some evidence to this affect.)

What is necessary is an examination of poverty rates as a function of local labor markets. What factors lead to high quality labor markets, ones with high proportions of good jobs and low poverty rates? A good beginning is to think of local labor market opportunity as comprised of both the quality and quantity of available employment. In labor markets where average earnings are high and jobs plentiful we would expect low poverty rates. This argument corresponds to the familiar notion that poverty is a function of economic underdevelopment and that economic growth will eventually eradicate poverty.

108

The JOB QUALITY + JOB QUANTITY = POVERT RATE argument is incomplete, in that it fails to take into account local structures of inequality. For a given level of employment and average wage we can observe different patterns of distribution. The data in Table 1 show how poverty rates can remain quite stable even as per capita income rises. It is necessary to incorporate some understanding of what factors influence the distribution of good and bad jobs, in addition to the level of economic activity. What factors contribute to local inequality? We can identify two global determinants of local inequality --**industrial structure** and the **relative power of labor.**

Industrial Structure

Some industries are more likely to generate high proportions of low quality, poverty level, jobs. Agriculture in particular, but also many of the emerging service industries provide many low wage jobs (Tomaskovic-Devey, 1983; Hodson, 1983). Conversely, employment in the Core Sector of the economy, where there is little market competition, and so firms tend to be stable and able to shift wage costs to consumers, has been associated by many researchers with good quality jobs (Tomaskovic-Devey, 1983; Hodson, 1983; Edwards, 1979; Gordon, 1972). In a more general sense large firms have been associated with higher productivity, protected markets and better quality jobs (Doeringer and Piore, 1971; Hodson 1984). The industrial structure of a locality is likely to influence poverty rates both through its effect on the average quality of jobs and the availability of poverty status jobs.[3]

The Relative Power of Labor

The relative power of labor compliments the local industrial structure in determining the ability of labor market entrants to demand from employers good quality jobs. In localities where the bargaining power of labor is weak much of the population will have no choice but to accept whatever jobs local employers offer. In such localities we can expect high poverty rates. The relative power of labor takes three forms --labor market "tightness", discrimination, and market control.

Labor Market Tightness Labor market "tightness" refers to the relationship between the number of available jobs and the number of job seekers. When there are more jobs than job seekers, wages rise and poverty can be expected to drop.

Discrimination In addition to the tightness of labor markets, certain groups (e.g. blacks, women) face discrimination from many potential employers and historically have had to accept generally lower wages. This discrimination can be the product of employer prejudice, or statistical discrimination in which the employer generalizes group attributes (black educational opportunity or female family responsibility) to all members of the status group. Discrimination not only lowers the wages of those who are discriminated against but an argument has been made that it also lowers the solidarity and so bargaining power of labor in general (Gordon, Edwards and Reich, 1982; Reich, 1981; Szymanski, 1976).

Market Control A final relative labor power concept is market control and refers to the ability of labor market participants to limit their exposure to market forces (Kreckel, 1980; Freedman, 1976; Althauser and Kalleberg, 1981). Unionization, powerful professional associations (e.g. American Medical Association), income supports extracted from the State such as the minimum wage or AFDC payments all represent resources that the labor force, or different fractions of the labor force can use to increase the quality of jobs or reduce their exposure to poverty.

In summary then we can understand poverty as being most directly a function of the availability of jobs, the proportion of jobs which pay low wages and the level of economic development. These three determinants of the local opportunity structure are in turn determined by the local industrial and labor market structure.

Diagram 1 summarizes this conceptual discussion of the antecedents of poverty rates in a local labor market. In the model, industrial structure and the relative power of labor are seen as

determinants of the overall quality and quantity of
available employment as well as the incidence of
low quality, poverty level jobs. The overall
availability of jobs and their quality are then
seen as determinants of the poverty rate in the
population.

Diagram 5.1 A Local Labor Market Conceptual Model
of Poverty Rates

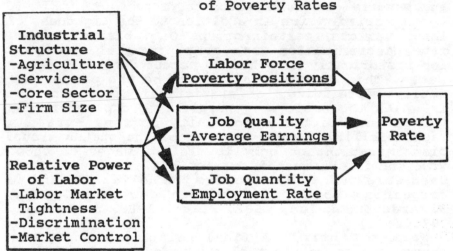

METHODOLOGY

To study fluctuations in poverty rates as a
function of the local opportunity structure
requires either the investigation of a cross-
section of localities or of a single locality over
time. This study will utilize a cross-sectional
approach. The data consist of information derived
from the 1980 Public Use Sample of the Census of
the Population for the 100 largest Standard
Metropolitan Statistical Areas (SMSA's) by the
author. SMSA's were chosen as the unit of analysis
for two reasons. Given current data collection
limitations the SMSA is the closest ecological unit
to the concept of a labor market available. The
SMSA is also the smallest ecological unit for which
some key indicators such as unionization rates and
firm size were available. The general methodology
employed here could be used on other available
ecological units such as counties, states or even

countries. The choice of ecological unit is bounded by both theoretical interest and data availability.

The dependent variable in this analysis is the poverty rate of persons in the SMSA. It is measured as the percent of the population whose 1979 household income fell below the federal poverty line for households of that size.

The first measure of **industrial structure** in this study is the percent of the labor force employed in Core industries (CORE). Durable manufacturing, utilities, communication, transportation and construction industry employment were summed and then taken as a percent of all employment to approximate the Core Sector concept. The proportion of employment in retail trade and personal services (SERVICE) is used as a measure of industries with high proportions of low wage jobs. Agricultural employment, although generally associated with poverty was not measured because of the urban nature of the sample. Finally data on average establishment size (FIRMSIZE) was added to the data set from the 1978 Census of Industry (U.S. Bureau of the Census, 1980).

Labor market tightness, the first **relative** labor **power** concept, was operationalized with two measures, the 1980 unemployment rate and the mean number of weeks of unemployment in 1979 for those who reported spells of unemployment. The **discrimination** concept was operationalized as the percent of the workforce minority and percent male. This study uses three very different measures of **labor market control** -- unionization, elite occupational shelters, and welfare shelters. Unionization was operationalized as the unionization rate of production workers in the mid-1970s (Freeman and Medoff, 1979). This indicator was used rather than the unionization of all workers because in preliminary analysis it was found to be more highly associated with both poverty rates and the intervening variables. Elite occupational shelters refers to the combination of high educational credentials and professional associations which some occupations use to control their labor market. The proportion of employment in an SMSA that could be classified as High Professional (Doctors, Accountants, Engineers, Scientists, Lawyers, University Professors) is the

second indicator of **labor market control**. The final
indicator of **labor market control** is the average
state AFDC payment in 1980 (U.S. Bureau of the
Census, 1981). AFDC payments vary tremendously from
state to state and provide non-market income to
raise some families above the poverty line and also
provide labor market bargaining resources for those
people at the end of the labor market queue. These
three measures, elite occupational shelters,
unionization, and AFDC payments tap resources that
are primarily available for different layers of the
job stratification structure. It remains to be seen
if all three provide direct or indirect resources
to limit poverty.

There are three **opportunity structure** concepts
in the theory developed in this paper intervening
between **industrial structure** and **relative labor
power** and poverty rates. They are Job Quality, Job
Quantity, and Labor Force Poverty Positions. Job
Quality is operationalized as the mean yearly
earnings of labor market participants in an SMSA in
1979 and is a measure of the level of overall
economic development in an area. Alternative
operationalizations such as mean hourly earnings
and mean hours worked per week were explored in
preliminary analysis but were less strongly related
to the dependent and other intervening variables in
the analysis. Mean household income was not used
because it is a household rather than labor market
concept and so not theoretically appropriate under
this model. The Job Quantity concept refers to the
availability of sufficient employment for the
population. The SMSA employment rate, calculated as
the percent of the total population employed is the
measure of Job Quantity. It differs from and is
superior to an unemployment rate in that it is a
pure measure of job availability, insensitive to
the age structure of, or the number of discouraged
workers in a locality. The final indicator is the
percent of employed people living in poverty, it
corresponds to the notion of low quality, poverty
level jobs.

The analysis utilizes weighted least squares
multiple regression.[4] The analysis strategy will
be to look first at the direct relationships
between **industrial structure** (Table 5.2, equation
1), **relative labor power** (Table 5.2, equation 2),

TABLE 5.2 WLS Regression of Poverty Rates Upon Industrial Structure and Labor Power and Opportunity Structure Variables for 100 Largest U.S. SMSA's in 1979.

	1^a	2	3	4
		Y = Poverty Rate		
Core	-.34(-.58)****			-.01(-.02)
Service	-.10(-.12)			-.01(-.00)
Firmsize	.08(.08)			.04(.04)
Male %		-.05(-.01)		-.06(-.05)
Minority %		.15(.35)***		.12(.27)****
Elite Professional %		-.25(-.11)		.01(.00)
Unionized Production Workers %		-.05(-.22)*		-.02(-.11)+
Unemployment Rate		-.08(-.06)		-.07(-.05)
Unemployment Duration		.47(.36)***		.16(.12)+
Mean AFDC Payments		-.00(-.01)		-.00(-.06)
Mean Earnings			$1.8\text{-}04^b$(.07)	-.00(-.03)
Employment Rate			-.22(-.32)****	-.21(-.31)****
Labor Force Poverty			1.25(.75)****	.98(.58)****
Constant	20.53	8.80	15.48	20.78
r	.574	.613	.839	.908
r^2	.309	.330	.696	.799

a. Metric Coefficient (Standarized Coefficient)
b. Scientific Notation
+   p = .10
*   p = .05
**   p = .01
*** p = .001
**** p = .0001 or below

and **opportunity structure** variables (Table 5.2, equation 3) and poverty rates. The full model of **industrial structure,** **labor power,** and **opportunity structure** variables will be explored in Table 5.2, equation 4. In Tables 5.3, 5.4, and 5.5 we will examine the relationships between **industrial structure** and **labor power** and **labor force poverty, job quantity,** and **job quality.** In these models reciprocal relationships between the opportunity structure measures are theoretically plausible and so two-stage weighted least squares are employed to produce the final estimates. Diagram 5.2 and Table 5.6 will present an overview of the significant relationships and facilitate a path analytic analysis of the process of poverty position generation. (Readers uncomfortable or unfamiliar with multiple regression type statistical analysis may want to skip to the Discussion Section.)

ANALYSIS

Poverty **Rates**

In Table 5.2, equation one we see the regression of poverty rates upon three **industrial structure** variables. The only significant relationship with poverty rates is the strong negative correlation (beta = -.58) of percent employed in the core sector of the economy (CORE) and poverty rate. Service employment (SERVICE) and mean establishment size (FIRMSIZE) are not significant and, in fact, their signs are both in the wrong direction.

Equation 2 reports the relationships between poverty rates and the **relative labor power** variables. Of the two labor market tightness variables --unemployment rate and unemployment duration-- only duration of unemployment is significantly and positively related to poverty rates (beta = .36). The unemployment rate coefficient is in the wrong direction and not significant. The analysis contains two discrimination indicators -percent labor force minority (MINORITY%) and percent labor force male (MALE%). MINORITY% has the predicted positive and statistically significant relationship (beta = .35) with poverty rates. The MEN% coefficient is in the

correct direction but not statistically
significant. All three market control variables
display the predicted negative relationship with
poverty rates but only the percent production
workers unionized (UNION%) is statistically
significant. Surprisingly, non-market income
support, targeted at poverty populations (MEAN
AFDC) has only the smallest of negative
relationships with poverty rates. Elite occupations
as a percent of local employment has a moderate
negative relationship with poverty rates which one
might expect to approach statistical significance
in a larger sample.

The **opportunity structure** variables in equation
3, display the predicted strong relationships with
poverty rates. All three variables --MEANEARN,
EMPLOYMENT RATE, LABOR FORCE POVERTY-- have the
predicted signs, but the coefficient for MEANEARN
is not statistically significant. The data in
equation 3 suggest that for every one percent rise
in employment rates a locality experiences almost a
quarter of a percent drop in the poverty rate and
for every one percent rise in labor force poverty
there is a resulting one and a quarter percent rise
in population poverty.

The full regression model is presented in
equation 4 of Table 5.2. Overall the model fits the
data well. As predicted the **opportunity structure**
variables provide most of the explanatory power in
the equation. Labor Force Poverty is the strongest
predictor in the equation (beta = .58) and displays
a nearly 45 degree slope (b = .98) with the
dependent variable. The Employment Rate continues
to display a negative, significant relationship
with poverty rates in this equation. Of the
industrial structure and **relative labor power**
concepts only three display continued strong
relationships with poverty rates over and above the
opportunity structure measures. Unionization rates
show a small negative relationship with poverty
(b = -.02, beta = -.11) and approaches statistical
significance with a probability below .1 but above
.05. Similarly, unemployment duration shows a
positive but statistical marginal relationship
with poverty rates (b = .16, beta = .12, and .10 <
p > .05). Most dramatic of the relative labor power
variables is MINORITY% which continues to display a

strong (Beta = .27) relationship with poverty rates over and above the opportunity structure variables. Of the remaining variables all are statistically insignificant.

Labor Force Poverty Rates

Table 5.3 contains the results of three regression equations of labor force poverty upon the industrial structure variables (equation 1), the relative labor power variables (equation 2), and both sets of predictor variables (equation 3). No specific predictions were made for these equations so I will simply summarize the significant relationships. In equation 1 percent employed in core industries (CORE) is negatively related (b = -.17, p = -.01) to labor force poverty. In equation 2 percent minority is positively associated with and percent unionized is negatively associated with labor force poverty. Surprisingly, in the two-stage solution reported in equation 3 percent male in the labor force is positively associated with labor force poverty (b = .16, p = .05). Percent minority displays a weak positive relationship (b = .06, p = .05) with labor force poverty in equation 2 but a stronger relationship (b = .11, beta = .40, p = .001) in the full model reported in equation 3. Finally mean labor force earnings (MEANEARN) has the strongest relationship with labor force poverty (b = -.001, beta = -.48, p = .0001).

Employment Rates

Table 5.4 reports the data for regressions of the job quantity indicator EMPLOYMENT RATE upon industrial structure variables (equation 1), relative labor power variables (equation 2), and pooled indicators (equation 3). Core employment is positively and highly significantly (p = .001) associated with employment rates in the industrial structure model but the relationship is reduced to non-significance

TABLE 5.3   WLS Regression of Labor Force Poverty upon Industrial Structure and Labor Power Variables for 100 largest SMSA's in 1979.

y = Labor Force Poverty Rate

	1^a	2	3^c
Core	-.17(-.47)****		-.10(-.28)*
Service	-.02(-.03)		-.001(-.00)
Firmsize	-.02(-.02)		-.02(-.04)
Male %		.08(.11)	.16(.20)*
Minority %		.06(.23)*	.10(.38)***
Elite Professional %		-.11(-.08)	-.02(-.01)
Unionized Production Workers %		-.03(-.23)*	-.002(-.02)
Unemployment Rate		-.04(-.06)	.10(.12)
Unemployment Duration		.11(.14)	-.03(-.04)
Mean AFDC Payment		.00(.02)	.001(.06)
Mean Earnings^b			-.001(-.49)****
Employment Rate^b			.10(.22)+
Constant	10.72	0.46	2.28
R	.471	.364	.637
R^2	.198	.068	.324

a. Metric Coefficient (Standardized Coefficient)
b. Predicted Scores, resulting from first stage of two-stage least squares analysis.
c. Two-Stage least squares.

+   p = .10
*   p = .05
**   p = .01
***   p = .001
**** p = .0001 or less

TABLE 5.4   WLS Regression of Employment Rate Upon Industrial Structure and Labor Power Variables for 100 Largest U.S. SMSA's in 1979.

	y = Percent Population in Labor Force		
	1^a	2	3^c
Core	.27(.31)***		.12(.14)
Service	.05(.04)		-.01(-.01)
Firmsize	-.32(-.21)*		.28(-.18)+
Men %		.22(.12)	-.12(-.06)
Minority %		.13(.21)*	-.18(-.28)*
Elite Professional %		.61(.18)*	.20(.06)
Unionized Production Workers %		-.01(-.02)	-.08(-.22)*
Unemployment Rate		-.18(-.09)	-.37(-.20)*
Unemployment Duration		-.83(-.44)****	-.38(-.21)*
Mean AFDC Payment		-.01(-.13)+	-.01(-.22)*
Mean Earnings^b			.002(.65)****
Labor Force Poverty^b			1.39(.43)**
Constant	61.18	59.75	34.9
R	.349	.598	.720
R^2	.094	.310	.452

a. Metric Coefficient (Standardized Coefficient)
b. Predicted scores from first stage of two stage least squares regression.
c. Two stage least squares regression.
+   p = .10
*   p = .05
**   p = .01
***   p = .001
**** p = .0001 or less

in equation 3. Mean establishment employment (FIRMSIZE) is negatively associated with employment rates (b = -.32, p = .05) in both the industrial structure and the pooled equation. Unemployment duration is negatively related to employment rate in both equations 2 and 3. The unemployment rate while not significantly associated with employment rates in the relative labor power equation, displays a moderate negative relationship in the pooled equation (beta = -.20, p= .05). While percent minority displays a <u>positive</u> relationship in the relative labor power equation(2), it is negatively related to employment rates in the full model (3). The three market control variables display interesting relationships with the employment rate. ELITE SHELTERS displays a positive significant association in equation two and a positive non-significant relationship in the pooled equation. Unionization rate in the SMSA is in the pooled equation negatively associated with employment rates (b = -.08, beta = -.22, p = .05). Welfare supports are also associated with a slight reduction in employment rates (b = -.01, beta = -.22, p = .05). Finally, mean earnings has a strong positive relationship with the employment rate (beta =.65, p = .0001) and labor force poverty displays a positive relationship as well (beta = .43, p = .01).

Mean Earnings

Table 5.5 presents the results of regressions of the mean labor force earnings in an SMSA upon the industrial structure and labor power variables. Core sector employment shows a strong positive relationship with mean earnings in equation one only. Core sector employment was, however, a major antecedent of labor force poverty and employment rates in the first stage of the two-stage least squares and so its impact is somewhat obscured in the final model. Percent minority also displays a strong positive relationship with mean earnings. The percent of employment in elite occupations also displays a significant positive relationship with mean earnings (b = 123.8, beta = .13, p = .10). The unemployment rate is positively associated with

TABLE 5.5 WLS Regression of Mean Labor Market Earnings Upon Industrial Structure and Labor Power Variables for the 100 Largest U.S. SMSA's in 1979

	Y = Mean Earnings		
	1[a]	2	3[c]
Core	97.6(.42)****		11.0(.05)
Service	-40.8(-.12)		9.8(.03)
Firmsize	37.1(.09)		-24.7(-.06)
Men %		30.9(.06)	42.9(.08)
Minority %		67.0(.38)***	89.4(.51)****
Elite Professional %		259.2(.27)**	123.8(.13)+
Unionized Production Workers %		20.6(.21)*	6.1(.06)
Unemployment Rate		123.0(.24)*	116.9(.23)**
Unemployment Duration		-163.6(-.32)**	9.5(.02)
Mean AFDC Payment		.86(.06)	2.1(.15)*
Employment Rate[b]			128.1(.42)****
Labor Force Poverty[b]			-548.8(-.62)****
Constant	11286	10015	2514
R	.468	.506	.836
R^2	.195	.200	.657

a. Metric Coefficient (Standardized Coefficient)
b. Predicted scored from first stage of two-stage least square analysis.
c. Two-stage least square regression.

+ $p = .10$
* $p = .05$
** $p = .01$
*** $p = .001$
**** $p = .0001$ or less

mean earnings (beta = .23, p = .01) as is mean
AFDC payment (beta = .15, p =.05). The employment
rate is positively associated with mean earnings
(beta = .42, p = .0001) and labor force poverty
displays a negative relationship (beta = -.62, p =
.0001).

Diagram 5.2. Path Diagram of Significant
Relationships (p = < .10) between Industrial
Structure, Relative Labor Power, and Opportunity
Structure Variables and Poverty Rates for the 100
Largest U.S. SMSAs in 1979-80 (Standardized
Coefficients).

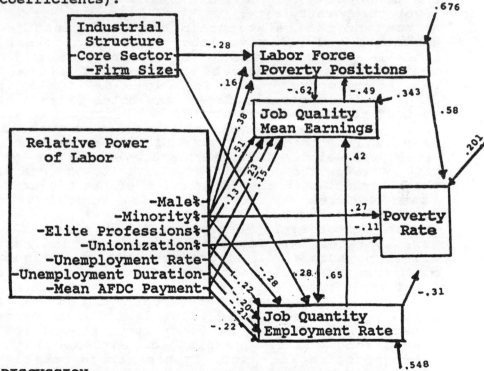

DISCUSSION

Diagram 5.2 presents a path model constructed from
the relationships reported in Tables 5.2 through
5.5. Only relationships with a probability of .10
or lower are reported. The numbers on the path
represent the relative magnitude and direction of
the relationship between two variables. Most of

the effects of the **industrial structure** and **labor power** variables upon poverty rates are mediated by the predicted **opportunity structure** variables -- labor force poverty, mean earnings and employment rate. Of these, only labor force poverty and the employment rate display direct effects upon poverty rates. Mean earnings does, however display substantial effects upon both labor force poverty and the employment rate. The percent of the labor force minority and percent of production workers unionized both display direct effects upon poverty rates. The larger the proportion of the labor force minority the higher the poverty rate. The larger the proportion of the labor force unionized the lower the poverty rate.

Most of the relationship between industrial structure and relative labor power and poverty rates is indirect, mediated by the intervening job characteristic variables. The significant relationships are present in Diagram 5.2. Table 5.6 displays the indirect, direct and total effects of each of the **industrial structure**, **labor power** and **opportunity structure** variables upon poverty rates. Significant indirect effects of core employment, elite professional employment and unionization upon poverty rates are understated because of the use of these variables in the first stage of the two-stage least squares estimation of the opportunity structure variables.

Core sector employment has no direct effect upon poverty rates, but has a negative (-.18) indirect effect because it is associated with both higher mean earnings and lower labor force poverty in a locality. Percent labor force male also has only a weak indirect positive effect upon poverty rates because it is associated with higher labor force poverty. This finding is contrary to theoretical predictions and is unexplained. Percent of the labor force racial minority has strong positive direct (.27) and indirect (.16 via both mean earnings and labor force poverty) effects upon poverty rates. This variable displays the second largest total effect (.43) upon poverty rates in this analysis and highlights the historical importance of racial discrimination in the

TABLE 5.6 Calculations of Direct, Indirect and
Total Effects of Independent Variables Upon Poverty
Rates.

Variable	Direct	Indirect	Total
Core		-.19	-.19
Male %		.09	.09
Minority %	.27	.16	.43
Elite Professional %		-.06	-.06
Unionized Production %	-.11	.06	-.05
Unemployment Rates		.05	.05
Unemployment Duration		.06	.06
Mean State AFDC Payment		.14	.14
Labor Force Poverty	.58	.26	.81
Mean Earnings		-.11	-.11
Employment Rate	-.31	.01	-.30

Source: Diagram 5.2

production of poverty positions in the United
States. Elite occupational composition has a small
negative indirect effect (-.06) upon poverty rates
via mean earnings. The presence of unusually high
concentrations of the very best jobs seems to have
a quite small influence (if any) on the incidence
of poverty. Unionization rates have contradictory
effects upon poverty rates. The direct effect of
unionization is to reduce poverty rates (-.11), but
the indirect effect is to raise them (.06), leading
to a small negative total effect (-.05). The
indirect effect is the result of the negative
relationship between unionization and employment
rates. Unemployment rates and unemployment duration
both show small indirect positive effects upon
poverty. It would seem that long spells of
unemployment, as well as, high rates of
unemployment are likely to undermine the labor
market power of low wage workers. Transfer payment
level (MEAN AFDC) has a very indirect effect upon
poverty rates mediated by its effects upon both
mean earnings and employment rates. These
relationships are, however, in different
directions. AFDC payment level is positively
associated with mean earnings but negatively
associated with the employment rate. One

interpretation is that high AFDC payments allow low
wage workers to withhold their labor until slightly
higher wage offers are made, thus increasing
overall earnings but also decreasing the number of
jobs offered by employers as wages rise. The net
effect on poverty rates is thus close to zero. It
should be realized, however, that AFDC payments in
even the most "generous" states are set to bring
families up towards the poverty line but not above
it.   If AFDC payments were high enough to lift
families out of poverty then we might expect larger
indirect effects and a direct effect upon poverty
rates as well.

The three opportunity structure variables
display substantial total effects upon poverty
rates. Labor force poverty is the single strongest
predictor (total effect = .81) of population
poverty with a direct effect of .58 and an indirect
effect, via employment rates of .26.   As poverty
level employment rises so does poverty in general,
at the same time earnings in general fall and
employment rates rise. Mean earnings shows small
indirect effects (-.11) upon poverty rates via both
the employment rate and labor force poverty.
Finally the employment rate is negatively related
to poverty directly (-.31) and has a slight
positive indirect relationship (.01).

In general then, we can conclude that the amount
of poverty in a locality primarily reflects the
availability of non-poverty level jobs, racial
discrimination, and the capacity of the working
class to protect itself through unionization.   The
level of economic development, measured as average
earnings does not reduce poverty directly but is
associated with more non-poverty level jobs.   Labor
markets characterized by large core sector firms,
low unemployment rates and short unemployment
duration, fewer minorities and more unions are also
likely to have fewer poverty level jobs.   Finally,
neither service sector employment nor the level of
AFDC payments has much to do with variations in
poverty rates across these SMSA's. The preceding
chapter by David Maume presents evidence that
service employment may have a slight positive
effect on the poverty rate for women but his
measure of the service sector including employment
in office related services such as banking and real

estate. Maume's research did show a negative effect of low wage service sector employment on the poverty buffer for high school dropouts. Sanders in the next chapter finds similar small effects of AFDC payments on poverty rates.

CONCLUSION AND POLICY IMPLICATIONS

This paper has argued for a structural understanding of poverty in which the incidence of poverty is a function of opportunity in a local labor market. Specifically the ratio of poverty positions (low wage jobs and insufficient jobs) generated by the labor market to community population will determine the extent of poverty in a locality. A theory of poverty rates was developed in which the local industrial structure and the relative power of labor were argued to influence an overall opportunity structure. Overall job quality (mean labor market earnings), job quantity (employment rate) and labor force poverty were seen as the ultimate determinants of poverty rates in the population.

The analysis largely upheld the model with the exception that both minority employment and unionization rates displayed direct effects upon poverty rates above and beyond their indirect effects upon local opportunity structures. The suggestion is that both racial discrimination and the collective organization of the working class can have dramatic effects upon the production of poverty level positions.

Population poverty rates are, of course, a function of both earnings and household size. Household composition, including the presence of a male wage earner and children, and household labor market activity, particularly the number of labor market participants, will greatly influence which families fall into poverty. The job quality and job quantity concepts developed in this paper are likely to act as conditional modifiers determining the likelihood and usefulness of multiple wage earners, divorce, and the poverty penalty associated with being in a female headed or minority household. Thus household composition, household employment activity, and the penalty associated with individual poverty "credentials" will be to some extent a function of the local opportunity structure. This is, of course, precisely the line of argument and data analysis in the preceding chapter.

The policy implications of this analysis directly oppose most poverty policy in the United States. If the goal is to reduce the incidence of poverty and all of its associated misery, then opportunity must be expended in areas of high poverty. More jobs is not enough, good jobs are required. The route to this goal would seem to include the elimination of poverty level employment and the historical legacy of racial discrimination. To accomplish the first goal a higher minimum wage, which after 40 hours of work provides a family of three enough income to be both above the poverty line and afford daycare is necessary. If such a minimum wage reduced employment then income transfer levels would have to be set high enough to lift the unemployed and underemployed out of poverty. The effects of discrimination are largely historical, and geographically concentrated in the southern United States. In the south United States racial antagonism between members of the working class have forestalled working class solidarity through unionization, kept income supports such as AFDC absurdly low, and overall produced mainly low wage labor markets. Recent investment activity in the south United States may result in higher wages and lower poverty rates. Higher minimum wages and national AFDC standards would also have the effect of eliminating the historical legacy of racism. It is not clear, of course, that all discrimination effects in this analysis are historical rather than current practice. Current racial discrimination in employment or in education, which is not only important for labor market entrants but also for potential capital investment, must be attacked through legislation and social movement activity. This study failed to find any significant relationship between the sex composition of the labor force and poverty rates. This is no doubt due to the fairly even geographical distribution of women and the low level of variation in the sex composition of the labor force across SMSAs.

Undoubtedly though, women's work is all too often poverty level work, part-time and minimum wage. Like racial minorities women must continue to pursue an aggressive social movement to increase the quality of traditionally female jobs and desegregate the labor force by sex.

NOTES

1 Of course, if government income supports were removed individuals would adjust their labor market behavior and so these rates are not accurate predictors of poverty without a welfare state.

2 I would go so far as to say if there are enough good jobs there will be fewer female headed households, because the economic pressure that is associated with family dissolution and teenage pregnancy will be reduced. Conversely, the cost of being in a female headed household drops as job opportunity rises and argument made in the previous chapter.

3 There is, of course, a literature on the determinants of job stratification within firms and industries (Baron and Bielby, 1980; Wallace and Kalleberg, 1982; Burroway, 1979, 1984; Hodson, 1983, 1984; Tomaskovic-Devey, 1983, 1986). The current argument does not focus on intra-organizational stratification processes. Instead it relies upon typical stratification patterns associated with industrial structure.

4 The weights used were population counts for the SMSA divided by the mean population of all SMSA's in the analysis. The weighting procedure was required to correct for sampling biases. The data was estimated by the author for each SMSA from a Public Use Sample of the 1980 Census of the Population. As such, each SMSA's data in the analysis is based on a different sample size, ranging from 4122 for the New York SMSA to 169 for Chattanooga, TN-GA.

128

BIBLIOGRAPHY

Althauser, R. and A. Kalleberg, 1981. "Firms, Occupations and the Structure of Labor Markets." in I. Berg (ed.) Sociological Perspectives on Labor Markets. (New York: Academic).

Baron, J. and W. Bielby, 1980. "Bringing the Firms Back In: Stratification Segmentation and the Organization of Work." American Sociological Review 45:737-65.

Becker, G., 1964. Human Capital (New York: Columbia University Press).

Burroway, M. 1979. Manufacturing Consent: Changes in the Labor Process Under Monopoly Capitalism. (Chicago: University of Chicago Press).

_____ 1983. "Between the Labor Process and the State: The Changing Face of Factory Regimes Under Advanced Capitalism." American Sociological Review 48:587-605.

Doeringer, P. and M. Piore, 1971. Internal Labor Markets and Manpower Analysis. (Lexington, MA: D.C. Heath).

Edwards, R., 1979. Contested Terrain (New York: Basic Books).

Freedman, M. 1976. Labor Markets: Segments and Shelters. (New Jersey, Alanheld and Osmun).

Freeman, R. and J. Medoff, 1979. "New Estimates of Private Sector Unionism in the United States." Industrial and Labor Relations Review 32:143-175.

Gordon, D. 1972. Theories of Poverty and Unemployment. (Lexington, MA: D.C. Heath).

Gordon, D., R. Edwards, and M. Reich, 1982. Segmented Work, Divided Workers: The Historical Transformation of Labor in the United States. (New York: Cambridge University Press).

Hodson, R., 1983. Worker's Earnings and Corporate Economic Structure. (New York: Academic).

_____ 1984. "Companies, Industries and the Measurement of Economic Stratification." American Sociological Review 49:335-348.

Kreckel, R., 1980. "Unequal Opportunity Structures and Labor Market Segmentation." Sociology 14:525-50.

Mincer, J., 1970. "The Distribution of Labors Income." Journal of Economic Literature 8:1-26.

Reich, M., 1981. Racial Inequality: A Political
    Economic Analysis (Princeton, NJ: Princeton
    University Press).
Szymanski, A., 1976. "Racial Discrimination and
    White Gain." American Sociological Review
    41:403-414.
Thurow, L., 1975. Generating Inequality (New York:
    Basic Books).
Tomaskovic-Devey, D., 1983. Good Jobs, Bad Jobs,
    No Jobs: The Stratification Consequences of U.S.
    Industrial and Occupational Structure and
    Change, 1960-1980. (unpublished Ph.D.
    dissertation, Boston University).
_____ 1986. "Organizational Stratification, the
    Relations of Production and Job Quality: A
    Theory of Positional Stratification." paper
    presented at Southern Sociological Society
    meeting in New Orleans.
U. S. Bureau of the Census, 1980. County Business
    Patterns, 1978:SMSAs U.S. Government Printing
    Office; Washington D.C.
------ 1981. Statistical Abstract of the United
    States, 1981, U.S. Government Printing Office.
Wallace, M. and A. Kalleberg, 1982. "Industrial
    Transformation and the Decline of Craft: The
    Decomposition of Skill in the Printing Industry
    1931-1978." American Sociological Review 47:307-
    324.

6

A Test of the New Structural
Critique of the Welfare State

Jimy M. Sanders

INTRODUCTION

According to the new structural critique of
poverty, "overly generous" welfare programs have
given rise to a class of citizens who <u>choose</u> to
live in poverty. The availability of transfer
payments and the antiwork and antifamily rules of
eligibility that govern their distribution
purportedly create powerful incentives for choosing
a lifestyle of single parenthood and unemployment.
Consequently, the incidence of poverty has
increased in recent years because large numbers of
Americans opt for a lifestyle of welfare-dependency
instead of low-wage employment. In effect, poverty
has become structural in determination in that
increases in poverty are largely endogenous to the
very welfare programs that were implemented to
curtail poverty.[1] This phenomenon allegedly
exists because of the rapid expansion of public
assistance between the early 1960s and mid 1970s
(e.g., Gallaway et al., 1985; Murray, 1984; Sowell,
1983).[2] This is, of course, a very different use
of the notion of structural poverty from that
presented in the last two chapters. In those
chapters structural poverty referred to the
existence of insufficient as well as low wage
employment. In this chapter, the idea of
structural poverty arises out of conservative
attacks on the welfare state and parallels the
historical distinction between the poor and paupers
discussed in Chapter One.

The purpose of this paper is to determine the extent to which these arguments accurately reflect our experience with public transfers and poverty during the past several years. The remaining sections of the paper consist of a brief background review of the critique that public transfers operate as a structural determinant of female headed families and poverty, an examination of the research evidence, an empirical test of the new structural critique of poverty, and a concluding discussion.

THE NEW STRUCTURAL CRITIQUE OF POVERTY

Those who contend welfare generates more poverty than it relieves have little quarrel with the observation that increases in public assistance reduce poverty among the poor. Rather, their position is that "overly generous" public transfers encourage increases in the number of poor people and hence, over the long run, the rate of poverty goes up. From this perspective, efforts to reduce poverty through welfare allocations are flawed for two fundamental reasons. First, the rise of female headed families is thought to be fueled by government regulations that discourage the presence of a prime aged man, especially an employed husband, in the household of a publicly assisted mother. Second, it is argued that public transfers reduce the incentive to work, particularly among those who are unlikely to obtain market-wages above the legal minimum. Were it not for the lure of a subsidized lifestyle of unemployment, many of these people would presumably be earning market-wages above the poverty level. As a result, we are purported to have more impoverished people today than if welfare benefits were less generous and consequently less attractive as an alternative to employment.

A number of widely read books seem to articulate the concerns and frustrations of many citizens and public officials who view the welfare system with serious misgivings and sometimes outright hostility (e.g., Gilder, 1980; Murray, 1984; Sowell, 1983; Kemp, 1979; Anderson, 1978; Friedman and Friedman, 1980; Mead, 1985). Much of the dissatisfaction with public welfare stems from the belief that taxes were steadily raised between the mid 1960s and early 1980s in order to foot the bill of an overly generous welfare system. Because this viewpoint is so widely held, the popular appeal of a punitive approach to "the welfare problem" has been gaining momentum (see the discussion of this process in Chapter Ten). According to this perspective, adult-recipients of income maintenance transfers deserve to be punished for their lack of employment and the production of children whom they cannot support. Increasingly, the underlying issue that motivates criticism of public assistance is the belief that many transfer-receiving adults choose to go jobless. They are, in effect, sponging off of taxpayers.

Aid to Families with Dependent Children (AFDC hereafter) is usually the focal point of controversy over the extent to which income maintenance transfers encourage acquiescence to a lifestyle of poverty and welfare-dependency (Halsey, 1982).[3] AFDC is the largest provider of cash transfers (other than Social Security). The total cost of AFDC was 16.1 billion dollars in 1984. This figure has grown rapidly since 1960 when it was one billion dollars. The number of AFDC recipients has also grown quickly. In 1960, there were approximately three million recipients per-month (parents and children). By 1984, there were 10.9 million recipients per-month (Statistical Abstract of the United States, 1986, 1984). AFDC guidelines often encourage recipients not to work and to avoid two parent households wherein at least one adult is employed fulltime (DiNitto and Dye, 1983). Therefore, AFDC is easily condemned as a prime example of public aid that contributes to habitual unemployment and family breakup. Father's absenteeism was the basis of AFDC eligibility for 87 percent of all recipient children in 1979 (Statistical Abstract of the United States, 1986).

Murray (1984) provides what is perhaps the most trenchant critique of AFDC. He concentrates on the socialization effect of growing up in an environment wherein many, perhaps most, neighbors, classmates, and friends come from households dependent on public assistance for long periods of time. In such neighborhoods, it is argued, young people are likely to accept as normative the avoidance of stable employment and two parent households in order to obtain government transfers. In this way, the new poverty of choice is thought to reproduce itself from one generation to the next. Subcultures emerge wherein work-values and self-sufficiency are not highly regarded. In effect, transfers reduce efforts among poor youths to acquire education and work-experience.

Thus the new structural critique of poverty leads to the conclusion that welfare programs such as AFDC should be drastically reduced. Since the availability of transfers is seen as an encouragement to welfare-dependency, cutbacks in public assistance will presumably motivate adults and teenagers to work and thereby demonstrate to children the importance of education for getting ahead. But does the research literature support the argument that "overly generous" AFDC transfers lead to increases in female headed families and poverty? We now turn our attention to answering this question.

THE STATE OF THE EVIDENCE

In one of the few research applications of the new structural critique of poverty, Gallaway and Vedder (1985) examine whether the relative generosity of states' AFDC programs in 1975 were related to percentage changes in the rate of poverty among children between 1969 and 1979. Using estimates of the marginal costs and revenues associated with raising a child in poverty, Gallaway and Vedder (1985) contend AFDC provides economic incentives to recipient-mothers for having several children. Their calculations suggest that, on average, the net profit per-child reared in poverty is 12.5 percent. Consequently, Gallaway and Vedder (1985) argue that states offering comparatively generous levels of AFDC transfers encourage increases in the rate of poverty among children. But these findings contrast sharply with much of the evidence.[4] A major review of the literature is provided by Danziger et al. (1981). The authors conclude that public transfers, including AFDC, account for modest declines in work-effort, but nonetheless are very effective in reducing poverty.

Numerous efforts have been undertaken to overcome the work-disincentives associated with AFDC. In 1967, the transfer tax rate on AFDC payments received by employed recipients was reduced from 100 to 67 percent for earnings above thirty dollars. The tax rate on AFDC transfers has increased since the 1981 Omnibus Budget Reconciliation Act (Fraker et al., 1985) back to 100 percent. Yet the real tax rate is often lighter than the intended rate due to underreports of income (Halsey, 1982). Also in 1967, the work incentive program, a forerunner of workfare, was created. But prior to passage of the Talmadge amendments in 1971, the opportunity to participate in a work incentive project was often reserved for only those deemed by welfare case workers to be most employable (Mink, 1978). By March of 1970, only seven percent of adult AFDC recipients were enrolled in work incentive projects (Gordon, 1978). The Talmadge amendments made it mandatory for all adult AFDC recipients to register for the work incentive program. However, exemptions were granted for numerous reasons including the presence of preschool aged children. As a result, many AFDC recipients remained unaffected by the work incentive program (Smith and O'Brien, 1978). During the 1970s, AFDC recipients in Seattle and Denver (1970-78) and Gary (1971-74) were included in the negative income tax experiment. AFDC recipients also participated in the supported work experiment conducted by the Manpower Demonstration Research Corporation starting in 1975.

Most studies find the tax rate on AFDC transfers is inversely related to work-effort (Moffitt, 1986; Danziger et al., 1981). But some researchers contend that the net effect of comparatively high transfer tax rates is to create a greater total volume of work since the number of people eligible for AFDC declines as the transfer tax rate becomes higher (Barr and Hall, 1981). Purportedly, the amount of work performed by former AFDC recipients more than offsets the reduction in work among those still receiving transfers.

Masters (1981) reports that the supported work program contributed to increases in post program earnings, although sometimes only over the short run, among 1,620 long term female recipients of

AFDC with poor work records and no preschool aged children. Auletta's (1982) sobering account of the experiences of AFDC participants in a supported work program operated by the Manpower Demonstration Research Corporation also suggests modest increases in employment can be achieved. Danziger's (1981) interviews of 34 AFDC recipient-mothers who completed a supported work program reveals that the women were often successful in obtaining steady employment. The main accomplishment of supported work, for these women, may have been that the experience instilled an improved sense of self-confidence. The lack of self-confidence is perhaps the main obstacle to successful participation in the labor market among AFDC recipient-mothers (Auletta, 1982). Chapter Eight explains in more depth why supported work has had more success than other training programs.

A survey of work incentive projects by Gordon (1978) identifies several examples of success, but many cases of failure are also found. By July of 1970, only nine percent of all work incentive participants had been terminated with a job (Mink, 1978). Approximately one-quarter of the employers of work incentive graduates received tax credits (Gordon, 1978). Initial findings from contemporary experiments of mandatory work programs in three states indicate employment among AFDC recipients, especially those with poor work histories, can be modestly increased over the short run (Friedlander et al., 1986).

Results of the negative income tax experiment are summarized by Robins (1985). The unusually high guaranteed levels of transfers provided by the experiment appear to have led to an overall reduction in work. Among female family heads, work-effort was initially estimated to typically decline the equivalent of between two and three 40 hour work-weeks annually. However, there are methodological problems with these experiments and the real amount of reduced work-effort is disputed. Moffitt (1981) reports that the actual reduction in work attributable to the Gary, Seattle, and Denver projects is closer to nine percent than the 25 to 30 percent reported in earlier analyses (e.g., Moffitt, 1979). The initial errors stem from underreports of income earned in the labor market.

Alternatively, Anderson (1978) offers a series of calculations that suggests the actual reduction in work attributable to the negative income tax experiment is larger than the 25 to 30 percent range initially reported.

The evidence in regard to the relationship between the rise of female headed families and AFDC transfers also cuts in many ways. The extent to which AFDC transfers contribute to the decline of two parent families is disputed. Bishop's (1980) review of the literature on employment, transfers, and marital instability includes seven studies that examine whether AFDC transfers encourage family breakup. A majority of these and other studies (e.g., Hutchens, 1979; Bahr, 1979) confirm such a relationship, but often the estimates are not statistically significant. This leads Bishop (1980) to conclude that the causal link between AFDC and the rise of female headed families has yet to be established. Ellwood and Bane (1984) find AFDC payments do increase the likelihood that young single mothers maintain their own household, but this tendency accounts for very little of the increase in female headed families since 1960.

In sum, the research usually indicates that AFDC transfers are associated with non-traditional family structure. However, it is not certain what part, if any, of the association reflects a causal relationship wherein AFDC contributes to the rise of female headed families. There is perhaps even less agreement on the question of whether AFDC transfers lead to increases in poverty. Most of the research indicates that AFDC has substantially reduced poverty since the early 1960s. However, the welfare system AFDC recipients participate in is fraught with a wide array of work-disincentives. Though many efforts have been made to moderate these disincentives, it is clear that substantial difficulties persist. In addition, proponents of the new structural critique of poverty find that comparatively generous AFDC transfers are related to increases in the rate of poverty among children. According to the new structuralist, this relationship exists because AFDC transfers encourage the rise of female headed families and diminish the importance of work-values and self-sufficiency. Of course, the research reported in the preceding two chapters showed that employment, per se, does not prevent poverty. This issue is ignored by the new structural critique of poverty. In the following section of this paper, I attempt to shed a clearer light on the extent to which the new structural critique contributes to our understanding of relationships involving AFDC, female headship, and poverty.

EXAMINING THE MERITS OF THE NEW STRUCTURAL CRITIQUE OF POVERTY

States play a decisive role in formulating and conducting AFDC programs. They are largely responsible for setting standards of eligibility, defining minimum basic needs, and determining the extent to which AFDC payments cover official levels of need.[5] Consequently, states are used as the unit of analysis in this study. I focus on the 1960s and 1970s.

An inconsistency emerges as soon as the observable data are applied to the new structural critique of poverty. In some respects the data conform to the critique, but in other respects the critique appears to be unsupported. In Figure 6.1, plots A and B reveal the extent to which the rate of poverty among families is inversely related to contemporaneous levels of monthly AFDC transfers per recipient family. A floor effect is suggested, such that beyond a certain point of generosity, AFDC transfers are virtually unrelated to the rate of family-poverty. Yet the simple linear relationship is strong in both 1960 and 1980. States most generous in their distribution of AFDC transfers tend to have the lowest levels of poverty. Despite this, the criticisms of AFDC reviewed above are also consistent with much of the data. Plot C shows the relationship between states' average monthly AFDC transfers per recipient family between 1960 and 1980 and changes in the rate of family-poverty over the same two decades. There is a strong pattern wherein states least generous in their provision of AFDC transfers experienced the greatest declines in poverty. Moreover, plot D indicates that states providing the lowest levels of AFDC transfers experienced

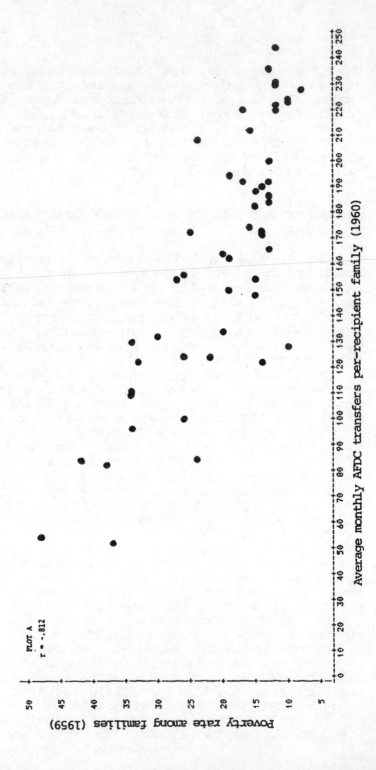

Figure 6.1 Scatter plots of AFDC transfers, family-poverty, and female headed families, 1980–1960.

TABLE 6.1 continued

PLOT B
r = -.716

Poverty rate among families (1979)

20 19 18 17 16 15 14 13 12 11 10 9 8 7 6 5

0 10 20 30 40 50 60 70 80 90 100 110 120 130 140 150 160 170 180 190 200 210 220 230 240 250

Average monthly AFDC transfers per-recipient family (1980)

Figure 6.1 continued

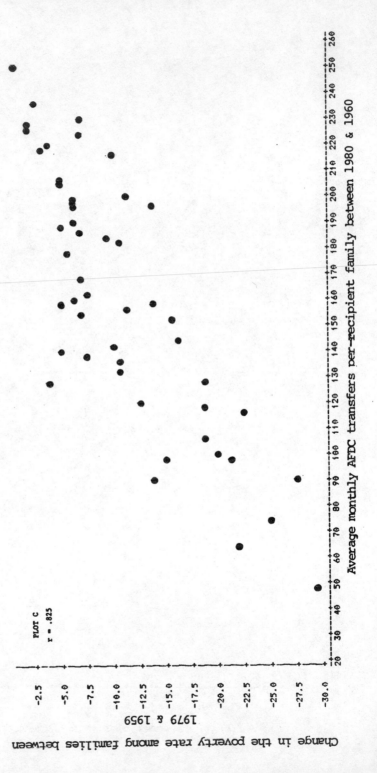

PLOT C
r = .825

Change in the poverty rate among families between 1979 & 1959

Average monthly AFDC transfers per-recipient family between 1980 & 1960

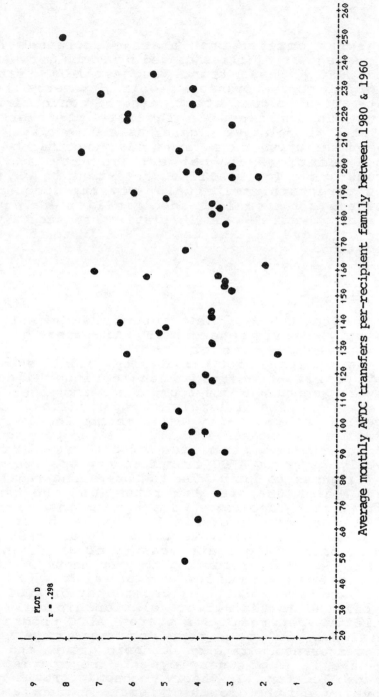

Average monthly AFDC transfers per-recipient family between 1980 & 1960

Change in the percentage of female headed families
between 1980 & 1960

PLOT D
r = .298

somewhat smaller than average increases in the percentage of families headed by women between 1960 and 1980. These trends suggest AFDC transfers mitigate contemporaneous levels of poverty, but the data are also consistent with the contention that long run increases in the rate of poverty are related to relatively generous AFDC outlays. Thus the descriptive data raise much uncertainty about the relationship between poverty and AFDC transfers. To establish the extent to which the new structural critique of poverty accounts for increases in female headed families and poverty, the hypothetical causal relationships contained in the critique must be tested. It is to this task I now turn.

Model

According to the new structural critique of poverty, overly generous AFDC transfers give rise to poverty through the following causal relationships. AFDC eligibility guidelines and the net profit associated with rearing children in poverty encourage disproportional increases in the number and size of female headed families. Because poverty is unusually high among female headed families, increases in such families push up rates of poverty among families and children. Further, overly generous AFDC transfers depress recipients' willingness to work, due to government regulations (e.g., high transfer tax rates) and the tendency for welfare-dependency to undermine the work ethic.

The proportion of families headed by women can be observed at the state level. In contrast, there is no direct aggregate measure of willingness to work. However, according to proponents of the new structural critique of poverty, the work disincentive effects of dependency on AFDC can be estimated as the direct relationship between the relative generosity of states' AFDC programs and changes in the rate of poverty if the contemporaneous rate of economic growth and change in the rate of unemployment are statistically controlled for. In theory, economic growth retards poverty and the growth of female headed families, while upswings in unemployment increase poverty and female headship.[6] In each equation, the dependent variable lagged 10 years is also controlled for. In this way, poverty and female headship are modeled as change, consistent with the theoretical arguments reviewed above.[7]

Each table reports three equations consistent with those presented in Footnote 6. Equation 1a is the structural-form equation with which estimates of the direct effects of AFDC transfers on poverty are obtained. Equation 1b is the reduced-form of equation 1a. A comparison of equations 1a and 1b reveals the extent to which the direct effects of AFDC transfers on changes in the rate of poverty are mediated by changes in the percentage of families headed by women. Equation 2 is the structural-form of the hypothetical process wherein AFDC transfers are related to changes in the percentage of families headed by women. The equations that pertain to poverty among families are estimated for both the 1960s and 1970s. The hypothetical processes reviewed above are examined separately for the two decades because contemporary criticisms of public assistance embrace the argument that the poverty inducing tendencies of welfare during the 1960s were pale in comparison to such tendencies during the 1970s (e.g., Gallaway et al., 1985). Due to limitations of the data, poverty among children is examined for only the latter decade. Descriptive statistics and the sources of the data are reported in an appendix. Fiscal data are analyzed in 1972 dollars to control for inflation.

FINDINGS

Tables 6.1 through 6.4 each report parameter estimates obtained with equations 1a, 1b, and 2. Table 6.1 considers changes in the rate of poverty among families during the 1960s. How well do these results adhere to the new structural critique of poverty? In equation 1a we see that the relative generosity of AFDC transfers is not directly related to changes in the rate of poverty among families during the 1960s. The possibility that a nonmonotonic relationship exists wherein AFDC transfers up to some level reduce poverty, but

TABLE 6.1 OLS parameter estimates of the determinants of changes in 1) the rate of poverty among FAMILIES and 2) the percentage of female headed families.   Circa 1970–1960.

	DEPENDENT VARIABLES					
	Poverty rate among families (1969)		Poverty rate among families (1969)		Percentage of female headed families (1970)	
Equation	1a		1b		2	
	b (SE)	B	b (SE)	B	b (SE)	B
Intercept	−.193		2.482		1.157	
Change in the percentage of female headed families (1970–1969)	.996 (.314)	.110	—	—	—	→
aRelative generosity of states' AFDC programs (per-recipient family, 1970–1960)	.640ns (.534)	.063	.642ns (.585)		.243ns (.201)	.065
Change in the rate of unemployment (1970–1960)	.013ns (.164)	.002	.047ns (.180)		.039ns (.064)	.030
Economic Growth (1970–1960)	−.088 (.027	−.167	−.126 (.026)		−.007ns (.013)	−.028
Poverty rate among families (1959)	.646 (.037)	1.188	.654 (.040)		—	—
Percentage of female headed families (1960)	—	—	—	—	.977 (.051)	.969
$\overline{R}^2$	.961		.953		.912	
Degrees-of-freedom	44		45		45	

aTo facilitate interpretation, the decimal point of the metric coefficients (b) and standard errors have been moved to the right two places

nsNull hypothesis not rejected at .05 level of significance, one-tail test.

transfers of greater value lead to increased poverty was also examined. Though Gallaway and Vedder (1985) argue that the relationship should be monotonic, a nonmonotonic specification is consistent with the arguments of Gallaway et al. (1985) for public aid in general. I found no evidence that a nonmonotonic relationship existed between the relative generosity of states' AFDC programs and changes in poverty during the 1960s. Further, the antifamily critique of AFDC is not supported in equation 2. The relative generosity of AFDC transfers in the 1960s is unrelated to changes in the percentage of female headed families. Hence the new structural critique of poverty offers a very faulty account of the determinants of poverty in the 1960s.

On the other hand, increases in the percentage of female headed families are directly related to increases in the rate of poverty among families. At the mean of the independent variable, the net increase in poverty is 1.25 percent.[8] But the most important determinant of poverty appears to be economic growth. The mean rate of economic growth between 1960 and 1970 is 42 percent. Economic growth of this magnitude translates into a decline in the rate of poverty among families of 3.7 percent. In contrast, changes in the rate of unemployment are unrelated to changes in the rate of poverty among families during the 1960s.

How is it possible that the rates of family-poverty and unemployment are unrelated? Poverty among families could be buffered from changes in the unemployment rate for any number of reasons. For example, during the 1960s, if the demand for workers in the "secondary labor market" adequately met the supply of poor people participating in the labor force and who had no recourse but to accept low wages, there would be no reason for changes in the economy-wide rate of unemployment to affect the rate of poverty among the working poor. Further, since most adult AFDC recipients do not participate in the labor force (DiNitto and Dye, 1983), changes in the rate of unemployment will have no bearing on their poverty status. Still, the performance of the economy, of which unemployment is one index, is usually believed to have considerable influence on poverty. Indeed, we find economic growth is the

most powerful suppresser of poverty. But net of
economic growth, we find unemployment to be
unrelated to the rate of poverty among families.

These relationships are re-examined for the
1970s in Table 6.2. For this period, the findings
are more consistent with the new structural
critique of poverty. The relative generosity of
AFDC transfers are directly related to both poverty
and female headship. A substantively large
interstate difference in average monthly AFDC
transfers per-recipient family of say $50
(approximately one standard deviation) is
associated with a net change of one-third of one
percent in the rate of poverty among families. In
equation 2, we see that a $50 interstate deviation
in monthly AFDC transfers per-recipient family is
associated with a net change of four-tenths of one
percent in the proportion of female headed
families. While these estimates are statistically
consistent with the new structural critique of
poverty, they nonetheless suggest that the
antifamily and antiwork impact of relatively
generous AFDC transfers during the 1970s were quite
weak in substantive terms.

The most powerful determinants of poverty among
families during the 1970s appear to have been
economic growth and the rise of female headed
families. When evaluated at the mean of the
independent variable, increases in the percentage
of female headed families are related to slightly
more than a one percent increase in the rate of
family-poverty. As economic growth slowed in the
1970s, its effect on contemporaneous changes in the
rate of poverty among families diminished. Family-
poverty was reduced only 1.25 percent by the mean
rate of economic growth during the 1970s. That the
estimated net effect of economic growth in the
1970s (b= -.045) is considerably smaller than the
effect in the 1960s (b = -.088) suggests that the
relationship between economic growth and poverty
may not operate independently of the pace of
economic growth or the absolute rate of poverty.
Danziger and Gottschalk (1986) and Gottschalk and
Danziger (1985) consider such possibilities and
conclude that probable rates of economic growth in
the foreseeable future are unlikely to effectively
reduce poverty.

TABLE 6.2 OLS parameter estimates of the determinants of changes in 1) the rate of poverty among FAMILIES and 2) the percentage of female headed families. Circa 1970–1980.

	DEPENDENT VARIABLES					
	Poverty rate among families (1979)		Poverty rate among families (1979)		Percentage of female headed families (1980)	
Equation	1a		1b		2	
	b (SE)	B	b (SE)	B	b (SE)	B
Intercept	1.237		2.589		-.066	
Change in the percentage of female headed families (1980–1970)	.376 (.111)	.134	—	—	—	—
[a]Relative generosity of states' AFDC programs (per-recipient family, 1980–1970)	.676 (.293)	.122	.809 (.322)	.147	.849 (.261)	.177
Change in the rate of unemployment (1980–1970)	.015[ns] (.074)	.008	.084[ns] (.079)	.043	.134[ns] (.086)	.078
Economic Growth (1980–1970)	-.045 (.015)	-.123	-.062 (.016)	-.169	-.028 (.018)	-.089
Poverty rate among families (1969)	.634 (.030)	1.143	.628 (.033)	1.133	—	—
Percentage of female headed families (1970)	—	—	—	—	1.235 (.067)	.943
$\bar{R}^2$	.951		.939		.909	
Degrees-of-freedom	44		45		45	

[a]To facilitate interpretation, the decimal point of the metric coefficients (b) and standard errors have been moved to the right two places

[ns]Null hypothesis not rejected at .05 level of significance, one-tail test.

What can we conclude about the new structural critique of poverty? Statistically, the critique is consistent with the data from the 1970s. Yet the total direct and indirect (via female headed families) effect of a substantively large interstate variation in AFDC transfers per-recipient family ($50) accounts for less than a one-half of one percent change in the rate of poverty among families. It is obvious that the new structural critique accounts for little of the actual changes in family-poverty and female headship that transpired during the 1970s.

The analyses reported in Tables 6.3 and 6.4 allow us to consider whether the new structural critique of poverty offers a better explanation of changes in the rate of poverty among children. Table 6.3 reports changes in the rate of poverty for children under 18 years of age. These findings are similar to those obtained for poverty among families during the 1970s. Again the new structural critique of poverty is statistically consistent with the data. However, metric interpretations of the estimates suggest the critique provides a weak account of the determinants of poverty. For instance, a standard deviation difference in annual AFDC payments per-recipient child ($293) is directly related to just over a one-half of one percent change in the rate of poverty among children. On average, the strongest effect on poverty is again attributable to economic growth. States averaged a 28 percent rate of economic growth during the 1970s which translates into a three percent decline in poverty among children.

Turning to Table 6.4, we see that the estimated relationships pertaining to poverty among children under 5 years of age approximate those estimated for all children.[9] In general, contemporary criticisms of AFDC appear to offer no better account of poverty among children than among families. In both cases, the explanatory power of the critique leaves much to be desired. The most powerful determinant of poverty identified in this study is economic growth.

TABLE 6.3 OLS parameter estimates of the determinants of changes in 1) the rate of poverty among <u>CHILDREN UNDER 18 YEARS OF AGE</u> and 2) the percentage of female headed families. Circa 1980-1970.

	DEPENDENT VARIABLES					
	Poverty rate among children under 18 years of age (1979)		Poverty rate among children under 18 years of age (1979)		Percentage of female headed families (1980)	
Equation	1a		1b		2	
	b (SE)	B	b (SE)	B	b (SE)	B
Intercept	4.290		5.828		-.115	
Change in the percentage of female headed families (1980-1970)	.442 (.203)	.099	—	—	—	—
[a]Relative generosity of states' AFDC programs (per-recipient child, 1980-1970)	.194 (.103)	.123	.226 (.106)	.144	.149 (.050)	.174
Change in the rate of unemployment (1980-1970)	.236 (.140)	.076	.314 (.141)	.101	.149 (.089)	.087
Economic Growth (1980-1970)	-.109 (.028)	-.187	-.132 (.027)	-.227	-.030 (.018)	-.093
Poverty rate among families (1969)	.674 (.039)	1.113	.677 (.041)	1.118	—	—
Percentage of female headed families (1970)	—	—	—	—	1.250 (.071)	.954
$\overline{R}^2$	.933		.928		.905	
Degrees-of-freedom	44		45		45	

[a] To facilitate interpretation, the decimal point of the metric coefficients (b) and standard errors have been moved to the right two places

ns Null hypothesis <u>not</u> rejected at .05 level of significance, one-tail test.

150

TABLE 6.4   OLS parameter estimates of the determinants of changes in 1) the rate of poverty among <u>CHILDREN UNDER 5 YEARS OF AGE</u> and 2) the percentage of female headed families.   Circa 1980–1970.

	DEPENDENT VARIABLES					
	Poverty rate among children under 5 years of age (1979)		Poverty rate among children under 5 years of age (1979)		Percentage of female headed families (1980)	
Equation	1a		1b		2	
	b (SE)	B	b (SE)	B	b (SE)	B
Intercept	6.255		8.351		−.115	___
Change in the percentage of female headed families (1980–1970)	.602 (.239)	.145	___	___	___	___
[a]Relative generosity of states' AFDC programs (per-recipient child, 1980–1970)	.278 (.121)	.191	.323 (.127)	.221	.149 (.050)	.174
Change in the rate of unemployment (1980–1970)	.224[ns] (.165)	.077	.330 (.169)	.114	.149 (.089)	.087
Economic Growth (1980–1970)	−.143 (.033)	−.263	−.175 (.033)	−.321	−.030 (.018)	−.093
Poverty rate among families (1969)	.647 (.046)	1.148	.650 (.048)	1.154	___	___
Percentage of female headed families (1970)	___	___	___	___	1.250 (.071)	.954
$\bar{R}^2$	.897		.880		.897	
Degrees-of-freedom	44		45		45	

[a]To facilitate interpretation, the decimal point of the metric coefficients (b) and standard errors have been moved to the right two places

[ns]Null hypothesis <u>not</u> rejected at .05 level of significance, one-tail test.

CONCLUSIONS

The evidence reported in this paper lends little credibility to the new structural critique of poverty. Yet the critique is statistically consistent with our analysis of the 1970s. That is, we do find statistically significant effects consistent with the thesis that, over the long run, comparatively generous AFDC transfers encourage acquiescence to a lifestyle of welfare-dependency and poverty. But these relationships are substantively weak and it is widely acknowledged that public transfers reduce poverty over the immediate short run. Thus the critical issue is the tradeoff between the short run diminution and long run incremental tendencies AFDC transfers exert on poverty.

The lack of annually reported poverty-data means we are unable to track short run associations between AFDC transfers and poverty at the state level. The data are more complete at the national level. Figure 2 provides an informative comparison of the descriptive relationship between poverty and 1) AFDC transfers and 2) social security retirement transfers for the United States as a whole. The graph displays the rates of poverty among children and among persons aged 65 or greater between 1959 and 1984. Average annual AFDC transfers per recipient child and average monthly social security benefits per retired worker (aged 62 or greater) are intermittently reported in 1984 dollars below the horizontal axis. These data may be found in the Statistical Abstract of the United States (1986, 1985, 1984, 1981, 1979, 1977).

The real dollar value of AFDC transfers per recipient child increased by 46 percent between 1960 and 1975. During this time, the number of child recipients of AFDC increased 242 percent. These policies appear to have had a large impact on poverty. Between 1960 and 1975, the rate of poverty among children fell approximately 10 percent. This decline in poverty was achieved despite the fact that 29 of the last 73 months of the period were marked by recession. Since 1975, the real value of AFDC transfers per recipient child has remained more or less unchanged. However, the pool of poor youths receiving AFDC

152

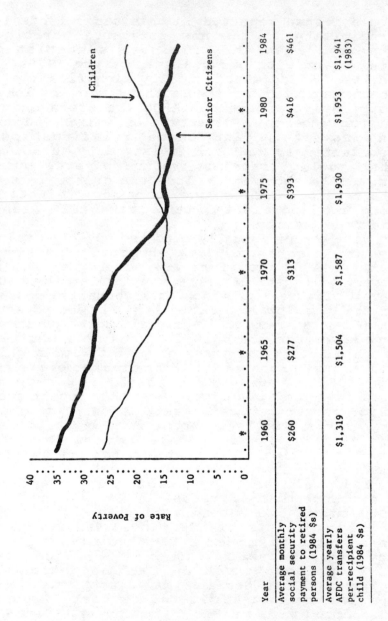

Figure 6.2 Transfer payments and poverty among the elderly and children, 1984–1959.

Year	1960	1965	1970	1975	1980	1984
Average monthly social security payment to retired persons (1984 $s)	$260	$277	$313	$393	$416	$461
Average yearly AFDC transfers per-recipient child (1984 $s)	$1,319	$1,504	$1,587	$1,930	$1,953	$1,941 (1983)

transfers has been reduced by 13 percent while the number of children living in poverty has grown by 16 percent (Statistical Abstract of the United States, 1986, 1979). What are the consequences of these developments? The rate of poverty among children increased roughly 5 percent between 1975 and 1984. As state AFDC programs expanded, poverty among children declined. Subsequent retrenchment in AFDC has coincided with increases in poverty among children.

While recent years have witnessed stagnation in AFDC benefits and a tightening of eligibility requirements, public transfers to the elderly have grown. During the 1970s, monthly social security payments per retired worker increased by one-third in real dollars. At the same time, the rate of poverty among seniors declined by more than nine percent. Between 1980 and 1984, social security payments to the retired grew another 11 percent while the rate of poverty among this segment of the population declined by three percent. Thus we see two divergent trends. On the one hand, transfers in support of the elderly are expanding and the rate of poverty among this segment of the population is declining. On the other hand, transfers in support of children are decreasing and the rate of poverty among this segment of the population is increasing.

Based on the available evidence, it is difficult to accept the argument that cutbacks in AFDC transfers will encourage work effort and traditional family structure to the point of pushing down the rate of poverty. It is more likely that reductions in AFDC transfers will portend increases in poverty. The immediate reductions in poverty resulting from augmenting poor people's income with AFDC transfers appear to more than offset the longer run counter tendency of AFDC transfers to induce some people into a lifestyle of welfare-dependency and poverty.

NOTES

1. The "new" structural critique of poverty is an old idea in the sociological literature. For instance, Simmel's (1908) structural analysis of

154

poverty, dependency, and the derogatory social
status of welfare-recipients proposes that the
unilateral transfer of resources creates a unique
social strata among the poor. When assistance is
offered and accepted under no expectations of (or
opportunity for) reciprocity, transfer-recipients
become distinguishable from the working poor who
maintain self-sufficiency. Hence the self-
sufficient poor are seen as contributors to the
social good whereas the welfare-dependent poor are
viewed as social parasites.

I would like to thank Elwood Carlson, Beth
Ghiloni, Bruce Mayhew, Miller McPherson, Patrick
Nolan, Ken Shin, John Skvoretz, Shelley Smith, Lynn
Smith-Lovin, Lala Steelman, Robert Stewart, and
Donald Tomaskovic-Devey for their criticisms and
suggestions.

2. Gallaway et al. (1985) report that
approximately 4.5 million Americans chose to join
the ranks of the officially impoverished between
1972 and 1978. In the ensuing five years, this
pool purportedly declined by more than one-half
because of reductions in the real value of public
transfers.

3. AFDC has a complex history. Its inception
occurred under the provisions of the 1935 Social
Security Act. Until 1950, the program was called
Aid to Dependent Children. Several papers that
consider the operation and effectiveness of AFDC
(and other antipoverty programs) may be found in
Haveman (1977). Block (1979) and Dobelstein (1980)
provide reviews of litigation involving AFDC
through the late 1970s. Historical reviews of AFDC
may be found in Patterson (1981) and DiNitto and
Dye (1983). See also the discussions in Chapters
One and Eight of this Volume.

4. The findings of Gallaway and Vedder (1985)
are consistent with the stereotypic view that
children provide a meal ticket for poor parents.
It is commonly believed that AFDC families are
large because of such economic incentives. In
fact, AFDC families tend to be small and they have
been declining in size for many years. In 1979, 70
percent of the families receiving AFDC transfers
had one or two children (Statistical Abstract of
the United States, 1984).

5. For example, in 1979 the state-determined level of monthly income necessary to cover all basic needs of a single mother with one child was as high as $482 (Vermont) and as low as $115 (Texas). Actual assistance provided to such families ranged from $390 (Hawaii) to $60 (Mississippi). Only three states (Vermont, Rhode Island, Alaska) met the non-binding minimum federal standards for food-allowances. Seven states (Connecticut, Delaware, Florida, Montana, Ohio, South Carolina, Texas) failed to provide for even one-half of these standards (Department of Health and Human Services, 1980). Patterson (1981) offers a historical account of interstate differences in AFDC programs.

6. These hypothetical processes are represented in the following equations.

$$P_t = B_0 + B_1(F_t - F_{t-10}) + B_2(R_t{}^1{}_{=}{}^0{}_1 A/10) -$$

$$B_3[((I_t - I_{t-10})/I_{t-10})](100) + B_4(U_t - U_{t-10}) +$$

$$B_5(P_{t-10}) + e_t. \tag{1a}$$

$$P_t = B_0 + B_2(R_t{}^1{}_{=}{}^0{}_1/10) -$$

$$B_3[((I_t - I_{t-10})/I_{t-10})](100) + B_4(U_t - U_{t-10}) +$$

$$B_5(P_{t-10}) + e_t. \tag{1b}$$

$$F_t = B_0 + B_2(R_t{}^1{}_{=}{}^0{}_1/10) -$$

$$B_3[((I_t - I_{t-10})/I_{t-10})](100) +$$

$$B_4(U_t - U_t{-10}) + B_5(F_{t-10}) + e_t. \tag{2}$$

P is the rate of poverty among families when A is the average monthly AFDC payment per-recipient family. P is the rate of poverty among children when A represents annual AFDC payments per-recipient child. The analyses conducted by Gallaway and Vedder (1985) reveal an inverse relationship between the net profit of raising a child in poverty and the age of the child. If this is correct, we might expect that economic

incentives to replenish the family's contingent to
young children would result in AFDC subsidization
being more strongly related to increased poverty
young children than children in general (but recall
note 4). Therefore, change in the rate of poverty
among children is analyzed separately for 1) all
children under 18 years of age and 2) only those
children under five years of age. F is the
percentage of families headed by women. The rate
of economic growth is operationalized as a
percentage change in per capita personal income
(I). U is the rate of unemployment.

7. The advantage of modeling change in this way
rather than operationalizing change scores on the
left side of the equals sign is that, if the
theoretical arguments dictating the specification
of the model are incorrect such that relevant
variables are omitted from one or more of the
equations, the effects of the missing variables
should be subsumed by the parameter estimate
associated with the lagged dependent variable.
Given the specification of a lagged dependent
variable, the same parameter estimates (with the
exception of the intercept) are obtained regardless
of whether the dependent variable (on the left side
of the equals sign) is measured as a change score
or simply the current level. It would be
preferable to use instruments rather than observed
values for lagged dependent variables to minimize
covariances between residuals and regressors.
However, when good instruments (highly correlated
with the observed variables for which they
substitute and uncorrelated with the residual) are
not readily estimated, the strategy of holding
constant a lagged observed dependent variable can
often be employed successfully (e.g., Hannan,
1979).

8. The descriptive statistics used to
demonstrate the substantive significance of the
parameter estimates may be found in the appendix.

9. Equation 2 in Table 6.4 is simply a
reproduction of equation 2 in Table 6.3. It is
reported in Table 6.4 for the convenience of the
reader.

BIBLIOGRAPHY

Anderson, Martin. 1978. Welfare: The Political Economy of Welfare Reform in the United States. Stanford, California: Hoover Institution.

Auletta, Ken. 1982. The Underclass. New York: Random House.

Bahr, Steven J. 1979. "The Effects of Welfare on Marital Stability and Remarriage." Journal of Marriage and the Family 41:553-60.

Barr, Nicholas and Robert Hall. 1981. "The Probability of Dependence on Public Assistance." Economica 48:109-23.

Bishop, John H. 1980. "Jobs, Cash transfers, and Marital Instability: A Review and Synthesis of the Evidence." Journal of Human Resources 15:301-34.

Block, Frank S. 1979. "Cooperative Federalism and the Role of Litigation in the Development of Federal AFDC Eligibility Policy." Wisconsin Law Review 1979:1-53.

Current Population Reports. 1985. "Money Income and Poverty Status of Families and Persons in the Untied States: 1984." P-60, No. 149. Department of Commerce, Bureau of the Census. Washington, D.C.: Government Printing Office.

_____. 1983. "Characteristics of the Population Below the Poverty Level: 1981." P-60, No. 138. Department of Commerce, Bureau of the Census. Washington, D.C.: Government Printing Office.

_____. 1981. "Characteristics of the Population Below the Poverty Level: 1979." P-60, No. 130. Department of Commerce, Bureau of the Census. Washington, D.C.: Government Printing Office.

_____. 1969. "Revision in Poverty Statistics, 1959 to 1968." P-203 No. 28. Department of Commerce, Bureau of the Census. Washington, D.C.: Government Printing Office.

Danziger, Sandra K. 1981. "Postprogram Changes in the Lives of AFDC Supported Work Participants: A Qualitative Assessment." Journal of Human Resources 16:637-48.

Danziger, Sheldon and Peter Gottschalk. 1986. "Do Rising Tides Lift All Boats? The Impact of Secular and Cyclical Changes on Poverty." American Economic Review 76 (supplement):405-10.

158

Danziger, Sheldon, Robert Haveman, and Robert
    Plotnik. 1981. "How Income Transfer Programs
    Affect Work, Savings, and the Income
    Distribution: A Critical Review." Journal of
    Economic Literature 19:975-1028.
Department of Health and Human Services. 1980.
    "Characteristics of State Plans for AFDC Under
    the Social Security Act Title IVA." Social
    Security Administration. Washington, D.C.:
    Government Printing Office.
DiNitto, Diana M. and Thomas R. Dye. 1983. Social
    Welfare: Politics and Public Policy. Englewood
    Cliffs, New Jersey: Prentice-Hall.
Dobelstein, Andrew W. 1980. Politics, Economics,
    and Public Welfare. Englewood Cliffs, New
    Jersey: Random House.
Ellwood, David and Mary Jo Bane. 1984. "The Impact
    of AFDC on Family Structure and Living
    Arrangements." Washington, D.C.: Department of
    Health and Human Services.
Fraker, Thomas, Robert Moffitt, and Douglas Wolf.
    1985. "Effective Tax Rates and Guarantees in the
    AFDC Program, 1967-1982." Journal of Human
    Resources 20:251-63.
Friedlander, Daniel, Barbara Goldman, Judith
    Gueron, and David Long. 1986. "Initial
    Findings from the Demonstration of State
    Work/Welfare Incentives. American Economic
    Review 76 (supplement):224-29.
Friedman, Milton and Rose Friedman. 1980. Free to
    Choose: A Personal Statement. New York: Harcourt
    Brace Jovanovich.
Gallaway, Lowell and Richard Vedder. 1985. "'Suffer
    the Little Children': The True Casualties of the
    War on Poverty." Pp. 48-63 in Hearing Before
    the Subcommittee on Monetary and Fiscal Policy
    of the Joint Economic Committee, Congress of the
    United States, Ninety-Ninth Congress, First
    Session, June 20. Washington, D.C.: Government
    Printing Office.
Gallaway, Lowell, Richard Vedder, and Therese
    Foster. 1985. "The "New" Structural Poverty: A
    Quantitative Analysis." Pp. 8-47 in Hearing
    Before the Subcommittee on Monetary and Fiscal

Policy of the Joint Economic Committee, Congress of the United States, Ninety-Ninth Congress, First Session, June 20. Washington, D.C.: Government Printing Office.

Gilder, George. 1980. Wealth and Poverty. New York: Basic Books.

Gottschalk, Peter and Sheldon Danziger. 1985. "A Framework for Evaluating the Effects of Economic Growth and Transfers on Poverty." American Economic Review 75:153-61.

Gordon, Jesse E. 1978. "WIN Research: A Review of the Findings." Pp. 24-88 in The Work Incentive Experience, edited by Charles D. Garvin, Audrey D. Smith, and William J. Reid. New York: Allanheld, Osmun and Company.

Halsey, Harlan I. 1982. "The Taxation of Transfer Income." Journal of Human Resources 17:558-80.

Hannan, Michael T. 1979. "Issues in Panel Analysis of National Development: A Methodological Overview." Pp. 17-33 in National Development and the World System: Educational, Economic, and Political Change, 1950-1970. John W. Meyer and Michael T. Hannan, editors. University of Chicago.

Haveman, Robert (Editor). 1977. A Decade of Federal Antipoverty Programs: Achievements, Failures, and Lessons. New York: Academic Press.

Hutchens, Robert M. 1979. "Welfare, Remarriage, and Marital Search." American Economic Review 69:369-79.

Kemp, Jack. 1979. An American Renaissance: A Strategy for the 1980's. New York: Harper and Row.

Masters, Stanley. 1981. "The Effects of Supported Work on the Earnings and Transfer Payments of Its Target Group." Journal of Human Resources 16:600-36.

Mead, Lawrence W. 1985. Beyond Entitlement: The Social Obligations of Citizenship. New York: Free Press.

Mink, George. 1978. "The Organization of WIN and Its Impact on Participants." Pp. 111-32 in The Work Incentive Experience, edited by Charles D. Garvin, Audrey D. Smith, and William J. Reid. New York: Allanheld, Osmun and Company.

Moffitt, Robert A. 1986. "Work Incentives in the AFDC System: An Analysis of the 1981 Reforms." American Economic Review 76 (supplement):219-23.
_____. 1981. "The Negative Income Tax: Would It Discourage Work?" Monthly Labor Review 104 (April):23-27.
_____. 1979. "Cumulative Effective Tax Rates and Guarantees in Low-Income Transfer Programs." Journal of Human Resources 14:122-29.
Murray, Charles. 1984. Losing Ground: American Social Policy, 1950-1980. New York: Basic.
Patterson, James T. 1981. America's Struggle Against Poverty, 1900-1980. Cambridge, Massachusetts: Harvard University Press.
Robins, Philip K. 1985. "A Comparison of the Labor Supply Findings From the Four Negative Income Tax Experiments." Journal of Human Resources 20:567-82.
Simmel, Georg. 1908. Soziologie. Leipzig: Duncker and Humblot.
Smith, Audrey D. and Gregory M. St. L. O'Brien. 1978. "The Carrot and the Stick." Pp. 152-66 in The Work Incentive Experience, edited by Charles D. Garvin, Audrey D. Smith, and William J. Reid. New York: Allanheld, Osmun and Company.
Sowell, Thomas. 1983. The Economics and Politics of Race: An International Perspective. New York: William Morrow.
State and Metropolitan Area Data Book. 1979, 1982, and 1986. Department of Commerce, Bureau of the Census. Washington, D.C.: Government Printing Office.
Statistical Abstract of the United States. 1986-1961. National Data Book and Guide to Sources. Department of Commerce, Bureau of the Census. Washington, D.C.: Government Printing Office.
United States Bureau of the Census. 1984. "Estimates of Poverty Including the Value of Non-Cash Benefits. Technical Paper 51. Washington, D.C.: Government Printing Office.
Wilson, William Julius and Robert Aponte. 1985. "Urban Poverty." Pp. 231-58 in Annual Review of Sociology. Ralph H. Turner and James F. Short, Jr., editors. Palo Alto, California: Annual Reviews.

APPENDIX

Variables (N=50)	Mean	Standard Deviation	Minimum	Maximum	Skewness
(Y1:A) Poverty rate among families, 1979	9.60	2.89	5.80	18.70	1.12
(Y1:B) Poverty rate among families, 1969	11.61	5.21	5.30	28.90	1.30
(Y1:C) Poverty rate among families, 1959	20.36	9.58	8.00	47.90	1.04
(Y1:A)-(Y1:B)	− 2.02	2.62	− 10.20	2.30	− .95
(Y1:B)-(Y1:C)	− 8.74	4.74	− 19.30	− 2.70	− .80
(Y2:A) Poverty rate among children aged 0-17 years, 1979	15.41	4.60	7.70	30.40	.98
(Y2:B) Poverty rate among children aged 0-17 years, 1969	15.89	7.59	7.80	41.30	1.30
(Y2:A)-(Y2:B)	− .49	3.75	− 10.90	6.30	− .67
(Y3:A) Poverty rate among children aged 0-4 years, 1979	17.18	4.28	8.00	30.20	.68
(Y3:B) Poverty rate among children aged 0-4 years, 1969	16.56	7.09	7.70	40.60	1.28
(Y3:A)-(Y3:B)	.62	3.99	− 10.40	8.10	− .54
(Y4:A) % of families headed by women, 1980	13.03	2.51	7.90	18.40	− .07
(Y4:B) % of families headed by women, 1970	9.95	1.92	6.20	13.50	.02
(Y4:C) % of families headed by women, 1960	8.69	1.90	4.70	12.80	.21
(Y3:A)-(Y3:B)	3.09	1.03	.90	5.50	.40
(Y3:B)-(Y3:C)	1.26	.57	.30	2.70	.50
(X1:A) Average annual AFDC transfers per-recipient child, 1980-70	840.04	293.29	211.96	1311.66	− .21
(X1:B) Average monthly AFDC transfers per-recipient family, 1980-70	158.11	52.30	46.37	251.43	− .11
(X1:C) Average monthly AFDC transfers per-recipient family, 1970-60	168.44	51.29	49.23	262.19	− .30
(X2:A) Economic growth, 1980-70	27.86	7.87	11.74	52.91	.67
(X2:B) Economic growth, 1970-60	41.68	9.88	25.27	67.45	.76
(X3:A) Change in the rate of Unemployment, 1980-70	1.94	1.47	− .80	5.60	.12
(X3:B) Change in the rate of Unemployment, 1970-60	− .38	.93	− 2.50	1.80	.29

Variables	Data Sources
Y1:A	Statistical Abstract of the United States (1984)
Y1:B	Statistical Abstract of the United States (1981)
Y1:C	Statistical Abstract of the United States (1972)
Y2:A & Y2:B	Statistical Abstract of the United States (1984)
Y3:A	Statistical Abstract of the United States (1984) and 1980 Census of the Population (1983)
Y3:B	Current Population Reports (1979)
Y4:A	State and Metropolitan Area Data Book (1986)
Y4:B & Y4:C	State and Metropolitan Area Data Book (1979)
X1:A	Statistical Abstract of the United States (1980-1970) and State and Metropolitan Area Data Book (1982)
X1:B	Statistical Abstract of the United States (1981-1971)
X1:C	Statistical Abstract of the United States (1971-1961)
X2:A & X2:B	Statistical Abstract of the United States (1981)
X3:A	Statistical Abstract of the United States (1981,1972)
X3:B	Statistical Abstract of the United States (1972) and State and Metropolitan Area Data Book (1979)

7

Fighting Poverty by Reducing Dependency: The Dilemma of Policy Assumptions

Michael Morris

At the core of most influential critiques of the American welfare state in recent years has been the claim that programs for the poor frequently exacerbate the very problems they are supposed to solve (e. g., Gilder, 1980; Mead, 1985; Murray, 1984). Specifically, it is charged that these programs foster dependency on government assistance, and thus lessen the likelihood that participants will ever escape poverty on their own. In this fashion the welfare state is depicted as actually contributing to the perpetuation of poverty. Indeed, even those who strongly support such programs usually agree with critics that a "genuine" or "permanent" solution to the poverty problem must be based in interventions that attempt to increase the economic self-sufficiency of individuals (e.g., Levitan, 1985).

This intellectual and political zeitgeist contains several basic premises and conclusions that warrant close examination. In particular, the issues of poverty reduction and dependency reduction appear to have been inadequately conceptualized by both welfare-state supporters and critics. A more thorough analysis strongly suggests that the dependency-reduction strategy does not have the ability to serve as the foundation of a successful, society-wide antipoverty policy. The assumptions that this strategy must satisfy are simply too great, in terms of both quantity and quality, to permit such an achievement. Much less problematical are the assumptions required by programs which provide direct economic assistance to participants. To the extent that this analysis is valid, a fundamental reorientation of our thinking about poverty policy's potentials and limits would seem to be called for.

POVERTY REDUCTION AND DEPENDENCY REDUCTION

Poverty and dependency represent distinct, though potentially related, social phenomena. In theory, a society could be characterized by high levels of both poverty and dependency, low levels of both, or be high on one dimension and low on the other. Within a social policy context, conservatives have traditionally been much more interested in minimizing dependency than in eliminating poverty. In fairness, however, it must be noted that most conservatives believe that reducing dependency is the most effective and efficient route to reducing poverty (e.g., Murray, 1984). In this regard it is possible to reduce poverty by both positive means (e.g., job/skill training, educational assistance) and negative ones (e.g., termination of welfare benefits). In the former case, individuals are actively assisted in becoming self-sufficient. In the latter, those who do not receive financial help from private sources will presumably develop the motivation and skills needed to support themselves in the labor market.

In contrast to conservatives, welfare-state supporters place greater emphasis on reducing poverty than on minimizing dependency, at least in the short run (e.g., Ellwood and Summers, 1986). Consequently, they endorse programs which provide immediate economic assistance but which, by their very nature, place participants in an economically dependent position vis-a-vis the government (e.g., AFDC, Food Stamps). Supporters frequently claim, however, that the well-being which results from reduced poverty can increase, in the long run, the ability of many recipients to become non-poor through their own efforts (e.g., Williamson, et al., 1975:205). In essence, then, it is being asserted that programs which increase dependency in the short run can, in the long run, help reduce dependency. Conservatives, of course, vigorously dispute the validity of this claim.

Two basic approaches to poverty policy are clearly discernible in the preceding discussion. The dependency-reduction strategy attempts to reduce poverty through indirect means, and in its positive version captures the spirit of the proverb: "Give a man a fish and you feed him for a day, teach him to fish and you feed him for life." The direct-assistance approach tries to reduce poverty directly through the provision of economic resources. In other words, it gives people fish.

Over the years countless studies have been conducted to evaluate the impact of programs representing these two approaches. While it is beyond the scope of this paper to examine this literature in detail, the findings encountered in such a review are consistent enough to be meaningfully summarized. The crux of this summary can be stated briefly: Direct-assistance programs have a significantly greater antipoverty impact on their participants than dependency-reduction programs have on theirs (Morris and Williamson, 1986). The former programs include those offering either cash or in-kind assistance, such as Social Security, Aid to Families with Dependent Children (AFDC), Supplemental Security Income (SSI), Unemployment Insurance, Food Stamps, subsidized housing, and Medicaid and Medicare. The most prominent dependency-reduction efforts include job/skill training, educational interventions (e.g., compensatory education), and social services (e.g., counseling, family planning services).

There are, of course, significant differences in the antipoverty performance of programs within the direct-assistance and dependency-reduction categories. For example, many dependency-reduction interventions do have some positive economic impact, and it can even be argued that a few are highly effective (e.g., the Job Corps, supported work for welfare mothers, contraceptive services for adolescents; see Forrest et al., 1981; Hollister et al., 1985; Long et al., 1981). Where direct-assistance efforts are concerned, Social Security is by far the most effective program, helping to reduce the poverty rate among the elderly from 35% in 1959 to 12% in 1984. AFDC, on the other hand, provides a level of support to participants that is painfully modest (Committee on

Ways and Means, 1985a, 1985b; Danziger et al., 1986; U. S. Bureau of the Census, 1986). Important as these within-group differences are, they should not obscure the basic point. Overall, direct-assistance programs outperform dependency-reduction ones in generating economic benefits for participants.

Critics of the direct-assistance approach claim that estimates of its positive economic impact tend to be very inflated. They maintain that most estimates fail to take into account the influences which these programs have on the labor supply, birth rates, and other factors related to low-income status (e.g., Plotnick, 1984). As Orr and Skidmore (1982:168) succinctly observe, "any receipt of cash or goods that is not a reward for work by definition makes work less necessary, because the recipient can enjoy a given level of consumption while working less than would otherwise be the case." To the extent that individuals respond to this incentive structure by actually working less than they would in the absence of the assistance program, some of the poverty that is "alleviated" by the intervention has in fact been created by it.

In a similar fashion, the availability of AFDC benefits might motivate some low-income females to avoid either terminating their pregnancies or putting their newborns up for adoption (see Phillips, 1981). Such a process would result in more families needing economic assistance than would have been the case had the program not existed.

The available evidence indicates that these behavioral responses to assistance are quite modest in magnitude (See Chapter Six and Morris and Williamson, 1986), and certainly are far less than those suggested or implied by some of the more publicized conservative analyses (e.g., Murray, 1984). Thus, it is highly unlikely that more refined estimates of antipoverty impact would significantly alter the major conclusion that direct-assistance is superior to dependency-reduction in fighting poverty.

Explaining Differences in Impact

Why is it that direct-assistance programs are found to have a greater antipoverty impact than dependency-reduction ones? One reason would seem to be methodological. The impact of most cash and in-kind programs on a participant's economic status is immediate and relatively easy to measure. The impact of most dependency-reduction programs is not. The economic benefits of the latter programs are usually not expected to be noticeable for some time. Indeed, in the case of educational interventions, it may be a decade or more before economic payoffs are supposed to occur. Assessing economic outcomes under these circumstances is an exceedingly difficult and imprecise task. As a result, evaluation studies may be underestimating the full impact of dependency-reduction programs on participants.

It is doubtful, however, that these methodological problems account for more than a small percentage of the differences in program efficacy that have been observed. A much more important reason would appear to be differences between the two strategies in the assumptions that must be met in order for them to have a significant antipoverty impact. Direct-assistance programs tend to involve relatively short chains of assumptions, with the individual assumptions in these chains being relatively easy to satisfy. In contrast, dependency-reduction interventions usually require relatively long chains of assumptions, with individual assumptions being relatively difficult to satisfy. both of these factors, the length of the chains and the severity of individual assumptions, appear to contribute to the differential effectiveness of the two strategies.

Consider, for example, a direct assistance program such as Social Security. In order for it to have a significant economic impact on participants, two conditions must be met:

1) The amount of assistance rendered must be non-negligible.

2)   This assistance must actually be received
        by participants (i.e., Social Security
        checks must be successfully delivered to
        them).

Compare these assumptions with those required by a
dependency-reduction programs such as skill
training for employment:

1)   Participants must possess or develop the
        motivation and ability necessary to learn
        the skills being taught.
2)   The model of skill training that is used
        must be educationally sound.
3)   Training must be at a sufficiently high
        skill level to qualify program graduates,
        in either the short or the long run, for
        jobs paying non-poverty wages.
4)   These jobs must actually be available in
        the communities where program graduates
        reside, or in communities they can move
        to.
5)   Graduates must have the ability and
        motivation to hold onto these jobs once
        they obtain them.
6)   The local, regional, and/or national
        economy must be vigorous enough to support
        the continued existence of these jobs.

It is clear that the length of the skill-
training assumption chain is much longer than that
of the Social Security one. This puts the skill-
training intervention at a disadvantage since, all
other things being equal, the greater the number of
assumptions required by a program, the lower the
probability that all of them will be met.   (The
only exceptions would be those unlikely cases in
which the probability of success for every
assumption was 100%).   Thus, even if each of the
assumptions associated with these two programs had
the same high probability of success (e.g., 90%),
the overall probability of skill training
generating significant economic benefits for a
given participant (53%) would still be much lower
than the corresponding probability for Social
Security (81%).

The vulnerability of lengthy assumption chains is perhaps most vividly demonstrated by the fact that five of the skill-training assumptions might have 100% probabilities of success, but the overall chances of the intervention succeeding would only be 20% if the sixth assumption had a 20% success probability. No chain is stronger than its weakest link, and long chains present more opportunities for weak links than short ones.

The extended time frame required by most dependency-reduction interventions, and the indirect route through which they are supposed to exert economic impact, are primarily responsible for their relatively long assumption chains. To the extent that both of these features are inherent to the dependency-reduction strategy, it is unlikely that the assumption chains associated with most of these interventions can be appreciably shortened.

The <u>nature</u> of dependency-reduction assumptions is also problematical. These assumptions frequently call for changes in the participant's motivation, ability, values, beliefs, or attitudes (e.g., the first skill-training assumption). Achieving significant change on these dimensions through social-policy interventions has traditionally been a very difficult task. In other words, the probability of satisfying these assumptions tends to be low when compared with the chances of fulfilling direct-assistance assumptions (e.g., successfully delivering a Social Security check).

Most dependency-reduction efforts also involve some assumptions that the program itself has no direct control over. These assumptions usually focus on the ability of the ability of the labor market to provide employment to motivated job-seekers (e.g., the fourth and sixth skill-training assumptions). If these assumptions had high probabilities of success in their own right, the fact that dependency-reduction interventions had little control over them would not be particularly problematical. For the most part, however, this appears not to be the case. It has long been recognized, for example, that local job markets frequently experience great difficulty in absorbing the graduate of skill-training programs. Indeed, this was one of the most common criticisms of training programs during the War on Poverty (e.g., Levin, 1977).

In contrast to the dependency-reduction approach, direct-assistance strategies tend to place much less emphasis -- at least in the short run -- on change-oriented assumptions and assumptions that are beyond their control. Thus, even if the assumption chains of the two types of programs were equal in length, there would still be reason to expect the direct-assistance strategy to have significantly greater antipoverty impact. Once again, it is unclear how change-oriented assumptions could be removed from most dependency-reduction programs; they seem to be inherent to the approach.

Those who expect the direct-assistance approach to reduce dependency in the long run must contend with the same assumption-related problems that affect the ability of the dependency-reduction strategy to reduce poverty; long assumption chains, change-oriented assumptions, and assumptions beyond the control of the intervention. For example, implicit in this expectation is the assumption that human needs are hierarchically ordered (Maslow, 1962). That is, the satisfaction of lower-order, survival-oriented needs via direct economic assistance is seen as motivating individuals to obtain the education and training necessary for personal development and upward mobility.

The empirical evidence in support of a hierarchical model of motivation is not nearly as strong as our intuition might initially suggest (Rauschenberger, et al., 1980; Wahba and Bridwell, 1976). Moreover, satisfying this hierarchical assumption simply opens the door to a whole set of additional assumptions that must be fulfilled if dependency is to be reduced, assumptions which frequently resemble those that were encountered when reviewing skill-training programs. Thus, achieving self-sufficiency at a non-poverty level through direct-assistance programs requires assumption chains that are no less intimidating than those associated with the dependency-reduction approach to fighting poverty. It should come as no surprise, then, that there is no strong empirical evidence demonstrating that direct-

170

assistance programs have a long-term positive impact on self-sufficiency. If an anything, the evidence suggests that there might be a slight negative impact on self-sufficiency in the long run (e.g., Bane and Ellwood, 1983; Hill et al., 1985).

POLICY IMPLICATIONS

The preceding analysis calls into question the widespread belief that the dependency-reduction approach is the most effective means of reducing poverty. However valuable this approach may be in other respects, as an overall antipoverty strategy its impact appears to be very limited when compared with the direct-assistance strategy. Moreover, given the myriad and difficult assumptions associated with this approach, it is doubtful whether specific dependency-reduction programs can ever be designed which will live up to the high expectations Americans have for them (Lewis and Schneider, 1985). In sum, it appears that a certain amount of dependency is the price society must pay if a major impact on poverty is to be achieved.

This does not mean, of course, that dependency-reduction programs cannot be improved in an incremental fashion. For example, evaluation studies indicate that increased contraceptive services for adolescents would significantly reduce the poverty resulting from female-headed households (Chamie and Henshaw, 1981; Forrest et al., 1981). The technology of birth control is such that proper application of the procedures involved virtually guarantees a "successful" outcome (i.e., the prevention of pregnancy). There are very few dependency-reduction programs that can make such a claim. Moreover, unlike many other dependency-reduction efforts, the successful practice of contraception requires a relatively low level of skill. Thus, the major obstacle for contraceptive programs is motivating eligible individuals to use the services available. Once participation is achieved, the probability of success is high.

Supported work programs for welfare mothers also deserve more widespread implementation. This approach does not emphasize skill training beyond the level that would normally occur in the course of learning an entry-level job as a new employee. Thus, supported work is less dependent on skill-training assumptions than are many other dependency-reduction interventions. In addition, AFDC mothers participating in supported work usually do so on a voluntary basis, and are highly motivated to leave the welfare rolls.[1] This increases the likelihood that any motivational assumptions associated with the intervention will be met.

Finally, the major focus of supported work is on aspects of the job-seeking, job-learning, and job-retention process that receive little attention in most dependency-reduction programs, even though they involve assumptions that have a powerful impact on the success of these interventions. Specifically, emphasis is placed on actively supporting participants in finding appropriate jobs, learning on-the-job skills, handling personal problems that could interfere with work performance, and becoming socialized to the work place (Tomaskovic-Devey, 1983). The assistance provided by supported work thus increases the probability that the employment assumptions associated with these issues will be fulfilled.

Because dependency-reduction programs having the demonstrated or potential effectiveness of contraceptive services and supported work for welfare mothers are rare, there is little reason to believe that the dependency-reduction strategy can ever serve as the foundation of a successful poverty policy in the United States, if success is defined in terms of achieving a very low poverty rate (say, 1% to 3%). Put another way, if poverty is defined such that the only way to solve it is through greatly increased self-sufficiency, then there is no realistic solution to the problem of poverty in America.

In this context it is frequently claimed that national economic growth has the ability to substantially reduce both poverty and dependency due to its positive impact on job creation (e.g., Gilder, 1980). This analysis of economic growth's role is incomplete, however. A major reason for economic growth's impact on poverty is that it

enables the government to increase the generosity
and availability of direct-assistance programs
which benefit those who are not equipped to take
advantage of the general expansion of job
opportunities accompanying growth (Crawford and
Jusenius, 1980; Gottschalk and Danziger, 1985).
Thus, even in the best of times there will be a
significant segment of the population which
requires special attention, a segment which is more
likely to benefit economically from direct
assistance than from dependency-reduction
interventions.

While there are certainly limits to any
society's ability to simultaneously redistribute
income to the lower class and maintain economic
growth, the available evidence indicates that the
United States could redistribute significantly more
income than it currently does without approaching
these boundaries (Burtless, 1986). A smaller
percentage of the U. S. national income is spent on
redistribution than in most other Western
industrialized countries. Moreover, this
relatively low level of redistribution does not
appear to have led to a relatively high level of
economic growth when the United States is compared
with these nations. There is also no consensus
among economists that, at a microeconomic level,
the impact of U. S. tax/transfer system on
individual work effort and savings has
substantially compromised overall economic
efficiency.

Against this background, it is important to
consider Burtless's (1986:47) contention that
"redistribution policy is ultimately political
rather than purely economic." Given our society's
ideological heritage, in which self-sufficiency is
enthusiatically endorsed and income redistribution
is viewed with great suspicion (Plattner, 1979;
Williams, 1970), it is uncertain whether the
powerful antipoverty potential of the direct-
assistance approach will ever be fully realized in
the United States. This uncertainty should not
obscure the fact that the dependency-reduction
strategy does not possess such potential. Thus, to
the extent that policy makers indulge their
preferences for dependency reduction at the expense

of programs which provide direct assistance, the fight against poverty will be characterized by more retreats than advances in the years to come.

NOTES

1. It is interesting to note in this context that ex-addicts, ex-offenders, and youth who have dropped out of school benefit much less from supported work than AFDC mothers (Hollister et al., 1985).

BIBLIOGRAPHY

Bane, Mary Jo, and David T. Ellwood 1983. The Dynamics of Dependence: The Routes to Self-Sufficiency. Cambridge, MA: Urban Systems Research and Engineering.

Burtless, Gary 1986. "Public Spending for the Poor: Trends, Prospects, and Economic Limits." Pp. 18-49 in Sheldon H. Danziger and Daniel H. Weinberg (eds.), Fighting Poverty: What Works and What Doesn't. Cambridge, MA: Harvard University Press.

Chamie, Mary, and Stanley K. Henshaw 1981. "The costs and benefits of government expenditures for family planning programs." Family Planning Perspectives 13:117-124.

Committee on Ways and Means, U. S. House of Representatives 1985a. Background Material and Data on Programs within the Jurisdiction of the Committee on Ways and Means. Washington, D. C: U. S. Government Printing Office.

Committee on Ways and Means, U. S. House of Representatives 1985b. Children in Poverty. Washington, D. C: U. S. Government Printing Office.

Crawford, Everett, and Carol Jusenius 1980. "Economic development policies to reduce structural unemployment." Pp. 141-195 in National Commission for Employment Policy, Sixth Annual Report. Washington, D. C: U. S. Government Printing Office.

Danziger, Sheldon, Robert Haveman, and Robert Plotnick 1986. Policy: Effects on the Poor and the Non-poor." Pp. 78-105 in Sheldon H.

Danziger and Daniel H. Weinberg (eds.), Fighting Poverty: What Works and What Doesn't. Cambridge, MA: Harvard University Press.

Ellwood, David T., and Lawrence H. Summers 1986. "Poverty in America: Is Welfare the Answer or the Problem?" Pp. 78-105 in Sheldon H. Danziger and Daniel H. Weinberg (eds.), Fighting Poverty: What Works and What Doesn't. Cambridge, MA: Harvard University Press.

Forrest, Jacqueline Darroch, Albert I. Hermalin, and Stanley K. Henshaw 1981. "The impact of family planning clinic programs on adolescent pregnancy." Family Planning Perspectives 13:109-116.

Gilder, George 1980. Wealth and Poverty. New York: Basic Books.

Gottschalk, Peter, and Sheldon Danziger 1985. "A framework for evaluating the effects of economic growth and transfers on poverty." American Economic Review 75:153-161.

Hill, Martha S., Sue Augustyniak, Greg J. Duncan, Gerald Gurin, Patricia Gurin, Jeffrey K. Liker, James N. Morgan, and Michael Ponza 1985. Motivation and Economic Mobility. Ann Arbor, MI: Institute for Social Research, University of Michigan.

Hollister, Robinson G., Jr., P. Kemper, and R. A. Maynard (eds.) 1985. The National Supported Work Demonstration. Madison: University of Wisconsin Press.

Levin, Henry M. 1977. "A decade of policy developments in improving education and training for low-income populations." Pp. 123-188 in Robert H. Haveman (ed.), A Decade of Federal Antipoverty Programs: Achievements, Failures, and Lessons. New York: Academic Press.

Levitan, Sar A. 1985. Programs in Aid of the Poor (5th ed.). Baltimore: Johns Hopkins University Press.

Lewis, I. A., and William Schneider 1985. "Hard Times: The public on poverty." Public Opinion 8 (June/July):1-7, 59-60.

Long, David A., Charles D. Mallar, and Craig V. D. Thornton 1981. "Evaluating the benefits and costs of the Job Corps." Journal of Policy Analysis and Management 1:55-76.

Maslow, Abraham H. 1962. Toward a Psychology of
    Being. New York: Van Nostrand Reinhold.
Mead, Lawrence M. 1985. Beyond Entitlement: The
    Social Obligations of Citizenship. New York:
    Free Press.
Morris, Michael, and John B. Williamson 1986.
    Poverty and Public Policy: An Analysis of
    Federal Intervention Efforts. Westport, CT:
    Greenwood Press.
Murray, Charles 1984. Losing Ground: American
    Social Policy, 1950-1980. New York: Basic
    Books.
Orr, Larry L., and Felicity Skidmore 1982. "The
    evolution of the work issue in welfare reform."
    Pp. 167-186 in Paul M. Sommers (ed.), Welfare
    Reform in America: Perspectives and Prospects.
    Boston: Kluwer-Nijhoff.
Phillips, Martha H. 1981. "Favorable family impact
    as an objective of income support policy." Pp.
    165-194 in Peter G. Brown, Conrad Johnson, and
    Paul Vernier (eds.), Income support: Conceptual
    and Policy Issues. Totowa, NJ: Rowman and
    Littlefield.
Plattner, Marc F. 1979. "The welfare state vs the
    redistributive state." Public Interest
    (Spring):28-48.
Plotnick, Robert 1984. "The redistributive impact
    of cash transfers." Public Finance Quarterly
    12:27-50.
Rauschenberger, J., N. Schmitt, and J. E. Hunter
    1980. "A test of the need hierarchy concept by
    a Markov model of change in need strength."
    Administrative Science Quarterly 25:654-670.
Tomaskovic-Devey, Donald 1983. Supported Work
    Success, Employment and Training Programs, and
    Labor Market Theories. Unpublished manuscript,
    Boston University, Center for Applied Social
    Sciences, Boston.
U. S. Bureau of the Census 1986. Characteristics
    of the Population Below the Poverty Level: 1984.
    (Current Population Reports, Series P-60).
    Washington, D. C.: U. S. Government Printing
    Office.
Wahba, Mahmoud A., and Lawrence G. Bridwell 1976.
    "Maslow reconsidered: A review of research on
    the need hierarchy theory." Organizational
    Behavior and Human Performance 15:212-240.

Williams, Robin M., Jr. 1970. American Society: A Sociological Interpretation (3rd ed.). New York: Alfred A. Knopf.

Williamson, John B., Jerry F. Borren, Frank J. Mifflen, Nancy A. Cooney, Linda Evans, Michael F. Foley, Richard Steiman, Jody Garber, Nancy Theberge, and Donna J. B. Turek 1975. Strategies Against Poverty in America. Cambridge, MA: Schenkman.

8

The Dynamics of Welfare Use: How Long and How Often?

Mark R. Rank

During the 1980's, the debate over the merits of the welfare system has become a topic of considerable concern. The Reagan Administration brought the issue to the foreground with the Omnibus Budget Reconciliation Act (OBRA) of 1981. The budget cuts that were directed at various welfare programs were both applauded and criticized by members of the political and academic communities.

The on-going debate, regarding the positive and/or negative effects of welfare programs is exemplified in the work of Charles Murray (1984) and Michael Harrington (1984). On one hand, Murray argues that the welfare programs of the 1960's and 1970's have encouraged dependency among the poor. Rather than helping low income families, welfare programs have kept the poor from rising beyond the ranks of poverty. On the other hand, Harrington argues that more, not less, government assistance is needed in order to combat recent poverty which has resulted from structural changes in the national economy. Rather than hindering the poor, welfare programs have provided valuable, albeit limited assistance.

Which is the correct viewpoint? Obviously the issue is both complex and politically charged. However, one way to begin to address this problem is to simply observe the process of families exiting and re-entering the welfare rolls. (Chapters Six and Seven address this same question in different but complementary ways.) By doing so, we can ask several important questions, such as,

"How long do families use welfare," "How likely is it that they will return having once exited," and "What proportion of households beginning a spell on public assistance will be off several years later?" By understanding the dynamics of welfare use, we are in a better position to assess the effects that such programs have on individual recipients.

PREVIOUS RESEARCH

Research analyzing the dynamics of welfare use has primarily focused on female headed families receiving Aid to Families with Dependent Children (AFDC). These studies have relied on either caseload samples (from California or New York) or the Panel Study of Income Dynamics data (See Chapter Four for use of the latter data source to answer a different question). In general, results indicate that most female heads using welfare do so for a fairly short amount of time (Boskin and Nold, 1975; Bane and Ellwood, 1983, Hutchens, 1981; Plotnick, 1983; Rank, 1985; Rein and Rainwater, 1978; Rydell et al., 1974). Although the estimates differ from study to study, the majority of recipients would appear to be on public assistance for less than three years.

In addition, a sizable amount of recidivism has been shown to exist (Bane and Ellwood, 1983; Boskin and Nold, 1975). Households tend to weave in and out of the welfare system, presumably as their economic and social conditions improve or deteriorate.

Rather than a static, locked in population, families on welfare (and specifically, female headed families) would appear to be much more dynamic in their use of welfare than the conventional stereotype would suggest. These findings parallel similar results for households in poverty (e.g., Duncan, 1984). Yet do such patterns hold for other types of households receiving welfare? This question is addressed by using a new data set which tracks various types of families receiving welfare over time.

DATA AND SAMPLING

The Data Base

In the early 1970's it was generally recognized
that there were a number of problems in Wisconsin's
administration of the AFDC, Food Stamp, and
Medicaid programs (Guy, 1982). In 1971 the
Wisconsin Department of Health and Social Services
initiated a project designed to produce a computer-
based information system in order to effectively
handle these problems. This system became known as
the Computer Reporting Network (CRN). By late
1978, a decision was made to implement the CRN
system statewide with distributed data processing
in the counties and a data base systems located in
Madison. As of September 1980, more than 99
percent of all cases in the state's 72 counties had
been loaded into the CRN system.
   Applicants for AFDC, Food Stamps, and/or
Medicaid are required to fill out a combined
application form. Their responses to these
questions are collected and reviewed by a county
case worker. The worker reviews the form for
accuracy and completeness. The information is then
keyed directly into a terminal from a county office
into the CRN system. Within a short period of time
a case determination is printed back to the county
office indicating the case eligibility and
benefits. Aside from new applications, workers at
the county level may also make changes to case
records already active in the data base. For
example, complete reviews of each case are required
at set intervals, and items that have changed will
be re-entered into the data base. Likewise, any
changes that have been reported prior to a case
review will also be entered into the system.

Sampling Procedure

A two percent random sample was drawn of all cases
that were participating as of September 30, 1980,
in one or more of the three programs. The total
number of eligible cases on the CRN system in
September 1980 was approximately 140,000 -
resulting in a sample size of 2,796 case heads (or
households). These households had been on welfare

for varying amounts of time. Some represented new
cases, others had been on for six months, and so
on. The two percent sample was built by combining
two simple random samples of 1 percent each.
These samples were generated by randomly selecting
two two-digit numbers and using these to select on
the last two digits of the case head's Social
Security number.

The cases were then followed at six month
intervals (through September 1983) by matching the
case head's Social Security number against the
entire end-of-month CRN file for each succeeding
interval beginning in March 1981. All analytical
files were stripped of personal identification
information (e.g., names, addresses, telephone
numbers, etc.) and the original Social Security
numbers were replaced with a unique identification
number to permit matching cases or individuals
across months. The sample includes September 1980,
March 1981, September 1981, March 1982, September
1982, March 1983, and September 1983. There is no
refusal rate, since case records rather than actual
individuals were sampled.

A small number of exits will not be picked up in
the analysis. If a case was receiving welfare in
March 1981, exited during June 1981, and came back
on in July 1981, this movement would not be
detected. Since the case is observed only in March
and September, it would be considered as being on
welfare during the entire six month interval. The
exit probability estimates are therefore
underestimated. However, in many respects this may
be desirable. Individuals who have returned to
welfare within several months have not really
escaped dependence. In addition, a sizeable number
of these terminations result from bureaucratic
regulations. For example, a household that did not
adequately report its income may be temporarily
terminated until the information is obtained. Or
an individual who receives three rather than two
monthly paychecks as a result of the number of
Fridays in a month, may also be temporarily
terminated. These cases are usually reinstated the
next month, and they represent exits only in an
administrative sense. By grouping the data in six
month intervals, much of this administrative
"noise" is reduced.

Throughout the analysis, the programs of AFDC, Food Stamps, and Medicaid are treated as a package. The concern lies in whether a family is receiving welfare or not, rather than whether they are receiving AFDC as opposed to food stamps. The reliance upon public assistance is the focal point of the analysis. However, the sample has been divided into household categories. By doing so, the population has also been roughly divided into program categories as well.

Household Categories

The welfare population contains several dominant types of households. These households participate in the welfare system differently (i.e., they are eligible for different programs). This analysis concentrates on four household categories: (1) female heads of household with children (no spouse present) including single females who are pregnant but without children; (2) married couples (with or without children); (3) single heads of household (no children or spouse present) and (4) elderly household heads (over age 65). Female heads constitute roughly 40 percent of the total sample, while married couples, singles, and the elderly each make up approximately 20 percent.

By dividing the sample according to household structure, the population has been roughly divided by program type. Consequently, 93.7 percent of female heads are on AFDC (63.7 percent are receiving AFDC, Food Stamps, and Medicaid; 30 percent are receiving AFDC and Medicaid), 97.5 percent of single heads are receiving Food Stamps and/or Medicaid, while 88 percent of the elderly are participating solely in the Medicaid programs. Married couples are fairly evenly distributed across the programs of AFDC, Food Stamps and Medicaid.

Three questions are addressed in the analysis: (1) How long do households remain on welfare before exiting; (2) How likely is it that they will return having once exited; (3) What proportion of households will be off welfare after several years? Each question can be answered through life table analyses.

The life table is a technique that demographers
and medical researchers have often used. Although
primarily found in mortality analysis, it can be
applied to other areas of research as well. Where
starting and terminal events can be defined, and
where the interval of time between these events is
of interest, the life table is often useful in
describing the patterns of a particular event
(e.g., death, birth, marriage). The discussion in
this chapter is based on life table and survival
analyses.

Methodology

We are interested in estimating how long various
types of households beginning a spell of welfare
will remain on before exiting. However, recall
that the sample selected in September 1980 was a
cross-section of welfare recipients. Some had been
on for one month, some for six months, and so on.
Therefore, a hypothetical or synthetic opening
cohort must be constructed in order to estimate how
long a case that begins a spell of welfare will
remain on.

There are three approaches which could be used
to construct exit probabilities over time for an
opening cohort. Within the September 1980 sample
there are a small number of cases that began their
spell of welfare in that month. These cases could
have been selected and followed over the three year
period of observation. The problem with this
approach is simply one of sample size. There are
too few beginning cases to estimate reliable exit
probabilities after one year.

A second approach would be to construct a
standard life table. If a case had been on welfare
one year prior to September 1980, they would be
considered passing through the 0-6 and 6-12 month
intervals without having exited. The entire sample
would therefore enter the 0-6 month interval, which
would represent the beginning six months of a
welfare spell. The problem with this approach is
that it downwardly biases the exit probabilities
during the early time intervals (i.e., 0-6, 6-12,
and 12-18 months). The reason for this bias is
that the sample contains a significant percentage

of cases that have already been on welfare for one or two years. Their counterparts who came on welfare at the same time, but subsequently exited before the sampling date of September 1980, are omitted from the analysis. This causes the early exit probabilities to appear lower than they actually are.

A third approach is used which solves the above problems of sample size and biased estimates. First, prior length of welfare use is calculated for the entire sample. Next, if a case had been on welfare for six months, as an example, they would not be included in the 0-6 month interval. Rather, cases are only included in intervals in which they are observed at the beginning and ending points of the interval. The above case would be included in the 6-12 month interval. If such a household had not exited during this interval, they would then be included in the 12-18 month interval, and so on. If they had exited during the 6-12 month interval, they would be eliminated from entering later intervals. Hence, the analysis is limited to explaining the first exit from welfare. By including only cases observed at both point A and point B in the probability estimates, no bias is introduced. Furthermore, the sample size on which these estimates are based is greatly increased, thus lending more confidence in the calculated probabilities. The sample size at risk will vary between intervals as a result of including only cases that are observed at the beginning and ending points of an interval. In this manner a set of exit probabilities for a hypothetical or synthetic opening cohort is constructed.

Households will be experiencing their welfare spells at differing chronological times. For example, a new case in September 1980 experiences the 6-12 month interval from March 1981 to September 1981. However, a case that had been on welfare for six months prior to September 1980 would experience the 6-12 month interval from September 1980 to March 1981. Period effects are distributed both across and within intervals, rather than solely within intervals.

In Table 8.1, column 1 shows the monthly intervals since the beginning of a welfare spell. The number of cases entering each interval is shown

in column 2, while the number of cases exiting from
welfare during an interval is found in column 3.
The cumulative proportion of exits is simply column
2 divided by column 3. The cumulative proportion
of exits is obtained by first calculating the
proportion of survivors (1 minus the proportion of
exits). The cumulative proportion of survivors is
then calculated by multiplying the proportion of
survivors through each interval. The proportion of
cumulative survivors through the 12-18 month
interval for female heads is .7474 x .8632 x
.8547 = .5514. The proportion of cumulative exits
is therefore, 1 -.5514 = .4486. Finally, the
median exit time is calculated for each of the five
subsamples. This represents the time point at
which the value of the proportion of cumulative
exits is .5. Consequently, 50 percent of the cases
analyzed will have exited from welfare at this
point. Linear interpolation is used to calculate
this value.

Looking first at the proportion of exits, there
is a general downward trend over time in the
likelihood of exiting from welfare. The longer a
household remains on welfare, the less likely they
are to leave. This is especially true for married
and single heads of household. The proportion of
single heads exiting during the first six months
interval is .5266, while the proportion who exit
during the last six month interval is .1398.
Several explanations for this trend are possible:
(1) there may be a settling-in effect occurring; or
(2) it may be that those remaining are severely
disadvantaged (e.g., low education, disabled, etc.)
and hence less likely to exit. In either case,
length of time is associated with lower exit
probabilities.[1]

Welfare Exits

In general, Table 8.1 shows that most households
beginning a spell of welfare stay on for a
relatively short amount of time. The median exit
time for female and elderly heads is 22 months,
while married and single heads have a median of 8.6
and 5.7 months. The idea that most families
beginning a spell of welfare will remain on

TABLE 8.1   LIFE TABLE ANALYSIS OF EXITING
FROM WELFARE
FOR A SYNTHETIC OPENING COHORT

Length on Welfare	Number Entering Interval	Of Exits	Proportion of Exits	Cumul Exits
Female Heads				
0-6	194	49	.2526	.2526
6-12	380	52	.1368	.3548
12-18	530	77	.1453	.4486
18-24	562	77	.1370	.5241
24-30	536	74	.1381	.5898
30-36	512	60	.1172	.6379

Median Exit Time - 22.08 Months

Married Heads				
0-6	151	63	.4172	.4172
6-12	251	82	.3267	.6076
12-18	238	56	.2353	.6999
18-24	300	46	.1533	.7459
24-30	185	37	.2000	.7967
30-36	155	27	.1742	.8322

Median Exit Time - 8.61 Months

Single Heads				
0-6	207	109	.5266	.5266
6-12	261	130	.4981	.7624
12-18	187	59	.3155	.8374
18-24	149	46	.3087	.8876
24-30	109	22	.2018	.9103
30-36	93	13	.1398	.9228

Median Exit Time - 5.70 Months

Elderly Heads				
0-6	72	15	.2083	.2083
6-12	229	40	.1747	.3466
12-18	296	45	.1520	.4459
18-24	304	44	.1497	.5261
24-30	287	32	.1115	.5789
30-36	283	38	.1343	.6355

Median Exit Time - 22.05 Months

Total Sample

0-6	624	236	.3782	.3782
6-12	1121	304	.2712	.5468
12-18	1251	237	.1894	.6327
18-24	1222	203	.1661	.6937
24-30	1117	165	.1477	.7389
30-36	1043	138	.1323	.7735

Median Exit Time - 10.33 Months

indefinitely, is clearly not supported by the data. Rather, most families would appear to be using welfare programs for temporary assistance.

However there are clear differences in the patterns of welfare utilization across household categories. The cumulative completed spell distributions are found in column 5. We can see that female and elderly heads have a slow but steady increase in the proportion who have exited over the first three years. They are more likely to use welfare over longer periods of time than either married or single heads of household. Single headed households show a dramatic percentage increase of exits during the first year, which then levels off during the next two years. Approximately three out of four single heads have exited from welfare within one year. Married couples also show a similar pattern, albeit less pronounced. The majority of single and married heads will use welfare relatively briefly, while elderly and female headed households participate over a somewhat longer time span.

Returning to Welfare

Having looked at the patterns of welfare exits, we wish to address the likelihood of returning to welfare given that an individual has left. To do so, a second life table was constructed (Table 8.2). The monthly intervals refer to the amount of time that has passed since the household has exited from welfare. Cases are eliminated from the analysis when they reach the end of the study

TABLE 8.2   LIFE TABLE ANALYSIS OF RETURNING TO
            WELFARE

	Number		Proportion of	
Length on Welfare	Entering Interval	Of Exits	Exits	Cumul Exits

Female Heads				
0-6	488	116	.2377	.2377
6-12	340	32	.0941	.3115
12-18	255	20	.0784	.3636
18-24	146	7	.0479	.3941
24-30	76	3	.0395	.4180

Married Heads				
0-6	398	62	.1558	.1558
6-12	320	30	.0938	.2350
12-18	265	24	.0906	.3043
18-24	163	11	.0675	.3513
24-30	94	4	.0426	.3789

Single Heads				
0-6	397	53	.1335	.1335
6-12	338	19	.0562	.1822
12-18	300	15	.0500	.2231
18-24	247	7	.0283	.2451
24-30	167	4	.0240	.2632

Elderly Heads				
0-6	312	17	.0545	.0545
6-12	257	9	.0350	.0876
12-18	206	3	.0146	.1009
18-24	145	3	.0207	.1195
24-30	78	0	.0207	.1195

Total Sample				
0-6	1595	248	.1555	.1555
6-12	1255	90	.0717	.2161
12-18	1026	62	.0604	.2634
18-24	701	28	.0399	.2928
24-30	415	11	.0265	.3115

(September 1983).   For example, if a household had
exited in March 1983 and remained off through
September 1983, they would be included (as a risk)
in the 0-6 month interval, but not in the 6-12
month interval.   Only cases observed at both points
A and B are included in the recidivism estimates
for each interval.[2]   As with exiting, there is a
time effect on the likelihood of returning to
welfare.   The longer a family remains off, the less
likely they are to return.   For female heads, 23.8
percent will reenter the welfare rolls within six
months.   However, after 24 months, only 4 percent
of those off will return within the next half year.
There is a substantial drop in the probability of
returning to welfare after six months.   This
pattern is true for all household groups.

A sizeable amount of recidivism is estimated to
occur within 2 1/2 years of having left a public
assistance program(s) (column 5). For female heads,
41.8 percent will have returned to welfare at some
point during the 30-month span.   Just as female
headed households are least likely to exit from
welfare,   they are most likely to return.
Approximately 37.9 and 26.3 percent of married and
single heads will have re-entered a welfare
program.   Only the elderly are unlikely to return
to welfare. Here, however, the explanation lies in
the manner of exiting. Approximately 70 percent of
elderly heads of household are leaving welfare
through death, which obviously results in lowered
rates of recidivism (see Rank, 1984).

PROPORTION REMAINING OFF WELFARE

Our final question combines the exiting and
recidivism estimates in Tables 8.1 and 8.2 to
obtain the proportion of households that will be
off welfare at the end of three years. By using
the exiting and re-entering rates, we can estimate
how many households beginning a spell of welfare
will be off three years later. This question of
course assumes that families can exit and reenter
the welfare rolls over the 3-year time span.

Table 8.3 presents the proportion of households
remaining off welfare over six month intervals.
Obviously these proportions will be lower than

those found in Table 8.1 because we have allowed
households to reenter welfare (as well as to exit
for a second or third time). After three years,
slightly less than half of all female heads will be
off public assistance. For married couples,
approximately seven out of ten will be off.
Eighty-four percent of single heads will no longer
be on welfare, while close to 60 percent of the
elderly will be off public assistance after a three
year period.

As with the exiting and recidivism rates, there
are clear differences across households in the
likelihood of being on welfare after three years.
Female and elderly heads are more likely to be
receiving welfare after several years than single
or married heads. Female heads have lower exiting
and higher recidivism rates, resulting in a larger
proportion being on welfare. The opposite is true
for single heads. That is, high rates of exiting
and lower return rates result in a smaller
proportion remaining on welfare after several
years.

DISCUSSION

The patterns of welfare use analyzed in this
chapter are important from a policy perspective.
The idea of an entrenched welfare class remaining
on public assistance for years at a time is simply
incorrect. Households using welfare will generally
do so for no more than one or two years. On the
other hand, many of those exiting will return to
the welfare rolls at some point in the future.
These families are likely to weave in and out of
poverty as their economic conditions improve or
worsen. For those who remain on welfare longer
periods of time, the chances of exiting decrease.
These are the individuals that may be locked in to
the welfare system. They represent, however, a
minority of the households beginning a spell of
welfare.

The implication of these findings is that
welfare programs tend to provide temporary
assistance to aid families over periodic times of
crisis. The fact that these spells may reoccur in
the future is indicative of the unstable position

that many welfare families undoubtedly occupy in
the labor force. That is, individuals in poverty
tend to accumulate in the secondary rather than the
primary labor market. Such occupations are
characterized by fast food chains, domestic work,
and so on.

One could argue that it is not necessarily that
welfare recipients choose not to work, but rather
the type of work available which keeps them close
to the poverty line (Goodwin, 1972, 1983 and
Chapter Four and Five of this volume) and therefore
in need of temporary welfare assistance. Policies
focusing on improving both available occupational
opportunities and skills for low income families
would provide greater economic stability for such
households in the future.

A second finding is that different types of
households participate differently in the welfare
system. Much of the previous research has focused
on female-headed families. Our comparison of
female heads with married, single, and elderly
heads, revealed that married couples and singles
are on welfare considerably shorter amounts of
time. On the other hand, the elderly when compared
with female heads, remain on public assistance for
identical lengths.

Clearly the structure of female- and elderly-
headed households puts them at a disadvantage in
the labor market. Female heads suffer several
disadvantages in the marketplace. The majority of
female-headed households have only one possible
wage earner, who often is unable to participate in
the labor force due to child-care responsibilities.
Furthermore, if she does enter the labor market,
her earnings are likely to be lower than her male
counterparts. Likewise, elderly heads are at a
severe disadvantage in the labor force. Most are
retired and unable to generate any income other
than social security, private pensions, or savings.
On the other hand, single and married household
heads tend to have greater resources at their
command as well as fewer constraints for entering
the labor market. The likelihood of exiting the
welfare system is therefore increased.

TABLE 8.3   PROPORTION REMAINING OFF WELFARE BY
            FAMILY TYPE

		Family Type		
Monthly Interval	Female Heads	Married Heads	Single Heads	Elderly Heads	Total Sample
0-6	.2526	.4172	.5266	.2083	.3782
6-12	.2948	.5426	.6920	.3352	.4880
12-18	.3614	.5993	.7470	.4225	.5469
18-24	.4068	.6213	.7959	.4971	.5915
24-30	.4511	.6609	.8230	.5415	.6277
30-36	.4815	.6898	.8426	.5944	.6582

By viewing the family as an economic unit, it
follows that different types of households will
vary in their patterns of welfare use (as we have
seen). Such a context is important from a policy
perspective.   It suggests that an individual's
flexibility and success in the labor market is
mediated partially through family structure.
Certainly other factors, such as human capital, and
labor market conditions, are important as well.
Nevertheless, the role of the family is critical in
facilitating welfare exits and presumably escaping
poverty.
     Social policy should recognize the importance of
this role. For example, the structure of female-
headed families puts them at an economic
disadvantage. Policies aimed at providing day care
assistance, better enforcement of child support
payments, and effective family planning services
would likely help such families achieve economic
stability.   In addition, policies directed at
reducing sex discrimination and the segmentation of
the labor market would also be beneficial to female
heads.
     In conclusion, social welfare policy should be
constructed with the recognition that households
using welfare do so in brief but occasionally
periodic spells. In addition, policy must
recognize that the welfare population is composed
of individuals living in various household

structures, and that such structures can facilitate or inhibit exiting and re-entering rates for the individual recipient.

NOTES

1 This relationship is examined in closer detail by Rank (1986). Once various demographic and socioeconomic characteristics are controlled for, using multivariate modeling, the length of time effect becomes nonexistent. Consequently, one could argue that the aggregate negative effect of welfare length on exiting is probably due to a demographic change in the composition of households, rather than an increased complacency on the part of welfare recipients. Those most likely to exit (i.e. those with smaller families, greater education, etc) do so quickly, leaving cases less likely to exit behind. The overall exit probabilities are thus reduced in the total population (as found in Table 1). However, one could plausibly argue that these individuals are also less motivated to exit from welfare. Unfortunately, this hypothesis could not be tested.

2 The populations found in Tables 8.1 and 8.2 are not completely identical. Households that had been on welfare longer than three years prior to September 1980, are not included in Table 8.1. In Table 8.2, individuals who had been on for more than three years could be included in the recidivism estimates. The result of this may be that the recidivism rates are slightly higher than had we limited ourselves to only the population in Table 8.1.

BIBLIOGRAPHY

Bane, Mary Jo, and David T. Ellwood. 1983. "The dynamics of dependence: The routes to self-sufficiency." Unpublished manuscript prepared for the Department of Health and Human Services, Washington, D. C.

Boskin, Michael J., and Frederick C. Nold. 1975. "A Markov model of turnover in aid to families with dependent children." Journal of Human Resources 10(Fall): 467-481.

Duncan, Greg J. 1984. _Years of Poverty, Years of Plenty_. Ann Arbor, Michigan: Institute for Social Research.

Goodwin, Leonard. 1983. _Causes and Cures of Welfare_. Lexington, Massachusetts: Lexington Books.

Goodwin, Leonard, 1972. _Do the Poor Need to Work?_ Washington, D. C: Brookings Institution.

Guy, Laura. 1982. _Computer Reporting Network Public Use Sample for Wisconsin Economic Assistance Recipients_, July 1981. Madison, Wisconsin: University of Wisconsin.

Harrington, Michael. 1984. _The New American Poverty_. New York: Holt, Rinehart, and Winston.

Hutchens, Robert M. 1981. "Entry and exit transitions in a government transfer program: The case of aid to families with dependent children." _Journal of Human Resources_ 16 (Spring):217-237.

Murray, Charles. 1984. _Losing Ground: American Social Policy, 1950-1980_. New York: Basic Books.

Plotnick, Robert D. 1983. "Turnover in the AFDC population: An event history analysis." _Journal of Human Resources_ 18 (Winter):65-81.

Rank, Mark R. 1986 "Family structure and the process of exiting from welfare." _Journal of Marriage and the Family_ 48 (August).

Rank, Mark R. 1985. "Exiting from welfare: A life table analysis." _Social Service Review_ 59 (September): 358-376.

Rank, Mark R. 1984. "The dynamics of welfare utilization: A longitudinal analysis of households receiving public assistance." Ph.D. dissertation, University of Wisconsin-Madison.

Rydell, Peter C., Thelma Palmeria, Gerald Blasis, and Dan Brown. 1974. _Welfare Caseload Dynamics in New York City_. New York: Rand Institute.

Wiseman, Michael. 1977. "Change and turnover in a welfare population." Institute of Business and Economic Research, University of California, Berkeley.

9

Health and Poverty in Single-Parent Families: The Consequences of Federal Policy Change[1]

Rosemary C. Sarri and Carol Crill Russell

Between 1980 and 1984 the number of people without health insurance in the United States increased by 22 percent from 28.7 million to 35.1 million persons, of whom nearly one-half are single women and their children (National Governors' Conference, 1986). Many of these families lost their health insurance and were thrust deeper into poverty when working women were terminated from Aid to Families with Dependent Children in 1981-1982. Provisions of the Omnibus Budget Reconciliation Act (OBRA) required that working women who were AFDC beneficiaries be terminated because it was argued they had demonstrated an ability to care for themselves and their children without government assistance. This chapter reports on the consequences for health and health care when single mothers attempt to cope with reduced income, lack of Medicaid for themselves and their children, as well as numerous serious family crises.[2]

In 1981 at the request of the Reagan administration the Congress passed the OBRA legislation that eliminated cash supplements, Medicaid insurance and eligibility for child care and work-related expenses for working women with children who were recipients of Aid to Families with Dependent Children. In addition, many lost Food Stamps, housing allowances and eligibility for emergency assistance and other special programs. Nationally, more than 442,000 families with 1.3 million children lost their benefits (GAO, 1985). From the numerous evaluations that have been completed regarding the impact of OBRA it is quite clear that the federal government and many state governments realized substantial savings even though AFDC is one of the smaller welfare programs. The General Accounting Office (1985) estimates that as of June, 1984, approximately six billion dollars had been saved since 1981.

Research by the Congressional Research Service (1984) indicates that over 550,000 persons were thrust into poverty because of the policy changes, and these persons were disproportionately single parent families and their children (U.S. House of Representatives, 1984). Moreover, despite the economic recovery, most of this population of working poor women and children has remained in poverty (U.S. Dept. of Commerce, 1986).

Why was this population of working single mothers targeted for benefit reduction? Perhaps the most obvious explanation arises from the long-standing resistance to welfare support for low-income women and children in the United States. Pearce (1982) documents that differentiating the "deserving" from the "undeserving" poor is the single most consistent theme of policy and program change in federal and state legislation in the twentieth century (see the discussion in Chapter One).

The writings of Martin Anderson and George Gilder provide ideological underpinnings for the changes implemented under OBRA. Anderson (1978) argues that poverty in the United States had been virtually eliminated and existing social programs were more than adequate for those truly in need. Moreover, the best welfare reform was "work" because guaranteed income reduced work effort. In turn, Gilder (1981) asserts that working-age, able-bodied poor people (especially women) should be weaned away from welfare programs, because of the "moral hazard of liberalism." He further argues that welfare programs "promote the value of being 'poor' and perpetuate poverty." (1981)

There is now substantial literature to indicate the consequences of poverty and income loss for health and well-being (Congressional Budget Office, 1979; Sidel and Sidel, 1978). Belle's study of AFDC recipients in Boston indicates that these women experience very high levels of stress, have frequent crises, and have relatively poor health overall (Belle, 1982). The inverse relationship between socioeconomic status and health problems is one of the most firmly and consistently established associations in epidemiological literature (Kessler, 1979; Kessler and Cleary, 1980; Langner and Michael, 1974; Thoits and Hannan, 1979). Dzede, et. al. (1981) found that both mental and physical health are related to poverty.

Low-income single-parent families experience a disproportionate number of crises because they lack resources for preventive action or to forestall the consequences of accidents that anyone can expect to encounter. This precarious situation creates further stress which in turn may result in additional crises (Belle, 1982). It has long been noted that poor people tend to view fate and luck as more critical in their lives than planning or saving. Such perspectives should be expected because the poor have limited or no ability to control many events which influence their well-being.

The guiding hypothesis for this study was that both objective (e.g. economic need) and subjective (e.g. perceived stress) factors influence the respondents' health and coping behavior.[3] However, it was expected that responses would be mediated by informal (e.g. kin, friends, and neighbors) and formal (e.g. social agencies) social networks as well as by the availability of resources such as health insurance associated with employment. We expected that coping behavior might be adaptive or maladaptive in terms of the family's subsequent well-being. Thus, when confronted by changes in AFDC policy that reduced benefits--how did women conceive of their options? What steps, if any, did they take to overcome the impact of their loss of income and to restore family well-being? How important in a woman's decision making was her need for Medicaid protection? Until recently most concern about the effects of welfare has focused on socio-psychological attributes of the recipients; almost no attention was directed to its consequences for the quality of these families' lives, (Sandelowski, 1981). We, therefore, sought to ascertain how women responded to these crises and negative conditions and then to examine their relationship to health and well-being.

METHODOLOGY

Representative, but not randomly selected, counties in Michigan and Georgia were surveyed in 1983, approximately 12 to 15 months after women were terminated from AFDC. Factors considered in the selection of counties included unemployment levels, rural vs. urban, and race because these variables are known to be associated with variable client careers in the AFDC population. Counties were selected as the critical unit for analysis because social services programs in both states are administered through county government, and some discretion remains at that level in decision making about health and welfare services. Respondents were randomly selected within each county from among the population of women terminated from AFDC in 1981 because they had been working at the time.

Respondents were initially contacted by mail to obtain their consent for participation in the study. All were interviewed in the respondents' homes. Each interview obtained information on welfare experience and attitudes, health, household composition, income and expenses, employment, education, marital experience, family background, parenting and child care, formal and informal social supports, and coping behavior. A total of 356 women in Michigan and 230 in Georgia, who had been terminated, were interviewed, but the sample reported in this paper only includes 486 single mothers who remained single from termination to the time of the interview, and were clearly terminated only because of the OBRA provisions that were applicable in both states.[4]

FINDINGS

There were a total of 1821 individuals residing in the 466 households reported on here. Of that total 68% in Georgia and 62% in Michigan were children under the age of 21. The median household size was four persons.

The median age of the respondents was 29 in Georgia and 33 in Michigan as Table 9.1 indicates; 37% in Michigan and 79% in Georgia were nonwhite.

The median school grade completed was Grade 11 in
Georgia and 12 in Michigan. Overall, Michigan women
were better educated because 80% in Michigan had
completed high school or its equivalent, and 27%
had some post-secondary education; 12% were in
school when interviewed.

At the time of the interview 77% in Michigan and
91% in Georgia identified themselves as single
parents because they were living apart even when
married, but there were further inter-state
differences. Forty-eight percent in Georgia and 26%
in Michigan were never married. There were more
women married, separated, and divorced in the
Michigan sample (56%) than in Georgia (43%).

While there were almost no differences in the
number of children in the households, children in
Georgia were younger; but, this is not surprising
given the differences in mothers' ages. Michigan
women were more likely to apply for AFDC at an
older age (24) and did so primarily because of
divorce, domestic violence and/or child abuse.
Women in Georgia first received AFDC at a median
age of twenty, primarily because of pregnancy or
childbirth as a single parent.

Questions about household mobility were asked
only in Michigan, but that revealed considerable
mobility subsequent to loss of AFDC benefits.
Nearly one-quarter moved at least once and 7 per
cent moved two or more times in 1982. Other
households had persons move out (23%) or persons
move in (29%). In sum, 53% of the households
experienced one or more of the mobility indicators
while 34% had two or more. When households were
recomposed, women most frequently moved in with
relatives, or if that alternative was not
available, women moved in with friends or sought
help from social agencies. Findings from the Robert
Wood Johnson Foundation national survey (1983)
indicate that 51% of families without health
insurance state that chronic illness led to a major
change in employment, housing or living
arrangements. This sample of low-income mothers
had similar experiences.

This sample of women were terminated from AFDC
because they were working and perceived to be
capable of taking care of themselves and their
children without government assistance. At the

time of the interview, 72.9% were employed (nearly 90% in the same job as when they were terminated) and 23.2% had returned to AFDC.

TABLE 9.1 PERSONAL AND SOCIAL CHARACTERISTICS OF WORKING FORMER AFDC RECIPIENTS

	Michigan N=279	Georgia N=207
Median Age in Years	33	29
% Non-White	37%	79%
Education:		
Less than Grade 12	22%	33%
High School Grad or GED	78%	47%
Some post-secondary	27%	10%
Currently enrolled	12%	0
Average No. of Children:		
In household	2.1	2.0
In AFDC Unit	1.8	2.0
Median Age of Children	12	9
Marital Status:		
Median age at first marriage	19	19
%Currently married	23%	9%
%Married one or more times	49%	43%
%Never married	26%	48%
AFDC Experience:		
Age at first grant	24	20
No. of times on AFDC	2.2	1.8
Household Mobility in 1982:		
%Moved 1 or more times	23%	N.A.
%Households with persons moving out	23%	N.A.
%Households with persons moving in	29%	N.A.
%Households with 1 or more mobility indicators	53%	N.A.
Household Composition:		
%Mothers and children only	84%	48%
%Mothers, children and other adults	16%	52%

HEALTH AND HEALTH CARE

When women in this study were removed from AFDC, they were presumed able to provide for themselves and their children, but removal from AFDC also meant loss of entitlement for Medicaid. Even though most worked full-time, one-third had no health benefits for themselves or their children. Because eligibility for AFDC disregards morbidity, single-mother families who are removed from AFDC on the basis of income and assets, and who also have high morbidity, confront critical questions about whether to seek medical care and how to pay for it. Only in Michigan was Medicaid available to "medically needy" families, based on high medical expenses and low income, but in actuality this program was available to very few of the working non-welfare poor population. Unless women were eligible for AFDC in Georgia, they could not receive any Medicaid assistance for themselves or their children. To gain insight into the impact of ineligibility for Medicaid on poor single-mother families with high morbidity, this chapter examines the relationships between:

1. morbidity of these mothers and their children
2. physician visits
3. refusal of treatment
4. health insurance
5. unreimbursed medical expenses
6. employment and welfare

Morbidity

For this chapter, morbidity is defined as the number of times a mother reports that she or her children had a disease or repeated infection in the previous year. The diseases include: arthritis, rheumatism, asthma/hayfever/ allergies, heart problems/angina, blood circulation/ hardening of the arteries, cancer, diabetes, epilepsy, gynecology problems, hypertension, kidney problems, liver problems, sickle cell anemia, and ulcer/frequent stomach pains. Additionally, morbidity includes accounts of the time the mother reports that she or her children had repeated chest

Table 9.2 MORBIDITY: COMPARISON OF MICHIGAN AFDC
AND NATIONAL HEALTH INTERVIEW SURVEY

Health Measures	% Women		% Children	
	AFDC[a]	NHIS[b]	AFDC[a]	NHIS[b]
Arthritis/Rheumatism	12.7	5.81	1.1	.74*
Asthma/Hay Fever/Allergies	26.6	2.65	21.9	7.61
Blood circulation problem	4.4		0.4	
Cancer	1.9		0.2	
Diabetes	5.7	.90	0.8	
Epilepsy	11.6	.32*	1.7	.23*
Gynecology problem	5.9	3.50	.8	.73*
Heart problem/Angina	13.3	4.12	2.3	.27*
Hypertension	13.3	5.71	0.8	3.55
Kidney problem	1.1	4.24	4.2	.38
Liver problem	35.0	.13	0.2	1.64*
Repeated colds/Strep throat	20.0		28.1	
Repeated ear infections	2.1		17.9	
Sickle Cell Anemia	13.3		1.7	
Tonsillitis/Tonsil enlargement	12.9		10.1	
Ulcers/Frequent stomach pains			1.9	

*Unreliable rate (high sampling error)
a   The AFDC sample reported here were all single
    mothers at   the time of the interview.
b   Source: L. Verbrugge, 1982, National Health
    Interview   Survey Analysis. Washington, D.C.:
    U. S. Department of   HHS, National Center for
    Health Statistics, 1979 Survey.

colds/strep throats, <u>repeated</u> ear infection, or
tonsillitis. In all, each mother could report up to
sixteen conditions of morbidity for herself and
each of her children.

The health conditions presented in Table 9.2
report the percentages of women and children
responding affirmatively to each measure.   It
indicates that 10-35% of the women report
incidences of arthritis/rheumatism, gynecology or
kidney problems, hypertension, repeated respiratory
infections, and ulcers or stomach pains.
Additionally, 1-9.9% report having asthma or
allergies, blood circulation or heart problems,
repeated ear infections, and tonsillitis.

The leading morbidity conditions for children are asthma/hayfever/allergies (21.9%), repeated colds (28%), repeated ear infections (17.9%), and tonsillitis or tonsil enlargement (10.1%).

Other conditions clustering at 5% or less are arthritis, blood circulation, gynecology, heart or kidney problems, or ulcers and stomach pains.

How do the levels of morbidity observed in the sample of poor single mothers from Michigan and Georgia compare with the general population of women and children in the United States? The closest set of comparable self-report data was collected in the 1979 National Health Interview survey.

With only preliminary analysis completed, the data indicate that this sample of former AFDC recipients has higher rates of asthma/hayfever/allergies, arthritis, diabetes, epilepsy, gynecology problems, hypertension, kidney problems, and liver problems. In fact, in many instances the magnitude of the difference is very large. Comparing children in the OBRA sample with the national sample reveals a pattern similar to those of their mothers. Children in the OBRA sample had higher rates of all illnesses except heart problems.

The morbidity percentages reported in Table 9.2 are important, but they do not indicate their impact on the lives of these mothers. Each of the physical conditions could have a major, moderate, or minuscule impact on a person's life. For instance, even a relatively benign condition such as tonsillitis can become life-threatening; and alternately, such a fearsome disease as cancer can become non-life-threatening if, for example, a tumor is completely removed, or the disease goes into a lengthy remission.

Therefore, it is postulated that not just the presence of an illness, but the presence of multiple illnesses affects a mother's need for health care and her ability to pay for the health care. Thus, in analysis, it was decided to count each report of an illness as one incidence of morbidity, irrespective of its actual or potential seriousness. Subsequently, scores were computed for women and children by adding incidences of

morbidity per person per household. The following
examples are presented to clarify this procedure
for the reader:

1. If a mother has both a liver problem and
   diabetes, then she has 2 incidences of
   morbidity.
2. If a mother has 3 children, 2 of whom have a
   liver problem, and 2 of whom have diabetes, then
   there are 4 incidences.

TABLE 9.3 Morbidity: Percent of Mothers, Children,
and Mothers/Children by Number of Morbidity
Incidences (N=474).

		Incidences of Morbidity			
	1	2	3	4+	TOTAL
Mothers	43.9	27.2	16.5	12.4	100.0%
Children	44.5	26.4	15.6	13.5	100.0%
Mothers/ Children	23.6	21.9	22.2	32.3	100.0%

From the morbidity indicators, counts were taken of
the number of reported incidences of illness. The
results for these mothers and their children are
presented in Table 9.3.

The mothers in this sample not only had to
contend with low-paying employment and at least
transitory loss of welfare benefits, but about 60%
experienced significant health problems of their
own during 1982. Fifty-six percent of the single
mothers in this sample reported at least one of the
sixteen illnesses reported in Table 9.2.
Furthermore, 12.4% of these women lived that year
with three or more of these conditions of physical
morbidity, as Table 9.3 indicates.

It is important to remember that in single
mother families the health of the mother's children
has a strong influence on her ability to support
her family without resources such as Medicaid or
insurance to pay for health care. Nearly 55% of
these households contained at least one child with
one of the sixteen illnesses reported above. Some
women are affected more severely by the ill-health

of their children. Table 9.3 also shows that 13.5% of households with a large number of illnesses contained children with three or more conditions.

Although the mother's health is critical, the health of her children may determine her ability to work and provide for her family. In most cases it is the total effect of her health plus the health of her children that provides the most accurate measure for determining the impact of ill-health on the family's ability to cope satisfactorily with assistance needs. For example, in some cases a sickly mother will not be able to provide for her children, even if they are healthy. In other cases, children with health problems may inhibit a healthy woman's ability to hold a job. In even other cases, moderate ill-health of both the mother and her children will combine to overcome her ability to pay for medical care. It is in the latter case, that of the "family's morbidity", or the combined morbidity of the mother and her children that is particularly important. When the family's health is considered together, there is a marked drop in the percentage of families experiencing no illness during the previous year, and a concomitant sharp rise in the percent of families reporting three or more incidences of illness. Only one family in five experienced no incidences of illness while one family in three lived through the year with three or more incidences of morbidity.

Physician Visits

For each of the sixteen illnesses reported for herself and her children in Table 9.2, the mother was asked whether she and/or her children visited a physician for that illness. Households without illness were deleted, and the remaining families were categorized as "Always Going to the Doctor" for each reported illness, or "Sometimes Go to the Doctor" for at least some reported illnesses. Percentages reported in Table 9.4 were calculated for Mothers, Children, and Mothers/Children together.

TABLE 9.4 PHYSICIAN VISITS OF MOTHERS AND CHILDREN

Families With Illnesses	Always go to Doctor	Sometimes Go to Doctor	TOTAL
Mothers(N=263)	58.9	41.1	100%
Children (N=259)	70.3	29.7	100%
Mothers/Children (N=355)	58.3	41.1	100%

These findings indicate that these mothers were more likely to take their children to a physician when the children were sick than they were likely to see a physician when they themselves were ill. Moreover, 41% of the mothers and 30% of the children did not visit a physician for at least some of the reported incidences of illness. This is cause for concern, because the illnesses included in this analysis are either serious or else are repeated colds and ear infections. Therefore, the measure of inconsistently going to the doctor represents a serious jeopardy of one's health. Information was not obtained as to whether health care was received from other providers such as nurses, or in schools in the case of children.

Refusal of Medical Treatment

One important obstacle to medical care that poor mothers must overcome is the refusal of physicians to treat them when they are ill. Physicians, hospitals, and clinics may currently refuse to treat patients both because the patient has Medicaid or because the patient does NOT have Medicaid. Medical establishments report refusing Medicaid patients because the payment is too low or because of the bureaucratic hassle involved in securing reimbursement from the government is too great.

Women in this sample were asked whether they had been refused medical treatment under various circumstances: whether they had Medicaid, had private insurance, or had no health insurance. The results show that about 11% of the women (52

families) have been refused medical treatment
because they did not have Medicaid. Of these
families, six reported 3-7 incidences of illness
for their children, and 12 reported 3-7 incidences
for the mothers. However, 10% were refused medical
treatment because the physician was not accepting
Medicaid patients. There was also a cluster of
sixteen mothers (3.4%) who have been refused
medical treatment, at one time or another, both
because they had Medicaid and because they did NOT
have Medicaid. When both types of refusal of
medical treatment are considered (i.e. with or
without Medicaid or other insurance), 82 families
(17% of the sample) were identified as having been
refused treatment. Of these, 17 reported 2
incidences and an additional 28 reported 3 or more
incidences of illness. Clearly, families with
major medical care needs are being turned away by
medical care providers.

Table 9.5 FAMILIES WITH SICK CHILDREN PERCENT OF
TIMES VISIT DOCTOR BY REFUSAL OF MEDICAL TREATMENT
(N=256)
VISIT DOCTOR WHEN SICK

Ever Refused	Always (N=180)	Sometimes[a] (N=40)	Seldom[b] (N=36)	Total (N=256)
Yes (N=47)	17.2	15.0	27.8	18.4
No (N=209)	82.8	85.0	72.2	81.4
TOTAL	100.0%	100.0%	100.0%	100.0%

a Sometimes = 1-74% of time.
b Seldom = 75-100% of time.

There are no strong relationships between having
once been refused treatment and whether a mother
visits the doctor when she is ill. However, Table
9.5 shows there were 36 families (27.8%) where the
children did not go to the doctor for most of their
incidences of illness, and in these families
mothers also reported higher rates of having been

refused treatment than for the sample as a whole.
Because of the correlational nature of these data,
it is impossible to determine the reasons why
mothers who have been refused treatment at least
once, do not take their children to doctors when
they become ill. It is probable that mothers, once
refused medical treatment, recall the experience
with anger, frustration, hopelessness, and
therefore, are reluctant to seek treatment, even
when children are quite ill.

Insurance/Medicaid Coverage

Single mothers who were removed from AFDC, lost
their entitlement to Medicaid, but 12 to 18 months
later 23% were again receiving AFDC and Medicaid. A
small number ineligible for AFDC, had applied
successfully for Medicaid under the medically needy
provision. In addition, the transition was eased
in some Michigan counties when they kept families
on Medicaid for four months after AFDC termination.
In Georgia, raising the "standard of need" resulted
in fewer AFDC terminations than otherwise would
have occurred. Women without Medicaid either paid
for their medical care through private or work-
related insurance benefits (45.6%), or had no
insurance of any type (31%). The latter obviously
must pay for health care out of their limited
personal income or not obtain treatment. The one-
fifth with Medicaid only were vulnerable to
reductions because of changes in eligibility
guidelines or in level in coverage, as has been the
pattern in recent years. Even those women with
work-related insurance usually had very limited
coverage for hospitalization only or else had high
deductibles. As a result, many were seldom able to
utilize such benefits. Most of these families
needed primary outpatient care, but that was
difficult for them to obtain. Health Maintenance
Organizations or similar services were few and far
between in 1982-1983 in both of these states.
There was a fortunate 1% who reported having both
Medicaid and private insurance.
    When we examine whether or not a mother seeks
treatment when someone in the family is ill, it is
clear that families with no insurance are least

likely to visit the doctor. Among those who have
illnesses, the following percentages do not see
doctors some of the time when they are ill:

        53.3% of those with no insurance
        39.3% of those with Medicaid only
        36.4% of those with other insurance

    Because we are interested in the relationship
between medical care and illness, a variable was
created, grouping women who had been refused
treatment at least once even when they had at least
some type of insurance, and those who had never
been refused. One might refer to this as the
"Medicaid Catch-22"! A total of 17.6% were refused
treatment at least once: 22.8% when they had no
insurance of any type, 25% when they had Medicaid
only, and 9% when they had some other type of
insurance. Apparently, physicians slightly prefer
to treat "charity" cases with no insurance than
those with Medicaid. In any event, doctor's
refusal to provide treatment is obviously a problem
for many poor single women.

Medical Expenses

When asked about the amounts of "out-of-pocket"
expenses for physicians, hospitals, prescriptions
and non-prescription drugs, the amounts were found
to be surprisingly high, as Table 9.6 indicates.[5]
None of these expenses were reimbursed by either
Medicaid or private insurance.

Table 9.6   Medical Care Expenses 1982 Uncovered By
                Insurance (in dollars)
                    (N=472)

Dollars	50	50-149	150-49	500-999	1000-1999	2000+
Frequency	103	135	148	56	17	13
Percent	21.8	28.6	31.4	11.9	3.6	2.7

Nearly half of the women had annual out-of-pocket
medical expenses exceeding $150 which is a sizeable
amount given their total annual income of $8976 in
Michigan and $6648 in Georgia. Both of these
amounts are well below the poverty level for their

respective household sizes. Medical bills also resulted in considerable indebtedness. The average amount owed by 55% of the Georgia single mothers who had debt was $492 whereas only 14% of the single mothers in Michigan had medical debts, but the average amount was $502. None of these women could afford this level of indebtedness, because they were unlikely to have sufficient income to be able to pay these bills--especially if their health was less than satisfactory. In this way, they were plunged even further into poverty with little likelihood of being able to escape regardless of their effort.

Among those who go to the doctor when someone is ill, single mothers are more likely to have medical expenses which are a larger proportion of their income. However, women who visit doctors for every illness (Table 9.5) are often not protected from medical expenses by Medicaid or other insurance. There are numerous deductibles and co-pay requirements. Thus, health care cost is a substantial part of family expenses--6% on the average for all families in this sample. However, it is also important to note that more than 25% of those with large medical expenses report that they do not visit physicians most of the time when a family member is ill. In this sample, families with 3 or more incidences of illness are less likely to go to a physician than those with a single incidence. However, this finding may reflect their own behavior in that people with frequent incidences may actually attempt to go to the doctor less often.

Women who are uninsured are as likely to have large as small medical bills, but those with Medicaid are far more likely to have small medical expenses. Although only one in four Medicaid-insured mothers has large medical expenses, this issue deserves further study because they are supposed to have most medical costs covered. However if we examine the medical expenses of women with varying types of insurance, we find that unreimbursed medical expenses above $150 or more are found in families:

> 64.8% of those with private insurance
> 44.8% of those with no insurance
> 25.2% of those with Medicaid

Obviously the private insurance group is in the worst situation, and these are not necessarily those with greater resources. However, many of these latter women had only catastrophic insurance or only that which covered "in-hospital" care. It is not adequate for families where high medical expenses could be anticipated.

Morbidity and health care expenses. All of the families in this sample had incomes that could only be categorized as survival level; moreover, a substantial percentage were in debt all of the time despite full-time employment. Clearly, medical expenses are always problematic and a burden, but they are likely to be most problematic for those with frequent illness.

Many women with frequent incidences of illness incur high medical bills. Approximately 15% had medical bills in excess of the amount paid by insurance. On the average, the excess was $500 or more. Visiting a physician results in high medical bills so it is not surprising that women do so for their children but not for themselves. The risk of refusal probably also influenced women not to visit doctors. One in five mothers (82) was refused treatment at least once whether or not she had Medicaid.

Table 9.7 indicates that families with high incidence of illness are more likely to have higher medical expense (more then $150). Conversely, those with no reported incidences of illness as reported in this chapter, are far more likely to have low medical expenses. Thirty-seven percent had expenses less than $50. The findings also indicate that 16% have medical expenses in excess of $500, largely because these expenses are not covered by any insurance. Among those with three or more incidences of illness, 26.1% had expenses in excess of $500 versus only 8% with no reported incidences.

Employment, Welfare and Race

Unemployed women, those on welfare, and those from minority groups are more likely to have frequent incidences of illness, but are less likely to visit a physician when someone becomes ill. Women on welfare reported that often they failed to visit a physician when they or a child was ill because they did not have money for transportation or child care for other children.

TABLE 9.7 HEALTH BY MEDICAL EXPENSES FOR SINGLE
            MOTHER FAMILIES
            Incidences of Illness

	None	3 or More	TOTAL
<$50	37.3	9.8	22.0
$50-149	33.6	24.2	28.6
$150-499	20.9	39.9	33.3
$500+	8.2	26.1	16.0
TOTAL	100.0	100.0	100.0

Unemployed mothers are more likely to have been refused medical treatment, and if they return to welfare, they still experience high rates of refusal of treatment by physicians. As a result, it is not surprising that employed mothers actually have more contact with medical care providers for every incidence of illness. As was noted earlier, this sample had the greatest need for outpatient primary health care; those who were employed and with insurance were best able to secure this care, although often at considerable cost.

No consistent relationships were observed between race and refusal of treatment, but non-white women reported visiting physicians less often even though they had higher incidences of illness. This pattern was observed for both mothers and their children. It is also noteworthy that this sample, especially in Georgia, was very disproportionately non-white (79%).

Much of the poor health of this sample of families is due to chronic illnesses that require prompt and continuing health care, but that need not necessitate a woman's being unemployed, although it may be essential that she have some welfare supplementation and health care insurance. Without such insurance, families with chronic illnesses have both increased out-of-pocket health expenses, increased debts, unstable income, and

increased probability of being refused medical
treatment. Because illness and lack of affordable
health care is so problematic for these families,
it is little wonder that so many reported that loss
of Medicaid was one of the most negative aspects of
being terminated from AFDC.

OTHER CRISES

Not only did these families have health problems,
they also had other serious crises with which to
cope. Having no money, no food, a serious illness,
death, job loss, family violence and problems of
their children was almost routine for these
families, as Table 9.8 indicates. Nearly nine out
of ten ran out of money at least once and 62
percent reported that they were without money seven
or more times. Half were without food at least
once and a quarter ran out of food more than seven
times. Several interviewers visited households in
which there was no food available and where
respondents were extremely anxious because of their
children. Many reported that they always ran out
of food at the end of the month when wages were
gone and emergency food was unavailable.
    Michigan respondents replied that the following
were the most serious problems experienced in 1982:
lack of money (28%); lack of food (10%); having
something bad happen to their children (14%);
having someone close die (9%); and own illness
(7%). Women with lower incomes experienced
somewhat more crises, particularly those involving
crime and lack of money, but the correlation was
not strong--probably because the income range for
the entire sample was limited relative to overall
need and because nearly all experienced several
serious crises during the year. Several reported
suicides within the family, serious fires, rape,
and other crises.
    The mean number of crises per respondent was
12.59 for the twelve to fifteen month time period.
Only 3 percent reported not having one or more of

TABLE 9.8   CRISES FOLLOWING TERMINATION[a]
                   (N=316)

		% Responding one or more times	Mean number of times
1.	Run out of money.	88.6	5.3
2.	Run out of food.	49.1	2.4
3.	Became seriously ill at least once.	39.9	.7
4.	Borrowed over $300.	36.8	.6
5.	Had someone important die.	34.6	.5
6.	Had problems with partner.	37.1	1.3
7.	Had furnace or major appliance break	32.6	.4
8.	Had something bad happen to child.	29.4	.5
9.	Been a victim of crime.	11.1	.1
10.	A Been to court or was arrested.	12.9	.2
11.	Had gas turned off.	8.6	.1
12.	Had electricity turned off.	7.3	.1
13.	Had something repossessed.	3.1	.0
14.	Had some other crises.	24.4	.4
Mean number per family.			12.6

a Since January, 1982, how many times, if at all,
have you _____? The time interval covered 12-18
months from the month of termination.

the crises which we asked them about. In a similar
survey of low-income women in Boston, Belle (1982)
reported that in a two-year period they experienced
an average of 14 serious crises which required
change and adjustment by the women. The Boston
study reported that the lack of money took the
greatest toll on mental and physical health; that
one-third did not have enough money for food; 48
percent had at least one child with a serious
school problem; and 23 percent rated their own
health as poor, (Belle 1982). These results then

are quite similar to the crises observed in the Michigan survey, again pointing to the fact that low-income women disproportionately experience serious crises and stress. The General Mills survey of a random sample of all United States' families in 1979 reported that, in order to cope with inflation, 75 percent of the single-parent families showed similar responses to these crises associated with reduced income (General Mills, 1979).

One might expect that families with large numbers of crises, especially frequent crises associated with lack of money or food, with illness, or with housing problems, would reapply for AFDC and would be relatively successful in being reinstated. Sixty percent of the Michigan sample did not receive any AFDC or Food Stamps after their initial termination in 1981-82. That group had the smallest mean number of crises (11.90). Those who subsequently received only Food Stamps had a mean of 12.06 crises while those who returned to AFDC had 15.17 and the highest mean number (15.67) occurred for those who were back on both AFDC and Food Stamps. Having to confront and cope with these crises was a major reason why most of the latter group chose to return to welfare even when they would have preferred to remain independent of it. However, two-thirds of the sample reported repeated efforts to obtain assistance from public and private agencies as well as from family and friends. It was the latter who most often provided need, material and non-material assistance.

DISCUSSION AND IMPLICATIONS

Overall, both subjective and objective indicators point to greater hardship for these families in the post-OBRA period. The findings correspond to those observed in several other state surveys. These women, all of whom had been terminated from AFDC at least once, perceived that their economic and social situation had declined substantially since 1982, and many reported being in almost continual crises. They felt themselves to be worse off than similar women in prior years in terms of their poor

health, increased indebtedness, problems of child
care, and other frequent crises. Their lives were
negatively affected by the OBRA cuts despite their
wholehearted and continuing work effort. Clearly,
this population is at high risk for extended
periods of income below the poverty level, and the
problem will be exacerbated as the number of
mother-only families below the poverty level
increases (Kamerman, 1985; APWA, 1985).

Americans pride themselves on efficiency and
often say, "An ounce of prevention is worth a pound
of cure." However, in the case of this sample of
low-income working single mothers, primary
prevention as a policy strategy seems to have been
wholly ignored. This strategy is particularly
problematic given the frequency and seriousness of
illnesses experienced by these families. They
encountered the greatest difficulty in attempting
to secure basic health care, and were often refused
treatment when they had Medicaid or other
insurance. On the other hand, those without
Medicaid also found it difficult to obtain
treatment. It is noteworthy that the proportion of
the poor and near poor covered by Medicaid dropped
from 63% in 1975 to 46% in 1983 (National
Governors' Conference, 1986). Unreimbursed medical
expenses were a frequent occurrence and a
considerable burden for single mothers in this
sample because they never had incomes large enough
to cover these costs. Analysis of the U.S.
Committee on Ways and Means (1985a) indicates that
fewer poor children in 1984 had Medicaid than in
the 1970's and that the poorer the child, the less
the Medicaid coverage.

Much of health care in the United States today
is geared toward cure and exotic high technology
treatment rather then primary prevention or on-
going care of chronic illness. In addition, the
system is being increasingly privatized with
insurance programs favoring those who are employed,
and medical care providers apparently feel free to
refuse to treat persons with Medicaid or no
insurance at all.

The Robert Wood Johnson Survey (1983) found that
one out of six uninsured persons in the United
States encountered difficulty in securing treatment
versus only one in twenty of those who had

insurance coverage. Overall, they observed that
the typical uninsured person had the following
characteristics: young, non-white, less education,
lower perceived health, single parents, part-time
work and low wages, employed in service industries,
and having a family income near or below the
poverty level. This sample of single mothers
resembles the typical uninsured person.
Particularly intolerable is the lack of health care
for so many millions of children. The Select Panel
on Children's Health (1980) has stated that it is
potentially disastrous for a society to rear a
generation of children in poverty and ill-health
when such is clearly avoidable. It is ironic that
such a situation prevails in one of the most
affluent countries of the world.

Poverty and poor health are a painful reality
for millions of American women and children--just
as it is for millions throughout the world. The
United States stands apart from other
industrialized countries of the world in that it
has only reluctantly extended income supports to
its needy citizens--even when those in need are
children, disabled, or ill--unable to care for
themselves. Rather than the "Great Society", it
might be more appropriate to refer to us as the
"Mean Society" because we have the resources to
eliminate poverty, but not the will to do so. Many
income support programs are gender-marked in that
they are far more punitive toward women than toward
men. They have explicit and implicit requirements
controlling the roles and behavior of women
regarding the socialization of the children, but
they are expected to fulfill these responsibilities
with insufficient resources and few means to effect
a change. It is no wonder then that the results
have been so disruptive for families. Current
proposals for Workfare programs are unlikely to be
any more effective unless they include
considerations of health and health care needs of
single mothers.

What then can be done to rectify an intolerable
situation that jeopardizes the well-being of
mothers and their children? First, physicians
should not be permitted to refuse patients with
Medicaid or other insurance. Second, those without
health insurance must be insured by the state for

primary as well as catastrophic care (Blendon,
Altman, Kilstein, 1983; Davis, 1975; Congress,
1979). Third, Medicaid and private insurance in
its current form must be extended into national
health insurance for all, preferably a national
system of health care. At present, Medicaid
neither guarantees access to medical treatment, nor
protects its recipients from inequitably high
medical costs. Because national health care will
be difficult to achieve politically, one strategy
might be to begin with comprehensive health care
for children and then gradually extend it to other
needy uncovered populations. Recent bills
introduced in the Congress by Senators Evans and
Durenberger contain provision for comprehensive
health care for children (U.S. Senate, 1986).

Fourth, many of the illnesses experienced by
these families are chronic and even with good
health care, some may be unable to work full-time
or to carry out their parental reponsibilities
fully. Therefore, women with serious chronic
illness should be eligible for disability
allowances insured by the federal government. Such
provision is likely to be far more cost effective
in the long run than waiting for these women to
become seriously ill before offering any relief.
Disability assistance is commonly provided to
professional and skilled workers; there is no
reason why such a program could not be developed
for single mothers.

Lastly, it was noted that most of these women
have very low wages. Most have lived far below the
poverty level for many years. In order to have
been eligible originally for AFDC they had to have
a total income below the state standard of need.
In many states that criteria is below 50% of the
poverty level. Raising the standard of need,
building in income-work incentives, and
implementing pay equity legislation would go a long
way toward reducing the impoverishment of poor
single mothers. Provisions of national health care
for these families would then enable them to be
autonomous and be able to function effectively, as
experience during the period 1968-1981 had begun to
demonstrate.

NOTES

1 The study on which this report was based was supported by grants received from the Ford Foundation, Shiffman Foundation, and the Ruth Mott Fund, plus additional special support from the Institute for Social Research and the School of Social Work of the University of Michigan. The study was completed collaboratively with the Center for the Study of Social Policy in Washington, who were responsible for field collection in Georgia. Responsibility for this report, however, rests solely with the authors of this chapter.

2   For further information on this study, see R. Sarri, (Ed.) 1984, The Impact of Federal Policy Change in AFDC Recipients and Their Families. Ann Arbor: University of Michigan Institute for Social Research.

3   The reason for the higher rates of heart problems for both the mothers and the children in the national sample, may reflect better health care in the general population.   Better health care would result in both improved detection and improved treatment.   In a sample of young poor women and children it is possible that heart problems go unnoticed, and therefore, result in higher rates of mortality, thus selecting out of sample (by death), mothers and children who would otherwise report heart problems.

4   There were several differences in implementing OBRA in Michigan and Georgia. Overall, Michigan had more liberal eligibility and higher benefits.   For example, Michigan had Medicaid for the needy regardless of their eligibility for AFDC.   However, the implementation of that benefit became increasingly restrictive in Michigan in the 1980's, particularly during and after the 1982 recession.   The AFDC caseload grew very rapidly, depleting the departmental funds. Thus, there was considerable effort to restrict new cases.

5. These expenses refer only to out-of-pocket expenses for medical care, and they do not include health insurance premiums.

BIBLIOGRAPHY

American Public Welfare Association 1985. _A Matter of Choice: Investing in Low-income Families and Their Children_. Washington, D.C.: American Public Welfare Association.

Anderson, M. 1978. _Welfare_. Stanford: Hoover Institute Press.

Belle, D. (Ed.) 1982. _Lives in Stress_. Beverly Hills: Sage.

Blendon, R. J., D. Altman, and S. Kilstein 1983. "Health insurance for the unemployed and uninsured." _National Journal_ 22, 22:1147.

Cass, B. 1986. The economic circumstances of single parent families in Australia: 1974-1985 some implication for child maintenance policies and the social security system. Canberra, A.C.T. Department of Social Security.

Congress of the U.S. 1979. _Health Maintenance Organizations in Cost-Effectiveness of Medical Technology_. Washington: GPO.

Congressional Budget Office 1979. _Profile of Health Care Coverage: The Haves and Have Nots_ Washington: GPO.

Davis, Karen 1975. _National Health Insurance: Benefits, Costs and Consequences_. Washington: Brookings.

Dzede, S., S. Pike, and J. Hackworth 1981. "The relationship between health-related stressful life events and anxiety: an analysis of a Florida metropolitan community". _Community Mental Health Journal_ 17: (winter) 294-305.

General Accounting Office 1985. _Evaluation of the Impact of OBRA on AFDC Recipients in Twelve Cities_. Washington: GPO.

General Mills 1979. _The American Family Report: Family Health in an Era of Stress_. Minneapolis, MN: General Mills.

Gilder, G. 1981. _Wealth and Poverty_. New York: Basic Books.

Kamerman, S. 1985. "Young, poor and a mother alone: Problems and possible solutions." in H. McAdoo and J. Parkam (Eds.) _Services to Young Families_. Washington: American Public Welfare Association.

Kessler, R. 1979. "Stress, social status, and psychological distress." Journal of Health and Social Behavior, 20:259-272.

Kessler, R. and P. Cleary 1980. "Social Class and Psychological Distress", American Sociological Review, 45. 463-478.

Kessler, R. and H. Neighbors 1986. "A new perspective on relationships among race, social class and psychological distress." Journal of Health and Social Behavior, 27 107-115.

Langner, T. and S. Michael 1974. Life, Stress and Mental Health. New York: Free Press.

Moynihan, D. 1985. Family and Nation. Godkin Lectures, Harvard University. Cambridge, Mass., April 8-9.

Nathan, R. and F. Doolittle 1983. The Consequences of Cuts: The Effects of the Reagan Domestic Program on State and Local Government. Princeton: Princeton University Press. National Governors' Conference 1986. "Today there are more than 35 million Americans without health insurance." Washington National Governor's Conference and National Conference of State Legislature, February.

National Institute of Health 1980. National Medical Care Utilization and Expenditure Report. Washington: Department of Health and Human Services.

Pearce, D. 1982. The Poverty of our Future: The Impact of Reagan's Budget Cuts on Women, Minorities, and Children. Washington, D.C. Center for National Policy Review.

Robert Wood Johnson Foundation 1983. National Health Access Survey, Washington, D.C.

Salamon, L. and L. Musselwhite 1986. Partners in the Public Service: Government and the NonProfit Sector in the American Welfare State. Washington, D.C.: Urban Institute.

Sandelowski, Margrete 1981. Women, Health & Choice. Englewood Cliffs: Prentice Hall.

Sarri, R. (Ed.) 1984. The Impact of Federal Policy Change on AFDC Recipients and Their Families. Ann Arbor: University of Michigan, Institute for Social Research.

Select Panel for the Promotion of Child Health
1981. Better Health for Our Children: A National
Strategy Vol. 1. Washington, D.C.: U.S.
Department of Health and Human Services, p. 31.

Sidel, Victor and Ruth Sidel 1978. A Healthy
State. New York: Pantheon.

Thoits, P. and M. Hannan 1979. "Income and
psychological distress: the impact of an income-
maintenance experiment", Journal of Health and
Social Behavior 20: 120-138.

U.S. Department of Commerce, Bureau of the Census
1986. Money, Income and Poverty Status of
Families and Persons in the United States: 1985.
Washington, D.C.: United States Government
Printing Office, Series P-60, No. 140.

U.S. House of Representatives, Committee on Ways
and Means 1986. Background Material and Data on
Programs Within the Jurisdiction of the
Committee on Ways and Means. Washington: United
States Government Printing Office, March 3.

U.S. House of Representatives, Committee on Ways
and Means. 1985. Children in Poverty.
Washington, D.C.: United States Government
Printing Office.

U.S. House of Representatives 1984. The Impact of
the OBRA Changes on Poverty in the U.S.,
Washington: GPO, July, p. 3.

U.S. Senate 1986. Congressional Record, October
24.

10

Ideology and Welfare Reform
Under the Reagan Administration

Susan Gotsch-Thomson

INTRODUCTION

In a recent article, Nathan Glazer (1984) argues
that the Reagan administration has been somewhat
unique in that it has a congruous set of
ideological beliefs that have been applied to a
number of social and political issues. The
conservative ideology of the Reagan administration
is not new, what is new is conservatism in a
position of power. Glazer traces several
conservative themes in Reagan's social policy:
changes in welfare that emphasize norms rather than
work incentives; the withdrawal of the federal
government from various programs; and an emphasis
on the "new federalism".

That the Reagan Administration sets a
conservative tone is little disputed. The nature
of this conservatism, Reagan's public statements
about welfare[1] and welfare reform, and the
symbolic content of these messages will be examined
in the first section of this chapter. Conservative
ideology sees the family as a crucial institution
in society, yet many of the welfare reforms have
had a negative impact on the economic well-being of
families with children. This contradiction will be
addressed in the second part of the paper. How
then can one politically reconcile a pro-family
ideology with anti-family results and make it
palatable to the American public? Glazer (1984)
has suggested that Reagan's ideology had to be
tempered because of political constraints, such as
strong middle-class opposition to changes in Social
Security. But the changes in welfare-related

programs made by the Reagan Administration have not been challenged by most Americans. Thus the final section of the paper will examine some of the reasons why this political acquiescence has occurred. There are many others (notably Miller and Tomaskovic-Devey, 1983; and Piven and Cloward, 1982) who have addressed the issue in terms of the economic and structural changes in American society that allowed for Reagan's success. While recognizing the crucial importance of such structural factors, the theme of the paper will be the ideology of the Reagan Administration, particularly in terms of its symbolic content (Edelman, 1964). Political symbolism provides us with a piece of the answer to why Reagan has been successful in, and lacked opposition to his changed welfare policies.

The concept of ideology used in this paper is taken from Dolbeare and Dolbeare (1976:2-3): Politics, and much of social life, involves the use of power to achieve goals amidst changing circumstances. Central to this process are beliefs about the present nature of the world and the hopes one has for its future. Such beliefs and hopes, when integrated into a more or less coherent picture of (1) how the present social, economic, and political order operates, (2) why this is so, and whether it is good or bad, and (3) what should be done about it, if anything, may be termed an "ideology". It is a series of images that describe and interpret what happens in politics from day to day. As applied to social problems such as poverty, ideologies shape the perception of what is problematic for society, why the problem exists and what should be done about the problem.[2]

IDEOLOGICAL ASSUMPTIONS OF INDIVIDUALIST-CONSERVATISM

A longing for the rugged individualism of the self-sufficient pioneer perhaps best describes the world view of the individualist-conservative.[3] Driven by the tenacity of self-interest, the individual works in an unfettered environment to meet needs, solve problems, and compete with others in a free market system.

Dolbeare and Dolbeare (1976:58) point out three aspects of individualist-conservatism that describes the kind of society seen as desirable and possible:

(1) a truly free market that allows "voluntary exchanges among mutually benefiting individuals"
(2) avoidance of coercion upon the individual, particularly government coercion
(3) a view of a "harmonious social system" based in the different but interdependent pursuit of goals by self-interested individuals freely competing with each other

Thus humans are seen as basically self-centered, competitive, and individualistic, all essential characteristics to the functioning of capitalism and the free market system. And the free market, as part of capitalism, is central to both economic and political freedom, as well as to self-fulfillment of individuals.

In such a freely competitive society of unfettered individuals, it follows that such individuals are ultimately responsible for their own social condition. Thus conservatives often define social problems in terms of personal or individual pathology while focusing on the deviant nature of conditions perceived as social problems.

There is, however, an important societal activity that the individualist-conservative cites as a cause of social problems, namely government intervention. Especially indicted is government regulation of business and federal support for certain social programs. By regulating business, the workings of the free market are hindered. And support for social programs is seen as fostering dependent individuals, who then become unable to care for themselves.

Solutions for social problems suggested by the conservative are likely to be two-fold: behavior modification or reform of the individual, or reduced government intervention into business and private lives. It is important to note that the conservative ideology in general tends toward inaction. This allows individual goals and the working of the free market to shape the outcome.

How this ideology is applied to the problem of poverty will now be examined in terms of the ideology and the Reagan administration.

CONSERVATIVE ELEMENTS IN REAGAN'S APPROACH TO POVERTY AND WELFARE

For conservatives, there is no inherent social problem in inequality. Poverty may be seen as a problem, but more importantly, can have problematic consequences. For many conservatives, the focus is on the problems with the welfare state rather than poverty per se. In looking at poverty, the conservative tends to concentrate on several aspects. Using a definition of absolute deprivation, many conservatives argue that the extent of poverty is overestimated. Secondly, the attention is on deviant values held by the individual rather than the structure of society. Third, they see the welfare system as part of the problem of poverty and dependency rather than a solution. And finally, the overarching theme is that state and local governments and private charities should be caring for the poor.

Restricted Definitions of Poverty

The conservative argues that various programs provide for "income-in-kind" such as subsidized housing, food stamps, and Medicaid. These in-kind benefits may bring many of the poor above the level of want. The argument is that if adjustments are made for the under-reporting of income, in-kind benefits, and taxes paid by the poor, the figures for poverty would be quite different.

The Reagan Administration's definition of need has focused on a restrictive definition of those who should receive social services -- only the "truly needy." As Reagan stated in his Radio Address of February 12, 1983:

So, let me repeat, far from trying to destroy what is best in our system of humane, free government, we're doing everything we can to save it by slowing down the destructive rate of growing in taxes and spending and by pruning non-essential programs. This way enough resources will be left to meet the requirements of the truly needy, and we will meet the challenge of fairness.

In keeping with the notion of the "truly needy," the Reagan Administration has begun to move in the direction of a changed definition of poverty, one that includes "in-kind" assistance in the income of the poor. A panel of largely conservative economists met in private session to consider how such benefits as food stamps, Medicaid, and housing subsidies could be calculated into the official definition of poverty (New York Times, April 23, 1984). This more restricted definition of poverty would result in a reduction in the numbers of poor.[4] Estimates are that if such noncash benefits were counted, the number of poor would be reduced by one-third to one-half (Focus, 1985b).[5] The movement toward a more restrictive definition of poverty by the Reagan Administration illustrates its conservative ideology.

Values and Poverty

The emphasis on cultural factors as a cause of poverty have been central to many explanations of the persistence of poverty. This "culture of poverty" approach, although originally meant to describe only a small portion of the poor (Lewis, 1966), has been applied to the poor in general by conservatives (Banfield, 1974). In this view, the poor are seen as placing a low or negative value on marriage. Also the inability to delay gratification, having lower aspirations, and fatalism become personality traits that are transmitted from parents to children. The consequence of these personality and cultural traits is that the poor are ill-equipped to escape from their poverty. Poverty is therefore perpetuated primarily because of the deviant values held by lower-class people. The poor are not prepared to take advantage of education, jobs, or other opportunities because they do not share the middle-class work- and family-oriented values of the wider society.   Economic poverty may be preventable, but lower-class values will continue to keep poor families at the bottom of the economic heap. The solution to poverty therefore includes attempts to change the values of the poor, or at least to compel them to abide by certain norms.

That Reagan espouses a "culture of poverty" viewpoint can be seen in his emphasis on the significance of values and norms -- particularly regarding deviant family forms, and the importance of work and commitment to work.

Glazer (1984) suggests that the Reagan approach has been to impose certain norms upon welfare recipients.   The change in AFDC regarding the financial responsibilities of step-parents toward step-children illustrates this.   Glazer (1984:87) suggests that Reagan hopes to: "promote [family] stability by imposing a norm -- i.e., that a man living with a mother and her children had an obligation to support the women with whom he lived as husband, the children with whom he lived as father."   The emphasis is thus on the American belief that parents and step-parents have a moral obligation to provide for children in the household. Thus the Reagan Administration has made it clear that it believes that welfare undermines a stable family by displacing the male and encouraging single women to have children in order to qualify for welfare.   Requiring step-fathers to financially support step-children links a moral obligation to support the children to sexual access to their mothers.

Another example of the significance of values concerns norms regarding the importance of work. Glazer (1984) suggests that Reagan has abandoned the notion that the government needs to provide incentives to work.   In 1981, the Reagan Administration made sweeping changes (some of which have since been modified) in Aid to Families with Dependent Children (AFDC) concerning work incentives and income.   For example, after the first four months of employment, all of the earnings of an AFDC recipient would be deducted from one's benefit's (where previously about 67 percent was deducted).   This would seem to undermine the incentive to work, a seeming anomaly

from a President who so strongly supported work.
But the contradiction is somewhat reconciled if one
recognizes that this is another example of imposing
a norm upon the poor, namely, that you should work
even if your benefits are cut (Glazer, 1984). In
addition, the Administration's emphasis on workfare
-- that welfare recipients must work in some
capacity in order to receive support -- has similar
conservative underpinnings.

Welfare as a Social Problem

Many of the deviant values held by the poor
(discussed above) can be worsened by the welfare
system, which is seen as a cause in the cycle of
dependency by the conservative.   Since
conservatives assume that human nature is
essentially selfish, and that people have to be
enticed to work, then welfare undermines the
motivation to work. In addition, conservatives are
particularly worried about the negative effects
that welfare has on the stability of families,
especially black families. Arguing that the family
is a vital economic institution, welfare is seen to
destroy that economic function. Because welfare
"competes" with the low earnings of the male head
of household, he often leaves the family and the
responsibilities it entails. The result is a cycle
of dependency on public hand-outs. Welfare
undermines individual responsibility, especially
with regard to work. But the dependency is seen to
be even more extensive. It involves loss of
ambition and autonomy for the individual who
depends on welfare; the result is weakened
character (Williamson, et al., 1981:69). This
concern with welfare dependency and its
consequences was the central theme of social
programs in Reagan's 1986 State of the Union
Address (February 8, 1986):

In the welfare culture, the breakdown of the
family, the most basic support system, has
reached crisis proportions -- in female and
child poverty, child abandonment, horrible
crimes and deteriorating schools. After
hundreds of billions of dollars in poverty

programs, the plight of the poor grows more painful. But the waste in dollars and cents pales before the most tragic loss -- the sinful waste of human spirit and potential.

We can ignore this terrible truth no longer. As Franklin Roosevelt warned 51 years ago, standing before this chamber, he said, "Welfare is a narcotic, a subtle destroyer of the human spirit." And we must now escape the spider's web of dependency.

The conservative also sees the "welfare bureaucracy" as part of the social problem of poverty. The expansion of welfare in recent years has been accompanied by a rapid expansion of government agencies and employees. The conservative argues that the result is an unwieldy bureaucracy characterized by waste and inefficiency. It is not surprising to the conservative that welfare fraud occurs, for they feel that the system itself fosters this lack of character and dishonesty on the part of the poor. An example of this type of fraud was given by Reagan (February 15, 1976, quoted in Green and MacColl, 1983:85):

> There's a woman in Chicago. She has 80 names, 30 addresses, 12 Social Security cards, and is collecting veteran's benefits on four non-existing deceased husbands. And she's collecting Social Security on her cards. She's got Medicaid, is getting food stamps, and she is collecting welfare under each of her names. Her tax-free cash income alone is over $150,000.

Reduce Federal Social Programs

In part to mitigate against such fraud, many conservatives would like to replace public welfare agencies with private or voluntary agencies. At the very least, they wish to reduce federal agencies by turning over their programs to state and local governments. But there is also an ideological commitment to reduce government intervention, especially at the federal level.

Reagan has repeatedly emphasized the need to increase private charities and reduce federal involvement in welfare programs. For example, his proposal to turn over more responsibility for welfare to the states was couched in terms of the "new" federalism and private enterprise. For example, fiscal 1987 budget proposed the "privatization" of compensatory education, housing vouchers, and the Federal Housing Administration (Congressional Quarterly, 1986c).

The reduction in federal spending on social programs is not seen as a punitive measure by conservatives. Rather, the Reagan administration sees that one of the most profound solutions to poverty (as well as other economic problems) is a strong, viable economy. Specially, his Administration has sought solutions to poverty in: first, a strong economy which will provide jobs to those who can work; and secondly, public assistance to those who cannot work (Robert J. Rubin, Assistant Secretary of the Department of Health and Human Services, reported in Focus, 1984:12).

In the long run, the solutions to poverty are found in a strong, viable capitalist economy. The notion of "supply-side" economics or the "trickle-down" theory of income distribution argues that jobs and increased wages are the direct result of a thriving economy. If businesses are allowed to keep most of their profits, the result will be greater investments which will benefit the entire society. Clearly this implies that government regulation of business be reduced, and tax policies be directed at reducing corporate taxes.

Thus to the extent that the Reagan Administration has defined the issues concerning poverty, it has focused primarily on the problems of the welfare system, particularly welfare dependency and its impact on the human character. Conservative solutions to poverty range from changing the deviant lower-class values of the poor, to tightening welfare programs, to stimulating the economy to encourage corporate investments. All of these have been suggested by the Reagan Administration. But what have been the impacts of Reagan's policies?

IMPACT OF REAGAN POLICIES

Before examining the impact of Reagan's welfare policies, a brief review of the changes is necessary. One of the most sweeping changes was the Omnibus Budget Reconciliation Act (OBRA) of 1981. The major changes concerning AFDC work incentives and incomes were (Focus, 1985a:2):

-- the $30-and-one-third earned income disregard was eliminated after four months of employment
-- even during the first four months, it was calculated on gross rather than net income
-- maximum allowable deductions were set for work expenses ($75) and child care expenses ($160 per child)
-- eligibility income limit reduced
-- assets eligibility limit lowered to $1000

Budget cuts have also accompanied these changes. For example, budget cuts affecting the poor would amount to $6 billion for fiscal year 1986, $11 billion in 1987, and $14.2 billion in 1988. The programs most affected are Medicaid, Community Services and the Legal Services Corporation, Supplemental Security for the aged, blind, disabled, Head Start, various housing and health programs for the poor, and the special food programs for poor children and pregnant women (New York Times, 1984). Some of Reagan's proposals also cut direct benefits to the middle classes, such as Guaranteed Student Loans, medicare and retirement for military and federal employees (Christian Science Monitor, 1985a), although these proposals have been less successful in Congress.

The evidence is mounting concerning the negative impact which OBRA has had on female-headed families, and recent studies show a continuing deterioration of these families (see Chapter Nine and Focus, 1986). In addition, there are related studies that show the impact of welfare on the well being of recipients. There seems no doubt that the brunt of the burden of changes have been and will continue to be borne by women and their children, especially minorities (Christian Science Monitor, 1985b, 1985c; Washington Post, 1985).

Even prior to Reagan's election, women and children were increasingly the victims of poverty. Sometimes termed "the feminization of poverty," many statistics showed the growing incidence of poverty among women, and therefore among their children (see especially Harrington, 1984; Scott, 1984). This was particularly evident for black and Hispanic women, though white women were also losing ground. By 1980, two out of three poor adults were women, and more than half the families who were poor were headed by women. Often the reason given for higher females rates is the increase in women who head families, but factors such as low wages for women and the impact of social programs may be more important factors.

Many welfare mothers work. Data from the Panel Study of Income Dynamics showed that, during a given year, about 40 percent of females who head welfare families worked (Erie and Rein, 1982). One of the major factors in their continued poverty stems from the low wages paid to them. According to Ehrenreich and Piven (1984), the major factor in low wages for women is occupational segregation. For example, women are concentrated in only 20 of the 420 occupations listed by Department of Labor, especially clerical and service. The average real hourly wage for service and retail trade actually fell in the late 1970's. This occurred even though there was greater demand for workers in clerical and service industries. And it is in exactly these areas where employment, and especially female employment, is likely to grow in the future.

There is some preliminary evidence that the effects of the OBRA reduced the standard of living for single parent (mostly female-headed) families, even though they had NOT reduced their work efforts. In a review of almost a dozen studies on the impacts of OBRA, Moffitt (reported in Focus, 1985a) found that most working AFDC recipients continued to work after the OBRA changes. The percentages of those dropping out of the labor force were similar to years prior to OBRA. Although most of the studies viewed only recipients, there seemed to be no work disincentive consequences of the new regulations, and welfare caseloads decreased--seeming to bear out what

Reagan had hoped for. However, Moffitt found that the changes had the greatest effect at lower income levels. To a small extent, the effects of OBRA increased weeks worked and real earnings, and lowered AFDC participation rates. But this trend increased successively at lower income levels-- among Reagan's "truly needy" rather than those at the upper levels of poverty income. In terms of well-being, there were several important consequences of the OBRA changes. Perhaps the most significant finding was that women were much worse off financially than they had been in the pre-OBRA period (Focus, 1985a). Despite increased monthly earnings from work, their overall average monthly income decreased by 6 percent (in a Michigan study) to 25 percent (in a Dallas study). Those who worked and got off of AFDC did better than those who did not work and received AFDC. Even for those who worked, increased earnings and food stamp benefits did not offset the loss of AFDC. In terms of needs, a study conducted in Minnesota (where monthly income declined by only 8 percent), researchers found that 44 percent of the respondents were short of food at some time, and 30 percent reported that their utility services were in jeopardy (either a threat or actual cut-off). Sarri and Russell in the preceding chapter report in depth on similar consequences of AFDC termination.

More recent studies reveal the continued deterioration of families with children headed by women (Focus, 1986). For all families with children during the period 1967-1984, mean family income grew (1967-1973), remained steady (1973-1979), and dropped (early 1980's) (Danziger and Gottschalk, 1986). The authors note that the general erosion of incomes of families with children can be traced to three factors: increased numbers of families headed by women, reduced real value of government transfers to the non-elderly poor, and reduced earnings of heads of families with children. That female-headed families experienced the most economic decline is apparent. For these families, the early (1967-1973) gains were small. And from 1973-1984, the mean real

income of these families declined by 7.8 percent
(for whites, 7.8%; blacks, 9.4%; and Hispanics,
13.3%).

Women heading families and experiencing the
impact of the budget cuts and economic changes
appear to suffer some negative psychological
consequences as well.   Prior studies had shown
that women who combined welfare and work felt
better about themselves than those receiving
welfare alone.   The results of OBRA lowered that
sense of security and well-being, to the point
where these women feel worse about themselves than
welfare women who do not work (Focus, 1985a).
Juxtaposed to the recent findings of Leonard
Goodwin (1983), these women may in fact experience
increased dependency in the future. Goodwin (1983)
found that a major factor which affected future
economic independence was higher expectations of
such independence, combined with success in the
world of work.

To summarize, the Reagan welfare budget cuts and
changes clearly appear to have a most severe impact
upon women and their children.   The tendency prior
to 1980 had been the deeper impoverishment of women
despite cash transfers.   Diminished funding and
tighter regulations can only increase their
poverty.   And, indeed, the preliminary analyses of
the effects of OBRA suggested that the well-being
of welfare mothers, particularly those who also
work, has decreased.   Although some of these
changes have been modified, the position of welfare
mothers is expected to show little improvement.
These changes have been virtually unopposed by the
American public, yet American values generally
reject increased impoverishment, especially among
children.   How has Reagan brought this about?

SUCCESS OF THE REAGAN ADMINISTRATION

We have seen that the rhetoric of the Reagan
Administration has been that of individualist
conservatism. Appeals to free enterprise, a social
"safety net" for the truly needy, the strengthening
of the family unit, and reduced government
intervention have been hallmarks of Reagan's
discussions of social policies concerning poverty.

However, the impacts of various policies such as tax cuts and social welfare spending, have been most detrimental to women and children.

A central question is how is it that Reagan was able to reconcile the rhetoric with the results, such that the American public has supported the winding down of the welfare state. I believe there are several possible answers to this question.[6]

First, Reagan has had some success in defining a "new ruling ideology." I will argue that the ideology is not really new, but rather builds on certain attitudes and values held by many Americans. What is new is the extent to which groups supporting the ideology have gained power. The crux of the ideology is based in modern conservatism (i.e., 19th century liberalism), particularly in areas that coincide with strongly held "American" values. As conceptualized by Miller and Tomaskovic-Devey (1983), the view that the welfare state should be diminished and businesses given more freedom is part of the ideology of "recapitalization of capitalism". And these views are not unique to conservatives. As Miller and Tomaskovic-Devey show, both neo-liberal and even some liberal politicians seem to have accepted this new "ruling ideology." Of the various elements of recapitalization, the third is most relevant to this paper.[7] As they state (1983:7): "The third drive seeks to teach ideological lessons -- expect less of government, there are no entitlements. Less government then means more capitalist activity." It is clear that Reagan's "new" ideology rejects the goals of greater equality, at least through government intervention, and therefore inherently tolerates poverty. But I would suggest that this "new" ideology also draws covertly on the underside of some American values, namely, classism, racism and sexism. An understanding of these symbolic messages concerning welfare provides one answer as to how Reagan has been able to make cuts in welfare spending.

Secondly, Reagan has not faced any organized opposition to the changes in welfare. In part, this is because he has been able to "write off" segments of the American population, both in terms of political support and in terms of bearing the

burden for spending reductions -- groups such as
women, children, minorities, and even labor. In
addition, he has not faced a coherent opposition by
liberals and the left.   The following sections
examine these issues in greater detail.[8]

Reagan Ideology

That Reagan appeals to many strongly held American
values is obvious.   His public rhetoric is
decidedly conservative in nature, rejecting liberal
values for reducing inequality and promoting
tolerance for "deviant" groups. Publicly, he seems
concerned about providing for those who are truly
in need.   On the surface, he appears to be an
individualist conservative, tempered by the
realities of politics.   But there are other
underlying messages in his ideology that make his
welfare reductions palatable, particularly to
people whose meaning systems about welfare include
elements of racism, sexism, and classism. Evidence
will be presented to show that persons holding
attitudes negative to women, blacks, and greater
equality were more likely to support Reagan.[9]
Not all supporters of Reagan manifest these
attitudes, but that he appeals to them will provide
some support for the argument that the "new"
ideology has gone beyond conservatism.
     The public statements made by the Reagan
Administration concerning poverty and welfare
contain messages that mesh well with the images
that many Americans hold about who welfare
recipients are and why they are poor.   He has
managed to paint a picture of the Great Society as
one of free handouts, particularly to the poor who
seem unwilling to make a contribution in return.
For some Americans, such as the white ethnics
studied by Jonathan Rieder (1985):

     [T]o utter the word liberal [is] as an
     expletive, signifying those who would leave
     families defenseless against the ravages of
     crime, those who would grant welfare to all
     that demand it, and those who would indulge
     the worst   instincts of children. (quoted
     in Lo, 1986:545)

In attempting to discredit liberalism and liberal social policies, Reagan has focused on welfare dependency and welfare fraud (see first section). His public attacks on welfare have not been aimed against children, and only indirectly against their mothers. His use of the term "able-bodied" suggests a picture of a male who needs to be encouraged to work. And indeed, his concept of a "safety-net" would suggest that children and the elderly would continue to receive assistance.

The rhetorical thrust of anti-poverty programs under Reagan is not to eliminate poverty but rather to provide subsistence for those in need and reduce dependency for those who can work. His statements about "helping" apply to the "truly needy" who will be provided a "safety net". There is a rejection of need to reduce inequality. Perhaps the most profound change in this commitment to equality can be seen in the new income tax laws (Philadelphia Inquirer, 1986: The Nation, 1986). Gone is the notion of progressively higher taxes for the wealthy. One of the central questions is to examine to what extent has the greatest support for Reagan (in terms of election results) been from those who LEAST espouse values central to an ideology supporting equality.

The data from the General Social Survey (1984,1985) show that persons holding such attitudes were more likely to vote for Reagan in 1980. Support for Reagan was highest among those who believed that: business profits benefit all, that the government has little responsibility to help people meet needs, that social welfare benefits are a disincentive to leaving poverty, and that business profits are distributed fairly. And the stronger the views, the more likely one was to have voted for Reagan in 1980. In almost all cases, Reagan supporters were twice as likely as Carter supporters to hold such attitudes (Table 10.1). Not surprisingly, self-identified conservatives were far more likely to have supported Reagan (data not shown). In addition, of those who voted for Reagan, 38.9 percent felt the government was showing too much concern for social welfare compared to 21.4 percent of those who voted for Carter.[10] Finally, one question directly addressed the issue of inequality: should the

government reduce income differences? Reagan
supporters were more likely to disagree with the
statement.[11] On a seven-point scale, 7.7 percent
of Reagan supporters, compared to 25.2 percent of
Carter supporters, most strongly agreed. In
contrast, 21.8 percent of Reagan supporters,
compared to 7.6 percent of Carter supporters, most
strongly disagreed (data not shown).

TABLE 10.1 Percent of Supporters of Reagan and
Carter Who Strongly Agreed or Strongly Disagreed
with Selected Ideological Beliefs
(Strongly Agree = S/A) (Strongly Disagree = S/D)

		Supporters of Reagan's	Supporters of Carter's
Business profits	S/A	30.8%	20.8%
benefit all:	S/D	3.2	10.1
Government	S/A	9.8	20.1
responsible	S/D	25.1	12.1
to meet needs:			
Social welfare			
benefits are	S/A	17.0	9.7
disincentive:	S/D	12.3	24.9
Business profits	S/A	7.6	4.3
are distributed	S/D	18.0	28.0
fairly:			

NOTE:All relationships significant at 0.003 or less

Source: Calculated from General Social Survey
(NORC), Spring 1984, Spring 1985 (white respondents
only)

Thus Reagan seems to have greater appeal for
those persons holding beliefs that government is
not responsible for reducing inequality, and
minimally responsible for welfare programs. Like

Reagan, they are more likely to see welfare as a disincentive to leaving poverty.

There is ample evidence of the underlying currents of sexism and racism in our society. Neither has been used directly as justification for reducing welfare. But I would suggest that they play a role in the public's acceptance of Reagan's cuts.[12] The public has images of welfare recipients as minority men who are too lazy to work, or single females (mostly minority) who engage in promiscuous behavior and often deliberately bear children in order to receive or increase their welfare benefits. These images make it easier for the public to accept budget cuts (Auclaire, 1984). The women are viewed as having few middle-class values (i.e. they are defined as immoral), and their children as potential troublemakers. In addition, the valuation of the traditional two-parent nuclear family (under conservative ideology) makes it easier to ignore those people who do not conform to such standards. These underlying currents of sexism and racism have become part of the symbolic content of the "new" ideology, especially as applied to poverty and welfare. In order to examine whether Reagan has had an appeal to those espousing traditional (stereotypical) attitudes about women, the election data from the General Social Survey were again examined.

Table 10.2 shows that these views were more common among those who voted for Reagan in both 1980 and 1984. By 1984, supporters of Reagan were considerably more likely than his opponents' supporters to agree with the following statements: women should take care of the home and not the country (Reagan, 28.0%; Mondale, 15.7%); would vote for a woman for President (Reagan, 75.9%; Mondale, 91.7%); and women are not emotionally suited for politics (Reagan, 47.4%; Mondale, 25.6%).[13] Here again Reagan supporters were generally twice as likely as others to oppose gender equality. Additionally, it is important to understand that these percentage differences had increased from 1980 to 1984.

In sum, the basis of this "new" ruling ideology is pro-capitalist (rather than laissez-faire) and against government intervention. But its success

TABLE 10.2:   Percentage of Supporters of Reagan and His Opponent Who Agreed with Selected Statements on Gender Equality

| | | Supporters of | |
	Year	Reagan	Carter/Mondale
Women should take	1980	-----	-----
care of home	1984	28.0%	15.7%
and country			
Vote for a woman	1980	78.7	84.9
for President	1984	75.9	91.7
Women are not	1980	46.7	38.4
emotionally suited	1984	47.4	25.6
for politics			

Source: Calculated from General Social Survey (NORC), Spring 1984, Spring 1985 (white respondents only)

in legitimating welfare curtailments may in part be due to the underside of the ideology which contains elements of classism and sexism.[14]

Writing Off the Powerless

In their classic argument, Piven and Cloward (1971) stated that one function of welfare was social control during times of economic crisis. As the economy contracted, welfare would be liberalized in order to subvert any revolutionary tendencies among those at the bottom. While their argument may well have had validity during previous economic cycles, Reagan was able to tighten welfare regulations during a severe recession without experiencing civil unrest.[15] How was this possible?

It is clear from the discussion in the second section that the groups hardest hit by policy changes and welfare reduction were children, female heads of families, and the working poor. Even before the Reagan reductions, welfare provided only a meager proportion of total transfer payments:

only 7.3 percent of 1980 income transfers went to
recipients of AFDC and food stamps who were not
elderly and not disabled (Focus, 1985c).   Evidence
shows that women benefit less than men from
transfer programs other than welfare, which
partially explains their higher rates of poverty.
For example, transfer payments reduced poverty
rates (in 1980) among white male heads of
households with children to 7.8 percent and among
similar nonwhite men to 16.9 percent.   In
contrast, the post-transfer poverty rates among
white and black women with children were 39.1
percent and 58.3 percent, respectively.   Yet it
was the programs that women are most dependent upon
that were cut by the Reagan Administration.   It was
not the well-being of men -- who are more likely to
engage in civil disorder -- that was threatened by
welfare reductions.   Particularly important is the
fact that the well-being of black male-headed
households improved (Focus, 1985c, 1986; Cassetty
and McRoy, 1983).   This might have reduced the
willingness of black men -- the major participants
in the urban uprisings of the 1960's -- to engage
in civil unrest.   The groups hardest hit by welfare
reductions -- women and children -- are those least
likely to engage in revolutionary activity.
Therefore Reagan could successfully ignore the
groups which were hardest hit by changes.   This may
provide one clue as to how Reagan avoided civil
unrest.
     Also, one may be able to safely ignore those at
the very bottom because there are few persons who
remain there year after year.   The results of the
Panel Study of Income Dynamics found that very
small proportions of the population remained in
poverty year-after-year from 1969-1978 (Duncan,
1984).   Although about one-fourth of all families
fell below the poverty line during at least one of
the ten years, only 0.7 percent were poor all ten
years, and 5.4 percent poor five or more years.
These "persistently poor" were disproportionately
found among two overlapping groups, namely, black
households and female-headed households.
     Thus the amount of mobility in and out of
poverty (though limited in the distance traveled)
suggests that most poor people are constantly
striving for upward mobility.

In addition, only a small proportion of the population depended upon welfare for survival during the decade (Duncan, 1984). One out of four families had received welfare in one or more years from 1969-1978 in the U. S., but only 2.0 percent received welfare all ten years, and 8.3 percent for five or more years. "Welfare dependents" were also more common among female-headed families, and particularly among black female-headed families. That only a small proportion of the population depends on welfare over time again suggests that this group can be safely ignored.

Thus the way in which the Reagan Administration can maintain social control while restricting welfare is related to the social characteristics of the persistently poor and welfare dependent, to their relatively small numbers, and to the existence of mobility in and out of poverty.

Opposition to Reagan Policies

The opposition to Reagan's policies has come largely from the left wing of the Democratic Party, which is greatly weakened.[16] As Michael Harrington (1986) points out, several important members of the Democratic Leadership Council are echoing Reagan in their criticism of the welfare system, notably former Governor Charles Robb of Virginia. I would contend that the existing opposition has met with little success because they have not fully understood why Reagan has been so successful. To the extent that Reagan can continue to parallel his "welfare ideology" with strongly held American values, the public will not oppose budget cuts, tighter restrictions, and the like. To the extent that oppositional forces can convince the public that indeed, the "safety net" is not there for many children (even if their mothers are viewed as undeserving) they may be more successful in defeating cuts in social spending. Children are symbolic of the future, and few Americans support programs that are detrimental to them. It is instructive that one program which the Reagan administration left untouched was Head Start, a program that serves "innocent" pre-school children. In contrast, the administration's fiscal

1987 budget called for the termination of the
Dependent Care and Follow Through programs, both
programs aimed at older children. The former is
designed to provide states with 75 percent matching
grants for childcare programs for "latch-key"
children, and the latter is a follow-up to Head
Start for older children. Perhaps these older
children are seen as less "innocent" and better
able to care for themselves. It is important to
note that some sign of opposition can be found:
both programs received funding from the House of
Representatives (Congressional Quarterly, 1986e).

In summary, we have seen that Reagan's attack on
dependency has led for welfare reform that would
reinforce the work ethic. The symbolic images of
welfare recipients that he has painted are those of
the "takers," the "able-bodied" who refused jobs,
the welfare mother who defies middle-class norms of
sexual morality. When combined with the call to
trim government spending, his "new" conservative
ideology has been successful. For both structural
and ideological reasons, there has been little
opposition to changes in welfare programs.

The meaning system that one may adopt from these
messages is laced with elements of sexism and
classism (and covertly, racism). Thus while
conservatives would normally be supportive of the
family, especially children, the images of welfare
families violate the conservative norm of a nuclear
two-parent family (preferably with the mother
staying at home).

It is crucial to understand that the single-
parent female violates a number of conservative
norms and values. Not only is she seen to be
sexually promiscuous, but her very independence
(even if it is based in dependence on welfare for
periods of time) is a threat to the two-parent
family, and particularly to the patriarchal family.
This normative message was stated clearly by
Charles Murray (1984): "single women who are unable
to support their children should not be supported
in such a way that allows them to set up an
independent household. Rather the
elimination/reduction of AFDC benefits would force
them to either marry or live with relatives."

Attitudes supporting gender equality are not yet embedded in the American value system. Nor have Americans come to terms with the relationship between gender equality and the family.

Reagan's messages concerning welfare heighten concern with the break-up of the traditional family form, and therefore mollify the opposition in regard to welfare changes.

Finally, Reagan has linked welfare with dependency and a reduced commitment to work. American values concerning equality have generally been couched in terms of "equality of opportunity," which stands in contrast to American values of individualism and success. The symbolic message concerning welfare seems to be that we have given people equality of opportunity and they have not made use of it. Reagan has succeeded in downplaying the importance of equality of opportunity (and seemingly eliminated commitment to equality of outcome), while raising the values of success and individualism to new heights.

These values complement an economy in need of increases in capital and productivity, and of a compliant, work-oriented labor force. They have gained hegemony due to structural conditions, but the symbolic content of the ideology has hastened the process. Political changes also require a change or revolution in thought (Gramsci, 1971). For those interested in changes, it is important to understand the content and symbolic messages of the ruling ideology.

NOTES

1 By welfare I refer to those programs aimed primarily toward the poor, chiefly AFDC, Medicaid and food stamps.

2 Much of the discussion of conservatism and its application to poverty is taken from Dolbeare and Dolbeare (1976) and Williamson, Evans, and Munley (1981).

3 Two different strands of conservatism can be noted. One places strong emphasis on individual self-satisfaction and has been termed individualist-conservatism (Dolbeare and Dolbeare, 1976). The other, organic-conservatism, sees

individual wants and needs as being subordinate to
the needs of society as a whole.   It is the
assumptions of individualist conservatism which
will be used in examining the rhetoric and results
of the Reagan Administration.
    4 It is interesting to note that including in-
kind benefits as income does not always result in
reductions in poverty. For example, when the value
of non-cash aid was included, the poverty rate
actually increased in some years (Wall Street
Journal, 1984).
    5 A study of the Congressional Budget Office
showed the following for 1976:   before any transfer
payments (such as welfare or Social Security), 25.5
percent of all households were below the poverty
line; after cash assistance, in-kind benefits, and
taxes,   only 6.9 percent of all households were
below the poverty line (Rodgers, 1979:28).
    6 Another factor that has been crucial to
Reagan's success has been the religious elements of
the New Right. This factor has been discussed at
length elsewhere (Tomaskovic-Devey, 1986) and will
not be covered in this paper.
    7 Clearly certain economic and structural
conditions are necessary for the dominance of any
ideology.   This has been discussed thoroughly in
Miller and Tomaskovic-Devey (1983), and Tomaskovic-
Devey (1986). The primary purpose of this paper is
to examine the components of the ideology -- the
symbolic content of the ideology which has gained
hegemony.
    8 Reagan has also highlighted an aspect of both
conservative and liberal ideology, which has served
to divert attention away from domestic issues --
that of anti-Communism. One could argue that one
impact of his rhetoric (and actions) is that
keeping international tensions at such a high peak
detracts from and takes precedence over discussions
of domestic policies.
    9 Data are taken from the General Social Survey
conducted in the Spring of 1984 and 1985 (National
Opinion Research Corporation).   The sample used
contained all white respondents for both years.
Other races were excluded because of the known
relationship between race/ethnicity and voting.
Various questions were asked concerning equality,
the role of government, and attitudes toward women

246

and blacks.   These questions were cross-tabulated
with respondent's Presidential vote in 1980 and
1984 (some data not available for 1984 election).
    10 The level of significance was 0.0000.
    11 The level of significance was 0.0000.
    12 Rieder's (1985) study also showed that people
in the   Italian community that he studied
associated liberalism with pro-black stances.   Thus
racial encounters and racial prejudice heightened
people's animosity toward liberalism.
    13 It should be noted that attitudes concerning
whether or not women should work outside the home
showed no differences with voting patterns.
    14 The data for attitudes toward blacks (blacks
shouldn't push, whites have right to segregated
neighborhood) showed few differences. However, the
differences were more pronounced for 1984:   12
percent of Reagan supporters, compared to 7.7
percent of Mondale supporters thought whites have a
right to segregated neighborhoods (and an eight
percentage-point spread for strongly disagree).
The factor of racism -- or perhaps benign neglect
-- needs to be examined more fully as a component
of the "new" ideology.   There appears some evidence
(Rieder, 1985) that some whites oppose liberalism
because of its perceived stance as pro-black.
    15 Piven and Cloward (1982) recognize this as a
historical argument that may be less relevant to
the current period.
    16 For a full discussion of alternatives to
recapitalization ideology,   see Miller and
Tomaskovic-Devey (1983).

BIBLIOGRAPHY

AuClaire, Philip 1984. "Public Attitudes Toward
    Social Welfare Expenditures." Social Work
    29:139-44.
Banfield, Edward C. 1974. The Unheavenly City
    Revisited. Boston: Little, Brown.
Cassetty, Judith H. and Ruth McRoy 1983. "Gender,
    Race, and the Shrinking Welfare Dollar." Public
    Welfare 41 (Summer):36-39.
Christian Science Monitor 1985a February 5, p.
    3ff.
_____ 1985b August 29, p. 1.

_____ 1985c September 13, p. 20.

Congressional Quarterly 1986a. "Children's Lobby: Investing in Tomorrow." January 11, p. 66.

_____ 1986b. "Deep New Cuts in Social Spending Proposed." February 8, p. 222-225.

_____ 1986c. "Democrats in Congress Open New Push for Child Care Aid." January 11, p. 63-67.

_____ 1986d. "Dozens of Programs Targeted for Extinction." February 8, p. 229-230.

_____ 1986e. "House Votes to Renew Five Social Programs." May 3, p. 971.

_____ 1986f. "Liberal Democrats Adapt to a Hostile Climate." August 9, p. 1797-1801.

_____ 1986g. "Reagan Pushes "Privatization" of Some Federal Functions." February 8, p. 231-232.

_____ 1986h. "Text of State of the Union Message." February 8, p. 274.

Danziger, Sheldon, and Peter Gottschalk 1986. "How Have Families with Children Been Faring?" University of Wisconsin: Institute for Research on Poverty Discussion Paper, No. 801-805.

Dolbeare, Kenneth M., and Patricia Dolbeare 1976. American Ideologies: The Competing Political Beliefs of the 1970's. Chicago: Rand McNally.

Duncan, Greg J. 1984. Years of Poverty, Years of Plenty. Ann Arbor: Survey Research Center, Institute for Social Research.

Edelman, Murray. 1964. The Symbolic Uses of Politics. Urbana, IL: University of Illinois Press.

Ehrenreich, Barbara, and Frances Fox Piven 1984. "The Feminization of Poverty." Dissent 31:162-170.

Erie, Steven, and Martin Rein 1982. "Welfare: The New Poor Laws." In A Gartner, et al. (eds.) What Reagan is Doing to Us. New York: Harper and Row.

Focus 1984. "Poverty in the United States: Where Do We Stand Now?" University of Wisconsin: Institute for Research on Poverty, Winter.

_____ 1985a. "Measuring the Effects of the Reagan Welfare Changes on the Work Effort and Well-being of Single Parents." University of Wisconsin: Institute for Research on Poverty, Spring.

248

_____ 1985b. Special issue: Summary of Conference at Williamsburg on "Poverty and Policy: Retrospect and Prospects." University of Wisconsin: Institute for Research on Poverty, Summer.

_____ 1985c. "OBRA Effects: An Update." University of Wisconsin: Institute for Research on Poverty, Fall and Winter.

_____ 1986. "The changing economic circumstances of children: Families losing ground." University of Wisconsin: Institute for Research on Poverty, Spring.

Glazer, Nathan 1984. "The Social Policy of the Reagan Administration: A Review." Public Interest 75:76-98.

Goodwin, Leonard 1983. Causes and Cures of Welfare. Lexington, MA: Lexington Books.

Gramsci, Antonio 1971. Selections From the Prison Notebooks. New York: International Publishers.

Green, Mark and Gail MacColl 1983. There He Goes Again: Ronald Reagan's Reign of Error. New York: Pantheon.

Harrington, Michael 1984. The New American Poverty. New York: Penguin Books.

_____ 1986. "Robbing the Poor: The Neo-Democrats Are Coming." Democratic Left 14 (May-August):8-9.

Lewis, Oscar 1966. "The Culture of Poverty." Scientific American 215(4):3-9.

Lo, Clarence Y. H. 1986. "Where Have All the Liberals Gone?" Contemporary Sociology 15:545-547.

Miller, S. M., and Donald Tomaskovic-Devey 1983. Recapitalizing America: Alternatives to the Corporate Distortion of National Policy. Boston: Routledge and Kegan Paul.

Murray, Charles 1984. Losing Ground: American Social Policy, 1950-1980. New York: Basic Books.

The Nation 1986. August 30, p. 1.

New York Times 1982. September 16, 1982, p. A1 ff., B6

_____ 1984a April 23, p. 1.

_____ 1984b December 14, p. B17.

_____ 1985c August 29, p. 14, A17.

Philadelphia Inquirer 1986. August 21, p. 1ff.

Piven, Frances Fox and Richard Cloward 1971. _Regulating the Poor: The Functions of Public Welfare_. New York: Pantheon Books.
_____ 1982. _The New Class War: Reagan's Attack on the Welfare State and Its Consequences_. New York: Pantheon.
Rieder, Jonathan 1985. _Canarsie: The Jews and Italians of Brooklyn Against Liberalism_. Cambridge, MA: Harvard University Press.
Rodgers, Harrell R., Jr. 1979. _Poverty Amid Plenty_. Reading, MA: Addison-Wesley.
Scott, Hilda 1984. _Working Your Way to the Bottom: The Feminization of Poverty_. London: Pandora Press.
Tomaskovic-Devey, Donald 1986. "The Protestant Ethic, the Christian Right, and the Spirit of Recapitalization." in Stephen D. Johnson and Joseph B. Tamney, (eds.) _The Political Role of Religion in the United States_. Boulder, Colorado: Westview Press.
Wall Street Journal 1984. February 24, p. 16.
_____ 1985 August 28, p. 44.
Washington Post 1985. December 26, p. D7.
Williamson, John B., Linda Evans, and Anne Munley 1981. _Social Problems: The Contemporary Debates_. Boston: Little, Brown and Company.

11

Poverty, Policy, and Politics: Implications of the Research Findings for Social Welfare Action

Donald Tomaskovic-Devey

Imagine the United States of America without a poverty problem. It probably is not too difficult to do. If you have trouble forming a mental picture of a U.S. free from impoverishment you might want to spend some time watching television, strolling through a college campus, or visiting a suburban shopping mall. In these places you will not find either the images or examples of poor people. You will not find the homeless, the sick and uncared for, the hungry, the isolated, the desperate members of a society marked by great inequality. Instead you will find the well dressed, well fed, well housed beneficiaries of an incredibly rich and successful society.

It will take some imagination to envision significant reduction, or better yet, elimination of poverty in the United States. Some of that imagination will be required in the design of economic and social policies that will be effective in reducing poverty. The research in this book provides a solid foundation from which to imagine effective anti-poverty policy in the United States. The previous ten chapters gave numerous insights into both how the impoverishment of twenty-eight million U.S. citizens is created, and what measures we can take as a society to reduce the level of poverty and lessen its burden. Somewhat more imagination and political courage are required if we as a nation are going to commit ourselves to the well-being of all our citizens.

This concluding chapter will require the reader to use some imagination. The first two sections will present a series of policy orientations and mechanisms (if not concrete proposals) for limiting poverty and reducing its consequences. It is my opinion that these policy orientations are technically correct (i.e., they will, within limitations, reduce and ameliorate poverty), and that they are achievable without placing undo stress upon the social fabric. Some of them, however, such as the elimination of low wage jobs, will strain the imagination of even the most politically naive reader. The third and last section of this chapter develops a political analysis of the barriers to and prospects for poverty reduction in the United States.

In Chapter Five I argued that poverty is a function of the ratio of households to good quality, non-poverty level jobs. The policy proposals outlined below first focus on household-level solutions to poverty, and then move on to an analysis of the labor market initiatives necessary to prevent poverty in the first place.

PREVENTING POVERTY -- HOUSEHOLD SOLUTIONS

Since poverty is definitionally a household phenomenon it seems logical to address poverty and social welfare initiatives at the household level. This logic can be misleading, however, and more structural poverty policies will be outlined in the next section. For a household to be counted among the poor under official definitions of poverty simply means that household income is lower than the poverty rate for a household of that size. Thus to reduce poverty requires an increase in income in poor households. Few would argue with this recipe for poverty reduction. Where the disagreement among policy makers lies is in the most appropriate means for raising the income of poor households.

Transfers Versus Training

There are two generic ways to raise household income. The first requires the direct transfer of income into the poor household. These income transfers can come from the state in the form of welfare payments, from absent fathers in the form of child support, or from family, community or church in the form of charity. The second method to increase household income is to increase the labor market income that household members earn. This requires that household members supply more hours of work to the labor market and/or earn a higher hourly wage than they currently do.

Historically U.S. policy makers have been uncomfortable with the direct transfer of income to the poor by the state. The fear of creating a dependent, "pauperized," population has often outweighed the desire to lessen the amount or consequences of poverty. Training programs have seemed more reasonable methods of reforming the perceived bad work habits and attitudes, and inadequate work skills of the poor, the unemployed, and the low-waged. Unfortunately, training programs do not work well at reducing poverty, as Morris argues in Chapter Seven. On the other hand, direct transfers of income have been successful at removing households from poverty. While this is true for the AFDC population in those few states where the combination of food stamps, AFDC and housing subsidies are high enough to lift households above the poverty line, it is overwhelmingly true for the elderly population. Americans over sixty-five years of age actually have a lower poverty rate than do those under sixty-five because the income-transfer program Social Security works.

Michael Morris in Chapter Seven provides a theoretical discussion that helps explain the superiority of transfers over training in the quest to reduce poverty. The success of income transfers requires only that the money actually be delivered to the poor household. Training programs make a whole series of dubious assumptions about the need and capacity to provide appropriate training, how labor markets work (that skills, experience, and motivation will be rewarded), and that there are, in fact, jobs available that pay adequate wages. The training programs that have shown some success short circuit the chain of dubious assumptions. Supported work for AFDC mothers is a good example.

By providing only higher waged jobs, with health
insurance and a period of supported supervision
during which participants learn skills on the job,
supported work programs have done better than most
training type programs.

If we want to reduce poverty in the short-term
then the most efficacious way is to increase the
level of transfer payments to households. Social
Security is a good example of a successful welfare
program. The Reagan administration's elimination of
the working poor from access to AFDC is an example
of how cutting back on transfers can increase the
amount of poverty in U.S. society. The simplest way
to reduce poverty is to extend benefits to more
poor households and at higher levels of support.
While these benefits must include income they can
be in kind services such as medical care as well.

Many conservative and liberal Americans fear
that extending benefits will reduce work effort and
create a dependent population. The research
reported by Jimy Sanders in Chapter Six and Mark
Rank in Chapter Eight demonstrate that dependency
creation is in fact a small threat. As Rank says,
"The idea of an entrenched welfare class remaining
on public assistance is simply incorrect." Much
more poverty is reduced by direct transfers than is
created by the small amount of additional
dependency that income transfers encourage. Because
the current levels of income transferred to the
non-aged poor are so low it is not clear what
dependency effect would be produced by raising all
household income levels up to the poverty line.
Perhaps more dependency would be created by less
harsh income supports, on the other hand it is not
inconceivable that all poverty could be eliminated
by increased transfers.

Husbands, Fathers and Child Support

Conservatives and liberals agree that income
transfers to poor families by agencies and persons
other than the government are a good thing. As
Teresa Arendell in Chapter Three discusses, for
many women the difference between being poor and
non-poor is access to male income. Husband-wife
households have much lower rates of impoverishment

than do female-headed households. Of course, the
whole household concept assumes that, while
individuals earn incomes, households consume them.
You only need one non-poverty level wage earner to
lift a whole household out of poverty. This
represents a transfer of income within the
household from the non-poverty wage earner to all
other members of the household. This is generally
considered a reasonable and even moral arrangement.
It is, in fact, an income transfer program which
creates dependency. Since typically female wages
are much lower than male wages, and women's work is
less likely to provide benefit packages that
include medical insurance and pension plans, and
children are barred from labor market participation
until their late teens, the husband-wife-child form
of family creates dependency of both women and
children upon men. The question for poverty policy
is what level of responsibility do husbands/fathers
have for their children and wives/lovers when
households dissolve through divorce or never form
in the first place?

Garfinkel and McLanahan in Chapter Two provide
some clear policy guidelines as to the extent of
responsibility men have to their families. The
primary responsibility is to children, who are
totally dependent upon adult support in any case,
and to whom a father should have a commitment which
endures beyond the often temporary relationship of
lover or husband. Low female wages are tied to
workplace organization, and so are not the
responsibility of husbands and must be remedied
through labor market initiatives (discussed below).
This understanding of the role of fathers is
consistent with current law but not with current
practice. Divorce settlements and paternity suits
can legally require child support payments, but
most women with children do not have this
protection. Most men who have court-mandated child
support responsibilities do not provide all of the
support to their children that they are supposed
to, and many provide none. Garfinkel and McLanahan
outline a proposal for automatic payroll deduction
to enforce child support payment. In a sense this
proposal shifts the burden of dependency from the
government to fathers, and does it with enforcement

procedures that minimize the chain of assumptions embedded in the policy. At this writing (June, 1987) the Ways and Means Committee of the U.S. House of Representatives is considering a Welfare Reform Act that among other initiatives would authorize states to collect child support payments from fathers by withholding from paychecks after a court order is issued. This is a weaker proposal than the one outlined in Chapter Two but recognizes the need for better controls over the incomes of absent fathers. Characteristically, the Welfare Reform Act has the support of Democrats but not Republicans, and is as concerned with reducing dependency on the federal government as it is with poverty reduction.

Labor Supply Problems

While income transfers within families, between fathers and their children, and between government and households can and do reduce poverty, fears of dependency, and the legitimate expectation that adult members of society work outside the home, force us to examine issues of labor supply. Since households can rise above the poverty line by increasing their earned income as well as through transfer receipts, any poverty initiative must examine the fundamental question of who is expected to work, and what barriers must be overcome to get them into the labor force.

Who should work? The central question a society must answer when deciding which classes of citizens should receive income transfers has to do with acceptable levels of dependency. Where dependency on income transfers is unacceptable then poverty amelioration must focus on initiatives to increase the labor market participation and earnings of the poor. (In the next section of this chapter I shall argue that job creation is a fundamental prerequisite for increased labor force participation.) Who should work? The cultural image of the welfare recipient as an able bodied male or a young woman having a series of children in order to live off of the state is simply false. Income transfer programs in the United States are primarily targeted at the elderly (social security) and families, generally single women, with young children. In a sense dependency among children and the elderly is seen as legitimate. Children are expected to be dependent, although there are clear public preferences for that dependence to be upon parents, particularly fathers, rather than the state. Mothers of small children have some moderate rights to public support in order to protect and raise their children. Among the elderly social security has assumed the status of a basic right of citizenship. Social security is available to all citizens over age 62 (65 for full benefits) and so is non-stigmatized. In addition, smaller populations, such as widows and the disabled are seen as having legitimate dependency rights as citizens.

It seems safe to conclude that the dependency of the aged, children, and the disabled upon the rest of society is reasonable. Of course, there are instances when populations who are not expected to be employed, do not require government transfers to survive. Their dependence is not totally focused on the government. Designing income transfer programs for the non-destitute dependent population is currently handled in two very different ways in the United States. Everyone over age 62 as a basic right of citizenship is entitled to social security support (although as Arendell points out in Chapter Three the adequacy of social security payments varies as a function of the number of years in the labor force and so tends to penalize women who have devoted significant periods of their life to childcare and home-making). Even rich people get social security. Children only receive welfare transfers when their parent or parents are desperately poor (one-half the poverty line in many states). Thus, children's access to state sponsored transfers is a function of household income but the access of the elderly to transfer income is a function of citizenship rights (although the level of support is a function of years in the labor force). To be consistent as a society we should either take social security away from all but the poorest of the elderly or provide income supports to all households with children. This latter course is the preferred mode in other advanced industrial

countries where child allowances are awarded to all
households for each child (Walker, 1984). This
practice has a positive political consequence, in
addition to increasing the well-being of all
children. It provides a non-stigmatized transfer
payment that acknowledges the importance of
children as present and future members of society.

Among healthy adults who should be expected to
work? Present AFDC regulations in most states
concede that the mothers of young children should
be exempt from work responsibility in order to care
for their children. To the extent that there is a
dependent welfare population, other than the poor
elderly, it is women with small children. They tend
to be dependent upon welfare until the children are
old enough to be in school full time. It is not
possible here to conclude whether or not these
women should work outside the home to support
themselves and their children or if their work as
mothers taking care of young children is
sufficiently important on its own. Certainly, if
women want to reduce their dependency on both men
and the state, they must do this through labor
markets and here we must examine the limitations on
labor supply that children pose.

Child Care. Someone must take care of small
children. For all women, but particularly single
women, finding good quality affordable child care
is a fundamental barrier to getting and keeping a
job. One of the reasons that welfare dependency is
greatly reduced after the youngest child is in
school full time is that the government, through
the public school system, becomes the primary
babysitter. If as a society we wish to lessen the
period of welfare dependency for single mothers of
young children then a societal level commitment to
quality child care is necessary. Child care must
either be subsidized for poor households in order
to encourage higher labor force participation or it
must, like social security and public schools, be
available as a basic public service and citizenship
right. Public child care need not be free, but it
also would better serve all citizens, particularly
the poor, if it was a non-stigmatized service.

Health Care. The United States is conspicuous
among advanced industrial societies not only for
the high cost of health care but also for the size

of the population without health care insurance
(see Chapters Three and Nine). The absence of a
national health insurance plan places a great
burden on the family incomes of many Americans.
The poorest families, those that qualify for AFDC,
also qualify for medicaid. Current rules however,
make both medicaid and AFDC unavailable to most of
the working poor. On its face this would seem a
great disincentive to labor supply, but most
households, even poor ones, do not plan to be sick.
Instead what we find is that illness, either among
adults or children, in the absence of health
insurance, encourages single mothers to leave the
labor force in order to get medicaid. For the rest
of the uninsured population, the absence of health
insurance lowers the likelihood of seeking medical
help for illness early on before it becomes
debilitating. Arendell in Chapter Three and Sarri
and Russell in Chapter Nine make quite clear the
critical health care burdens imposed on the poor.
The United States spends more on health care per
capita than any other nation in the world, but
leaves its low income population, with very little
health care at all. Free health care to all low
income Americans would reduce substantially the
burdens of poverty and prevent the potential
debilitating illness that may in the long term
create greater dependencies. Free health care to
the poor may not be easy to implement both because
of potentially high costs and the tendency of
medical doctors to refuse to treat poor patients,
both with and without medicaid insurance (see
Chapter Nine for evidence to this effect). National
health insurance for all citizens may be a more
practical avenue to insuring medical care for the
poor (and the aged) than specialized, and
potentially stigmatized, health insurance schemes
such as medicaid.
    Work Requirements. Current proposals for
welfare reform include requirements that welfare
mothers with children over age three work. The
Democrat backed Family Welfare Reform Act (June
1987) proposes to provide for transitional child-
care assistance and medicaid benefits, for welfare
mothers moving into low wage jobs. While this
proposal may not be enacted it does signify a

sensitivity to the fundamental constraints on labor
supply that health insurance and child-care pose.
The target jobs, however, remain low waged ones and
so the potential for employed poverty replacing
unemployed poverty, of independent poverty
replacing dependent poverty is quite high. These
work requirements parallel those already in place
for the unemployed who must demonstrate that they
are looking for work and are prepared to accept
employment if they are to continue to receive
unemployment compensation. Laws mandating labor
force participation are, however, naive responses
to poverty and welfare dependency in the absence of
more fundamental examinations of the role of
employment opportunity in creating poverty in the
first place.

PREVENTING POVERTY -- LABOR MARKET SOLUTIONS

Many of the articles in this volume have stressed
that poverty is not only a function of the absence
of employment but also of the wages attached to
available jobs. Increasing labor supply through
child care and health care provision or making job
searches mandatory for welfare recipients, will not
reduce poverty or even the need for welfare unless
enough jobs are available, and the available jobs
pay non-poverty level wages.

The Quality and Quantity of Jobs

David Maume in Chapter Four and this author in
Chapter Five make clear that the amount of poverty
in a locality is fundamentally conditioned by the
number and types of jobs available. Some jobs
typically pay non-poverty level wages (these
include unionized jobs, jobs in core sector firms,
and jobs in high waged labor markets) and some
industries (non-core) and localities (ones with
high unemployment rates and high levels of racial
discrimination) typically produce more poverty
level employment and lower levels of employment
overall. When Michael Morris in Chapter Seven
argues that training programs don't work because of
their long chains of dubious assumptions, one of

the fundamental weak links is the assumption that
increasing labor supply and/or the qualifications
of the currently poor will reduce poverty. In the
absence of enough non-poverty level jobs the best
that can be expected of training programs is that
they move some people out of poverty while others,
who otherwise would have held the limited non-
poverty level jobs, fall into poverty.

In order to fight poverty effectively and reduce
dependency we need as a society to increase
employment in good quality jobs. The analyses in
Chapters Four and Five suggest historical such as
racial discrimination, the level of union
organization among the working class, and
industrial structure causes of low waged and
inadequate jobs. Government policy should be
focused on increasing the supply of good quality
jobs.

Low wage jobs can be eliminated by setting a
higher minimum wage. Currently a family of four
must work about sixty-three hours per week at the
minimum wage just to approach the poverty line.
Raising the minimum wage from $3.35/hour to
$5.25/hour would reduce the level of required work
activity to forty hours per week per household.
Forty hours of paid work are quite reasonable by
U.S. standards for husband-wife families and are
even attainable for single parent families with
access to affordable child care.

The elimination of low wage jobs must be matched
with government policy focused on job creation.
Many economists fear that raising the minimum wage
will eliminate jobs, and they are probably correct
in the all else equal world of laissez faire
markets. In the U.S. we have a seemingly permanent
high unemployment rate. In 1987 after four years of
economic growth the unemployment rate still hovered
near seven percent of the labor force, about where
it was in 1979-80 when Ronald Reagan made it a
prominent indicator of economic misery. In the
U.S. it has been public policy since 1979 that
inflation, rather than unemployment, should be the
central focus of macroeconomic policy (Miller and
Tomaskovic-Devey, 1983). In fact, through
manipulations of the money supply, unemployment is
used as one of the primary mechanisms to fight

inflation. Other western nations, including Sweden, Switzerland, Austria, and Japan have managed to control both inflation and unemployment through macroeconomic and institutional regulation of their economies (Therborn, 1986). In those nations citizenship rights to employment are treated as seriously as employer's rights to property and profit. Clearly both the raising of the minimum wage and efforts to reduce unemployment and create jobs as anti-poverty mechanisms have profound implications for the general operation of U.S. labor markets and the distribution of income between employers and employees generally. There are, however, clear political impediments to increasing the quality and quantity of jobs and they will be discussed below.

Sex-Segregation in Employment and Female Earnings

Poverty is disproportionally concentrated among women and their dependents. The low waged jobs that are generally available to women in the labor market often make them dependent upon male earnings to escape poverty. One of the fundamental causes of women's low labor market earnings is sex-segregation in employment and the status assumption that most employers (and many employees) make that women's work is worth less. (In addition, women because of traditional family responsibility often work fewer continuous years and more part-time hours in the labor force. The poverty reduction policies associated with labor supply are discussed above.) Women and men rarely are employed in the same job in the same firm. Typically female jobs tend to get lower wages even when they are performing comparable tasks to jobs that are typically filled by men. The elimination of sex-segregation practices in employment would, over the long term tend to reduce the institutionally grounded lower pay associated with female labor.

The policy initiative referred to as "comparable worth" or "equal pay for equal work" has the potential to reduce some of the male-female wage disparity. Comparable worth proposals tend to focus on formal job evaluations in which jobs are ranked in terms of their education and skill

requirements, training times, and task
difficulties. After ranking, jobs that require
comparable levels of skill and training should be
paid comparable wages. In practice this tends to
raise women's wages to the level of men doing
similarly skilled work. Under comparable worth
proposals sex-segregation in employment could
remain, but the earnings penalty associated with
being in a female job would be eliminated.
Comparable worth does not address sex-segregation
that exists across types of firms (males tend to
hold the high wage wholesale sales jobs and females
the low paid retail sales jobs) nor sex-segregation
which is consistent with skill disparities (lawyers
and legal secretaries in law firms) but it does
provide one policy initiative to lessen
institutionalized sex discrimination and so would
probably reduce the poverty vulnerability of women
employed in large firms with many types of sex-
segregated jobs.

Industrial Policy

In the United States industrial policy and poverty
policy are rarely, if ever, discussed together.
Current U.S. industrial policy is largely targeted
at encouraging capital investment, particularly in
manufacturing and export industries. Policy
mechanisms for this type of industrial policy tend
to be tightly linked to the tax code. Corporations
are given tax breaks for desired investment
behavior. A second form of industrial policy which
is almost never discussed as such also exists in
the U.S., and this is government procurement, most
notably military spending. The largest consumers of
goods and services in the U.S. economy are the
federal and state governments. Every time the
state or federal government enters into a purchase
agreement they are encouraging economic development
in the area(s) where vendors locate their
businesses. Pork barrel military projects locate
weapons contracts and military bases where powerful
congresspeople and industrialists lobby for them to
be. If both the explicit and implicit industrial
policies of the U.S. government were reoriented to
take poverty reduction goals into account a whole

new and potentially effective method of poverty prevention could be established. Vendors should be given preference for government contracts (this initiative is just as applicable on state and federal levels) when they locate production facilities in areas with large poverty populations or when they deliberately hire from among poor populations. Similarly, decisions about military base location and military spending could be influenced by the level of local need. And finally, the industrial policy built into the tax code could be redirected to focus on job creation and domestic employment. This discussion is expanded in Miller and Tomaskovic-Devey (1983).

Labor Market Policy

The two central labor market policies to reduce the of poverty and lessen dependence have already been discussed. They are to raise the minimum wage in order to reduce the relationship between low wage employment and poverty, and to pursue full employment policies to insure the availability of jobs. Current labor market policy pays lip service to employment creation but in fact unemployment is the main policy tool in the successful fight against inflation.

The policy not to pursue is skill training for nonexistent jobs. Training programs are particularly wrong-headed when they endeavor only to teach proper work habits and establish some employment history in localities that offer little in the way of non-poverty level employment. These cheap efforts at upgrading the human capital of the currently unemployed or low waged ignore the central importance of job placement, job availability and on-the-job skill training. Skill training programs only make sense if they are linked to real jobs where the demand for skilled labor exceeds current supply.

PREVENTING POVERTY -- POLITICAL ACTION AND REACTION

At this point the reader has been advised that effective poverty reduction and amelioration policies should include raising the minimum wage substantially, a full employment economy, more generous transfer payments, child allowances for all households, payroll deductions of child support from absent fathers' earnings, subsidized child care, nationalized health insurance, comparable worth job evaluations, the long-term elimination of sex segregation in employment, and national and state level industrial policies targeted at poverty reduction. This is, of course, a theoretical wish list with little current potential for being fulfilled. Some of these proposals are likely to be adopted in some form over the next few years (e.g. higher minimum wage, payroll deductions for child support, child care and health insurance subsidies for the currently dependent poor), although they will be enacted in modified and less generous forms than set out here. Others (a full employment economy and targeted industrial policies) are not yet visible in U.S. political discourse, but are currently practiced in one or more industrial countries in Europe, and so are socially and economically possible if not politically practical (Therborn, 1986; Walker et. al. 1984). Still others (comparable worth and the elimination of sex-segregation in employment) are nowhere widely practiced but have political support in the United States among some feminist and labor union organizations. Thus all of the proposals are feasible at some level of implementation, but face very real political barriers.

Nowhere in mainstream U.S. politics is there a political explanation of poverty which focuses on the quality of jobs nor is there a political commitment to eradicate poverty. There is a political commitment among some Democrats to lessen poverty while lessening dependency. Among Republicans the commitment tends to be limited to lessening dependency. This is why policies likely to be enacted are largely limited to ones that enhance labor supply among the AFDC population and shift dependency from the government to absent fathers. These are good policies but they do not address the creation of poverty through normal labor market operation. While it is likely that the minimum wage will be raised before the next presidential election, with Republicans and Democrats trying to gain votes in the process, it

is unlikely that it will be raised high enough to
seriously confront the reality of employed poverty,
nor will it be indexed to inflation in order to
preserve the social benefits of a higher minimum
wage.   The goal of poverty prevention remains
politically subservient to other goals such as
international competiveness, the profitability of
private businesses, U.S. military preparedness, and
the reelection of incumbent legislators (Miller and
Tomaskovic-Devey, 1983).

Political Issues Associated With Redistributing Income

To eliminate poverty will cost money.   Raising
transfer payments will effect the federal budget.
Taxes will have to be raised, spending elsewhere in
the budget cut, or deficits enlarged in order to
accommodate increased social welfare spending.
Preventing poverty through labor market and
industrial policy initiatives will transfer income
from employers to low-wage employees and
potentially from higher wage employees to low-wage
employees as well.   If low-wage jobs are replaced
with better paying ones the price of services
typically performed by low-wage workers (e.g. take-
out-food, retail sales) will go up and so increase
costs of services for middle-class households.   If
comparable worth laws are enacted and enforced,
income will be redistributed from employers to
female employees and potentially from men to women.
Since blacks are disproportionally found in low-
wage jobs, a higher minimum wage may redistribute
income from white to black households. All social
and economic policies redistribute income and
poverty policies are no exception (Thurow, 1983).
The political problems is in forging policies that
redistribute income without strong opposition.
    The Reagan administration was able to
redistribute income from low-income households to
middle class and upper class households by changing
tax laws and welfare eligibility rules with the
political promise that these changes would lead to
economic revitalization. On the other hand, the
Reagan administration has generally failed in its
effort to cut social security payments (although it

has been able to decrease medicare coverage
somewhat). The difference in success is a function
of the level of political opposition to its
policies. Corporations and middle class households
embraced the income enhancing effects of tax cuts
and were not particularly troubled by the reduction
in income to the already low income. The poor did
not mount an effective protest to changes in
transfer eligibility, but the elderly, with support
from a broad cross-section of society, successfully
defended social security.

If we look at the two periods of expansion in
the U.S. welfare state, the "New Deal" of the
1930's and the "Great Society" of the late 1960's
we can see two circumstances under which the poor
have had more political success. During the great
depression there was a great deal of political
unrest, people with jobs were struggling to make
ends meet, and even the better paid and securely
employed could visualize themselves as poor. There
was broad popular support and mass agitation and
protest behind political proposals to expand the
role of the state in guaranteeing the income of at
least some sections of the population. The 1960's
we also saw political agitation, much less than in
the 1930's, but we also were an incredibly rich
nation, where government income threatened to
overwhelm the ability of the federal government to
spend. In this period the cost of an expanding
welfare state could be born by a redistribution of
the income generated by growth, rather than
directly reducing anyone's current income.

In the present period none of these factors are
present. There is no broad social movement by the
poor, the mass of the population does not identify
its interest with the poor, and because we have a
slow growth economy both employers and the middle
classes might have to lose income for the poor to
gain.

The "Undeserving Poor" versus "Citizenship Rights"

In surveys very few people describe themselves as
poor, even when their income qualifies them for
such a designation. Poverty as we have seen is very
much a life-cycle phenomenon, with the very young,

single women, and the elderly with interrupted work histories (and so low social security benefits) most at risk. And among these groups it is only the elderly poor who can be characterized as permanently poor. The social imagery of poverty as the result of personal habits associated with minorities and sexually immoral women is a distortion of reality. It is, however, a convenient distortion for those who stand to lose by reductions in poverty (employers and better off households) because it allows poverty to be socially isolated among other, less deserving groups.

The United States is a profoundly divided society on the basis of race and class. Personal failings are the preferred explanation for economic and social hardship and there is, presently at least, very little compassion across race and class lines for the less well off. The white middle class is content to take its jobs and its tax breaks and run. Employers show even less concern for the poor, whose income mobility would directly threaten their profits by increasing labor costs. What is lacking is a notion of citizenship rights. The moral indignation that Americans feel toward nations that challenge the international prestige of the United States is not reproduced internally with a nationalist commitment to our fellow citizens. When a U.S. airplane is hijacked by terrorists from the Middle East it is interpreted as a national humiliation that requires strong responses. Twenty-eight million poor in the richest nation on earth is not interpreted as a national humiliation, rather it is a reflection of inadequate human capital and cultural inferiority among the poor themselves.

The assumption that the poor are undeserving leads to a stigmatization of policies to ameliorate poverty. All poverty policies it would seem must reduce dependency and stigmatize recipients in order to discourage participation. Social programs such as social security and public education are available to all citizens and are non-stigmatized even though they may reduce poverty and certainly redistribute income. It is for this reason that I have suggested that child allowances, child care subsidies and health insurance should all be

general population, rather than poverty population,
policy initiatives. Policies targeted at the poor
are stigmatized, they are less than citizenship
rights, closer to charity, and the Reagan
administration has demonstrated quite clearly that
in the next political moment that they may be
reduced or even eliminated.

The stigma associated with poverty, the
assumption that the poor are primarily responsible
for their poverty, and the ideological centrality
of individualist notions of free market economies
all combine to make the structural antecedents of
poverty invisible in the United States. Poverty is
associated quite strongly with male-female and
black-white inequality as well as with the
functioning of local economies. Poverty is created
by forces in the society that the individuals who
are currently poor have no control over.   In the
absence of a notion of citizenship rights or a
strong social movement among the approximately
fifty percent of working Americans who are likely
to be poor sometime in their life, it is unlikely
that serious political attention will be paid to
policies designed to prevent poverty from being
produced by the normal social and economic
functioning of U.S. society.

In Chapter Ten, Susan Gotsch-Thomson argued that
the Reagan administration had exploited and
exacerbated sex, race and class divisions in the
United States in the process of attacking and
rolling back the welfare state. Political
coalitions to expand the effectiveness and
commitment of anti-poverty policy will need to
bridge those ideological divisions. I cannot argue
that such coalitions are likely to emerge and be
effective in the short-term. It is possible,
however, to point out who the key groups would have
to be.

Those groups most at risk to be poor must
spearhead any political movement to strengthen the
commitment of the United States as a society to its
most vulnerable. We are not in a period of strong
economic growth (like the 1960's) that makes "cost-
free liberalism" a promising route. Instead
notions of citizenship rights and fairness must be
made politically fashionable. The major
organizations of the civil rights, women's and

union movements must work together in this effort. The Democratic party must be encouraged to renew its relationship with the less fortunate and powerful. Although there has been some movement in this direction, spearheaded by the activities of Presidential candidate Jesse Jackson and his Rainbow Coalition, the poor and the working class remain marginal to the Democratic party. Neither the women's movement or prominent union organizations have moved strongly toward political coalition. Future political organization around the notions of citizenship rights and the quality of employment opportunity is necessary if effective poverty prevention policy is to be developed and implemented in the United States.

BIBLIOGRAPHY

Miller, S. M. and Donald Tomaskovic-Devey 1983. Recapitalizing America: Alternatives to the Corporate Distortion of National Policy. Boston: Routledge & Kegan Paul.

Therborn, Goran 1986. Why Some Peoples are More Unemployed Than Others: The Strange Paradox of Growth and Unemployment. London: Verso Books.

Thurow, Lester C. 1983. Dangerous Currents: The State of Economics. New York: Random House.

Walker, Robert 1984. "Resources, Welfare Expenditures and Poverty in European Countries." in Robert Walker, Roger Lawson and Peter Townsend (eds.) Responses to Poverty: Lessons From Europe. Cranbury, New Jersey: Fairleigh Dickenson University Press.

Walker, Robert, Roger Lawson and Peter Townsend (eds.) 1984. Responses to Poverty: Lessons From Europe. Cranbury, New Jersey: Fairleigh Dickinson University Press.